Piggyback Rides
aɴd Slippery Slides

How to Have Fun
Raising First-Rate Children

Piggyback Rides
and Slippery Slides

How to Have Fun
Raising First-Rate Children

Lynnae Allred

Lynnae W. Allred

CFI
Springville, Utah

ISBN 13: 978-1-59955-053-4

Published by CFI, an imprint of Cedar Fort, Inc., 2373 W. 700 S., Springville, UT, 84663
Distributed by Cedar Fort, Inc., www.cedarfort.com

LIBRARY OF CONGRESS CATALOGING-IN-PUBLICATION DATA

Allred, Lynnae Whiting, 1966-
  Piggyback rides and slippery slides : how to have fun raising first-rate children / Lynnae Whiting Allred.
    p. cm.
  ISBN 978-1-59955-053-4
  1. Play—Psychological aspects. 2. Child rearing. I. Title.

  BF717.A43 2007
  649'.5—dc22

                          2007017742

Cover design by Nicole Williams
Cover design © 2007 by Lyle Mortimer
Edited and typeset by Kimiko M. Hammari

Printed in the United States of America

10 9 8 7 6 5 4 3 2 1

Printed on acid-free paper

In order to develop normally, a child requires progressively more complex joint activity with one or more adults who have an irrational emotional relationship with the child. Somebody's got to be crazy about that kid. That's number one. First, last, and always.

—Urie Bronfenbrenner

Contents

Chapter 1

Playing with Our Children

I remember Grandma's pink Melmac cups well. They are connected to many happy childhood memories. On cold winter mornings, they were filled with hot cocoa for breakfast. During Thanksgiving dinner, they held Sprite mixed with Concord grape juice pressed from Grandma's own vines. There was always a pink Melmac cup next to the stubbly brush Grandpa used for lathering up his face before he shaved. At night, after the milking was done, Grandpa would put his dentures in the cup to soak. But my most vivid memory of pink Melmac cups was the day when Grandma got them out so we could have a tea party.

Grandma had spent a busy morning gathering the eggs, straining the cream from the top of the milk before she situated it on the stove to pasteurize, and setting the sprinklers outside to water the rosebushes. But now the housework was in order, and she had a few minutes to make memories with me. She put the piano bench in the middle of the living room and covered it with an eyelet-edged pillowcase. She got out her gravy boat (the one with the wheat sheaves painted on the sides and only a tiny chip out of the handle) and filled it with fresh whole milk Grandpa had brought in from the milking barn just that morning. She put out two of her best china saucers, got one of those pink Melmac cups out of the cupboard for each of us, and then put three chocolate wafer cookies on each plate. I'm sure our party lasted only a few minutes, but thirty-five years later, I can remember how grown-up I felt pouring my own milk out of the only "teapot" Grandma owned.

I also remember the day my mother taught me to play school. I don't know why she set aside her own agenda for the day. I would guess that one or two of my younger sisters joined us, but I don't remember anyone but Mom being there. My little table and chair were my desk, and she gave me a shoebox full of school supplies to use—some unbroken crayons she had managed to scrounge from the bottom of the diaper bag, a brand new pencil with no bite marks on the eraser, a few pieces of her special bonded typewriter paper (not the leftover "scratch" paper that already had writing on one side that I was usually allowed to use).

She equipped herself with a small bell to ring at "recess" time and a large sheet of butcher paper, which she taped to the door of my toy cupboard. She sat next to the cupboard and began to write. School was in session.

I have often wondered why these two events stand out so clearly in my memory. I suppose part of the reason is that they were a little bit out-of-the-ordinary. It wasn't because Mom and Grandma never set aside time just for me, because both of them spent one-on-one time with me frequently. It wasn't just because they set aside their own busy agendas to do something for me, either. There were hundreds of times when each of them did that. I think the reason these two incidents have had such a powerful hold on my memory is that in each case, an adult stepped out of her everyday adult role and became a playmate. There were no "ulterior motives" that I knew of—Mom wasn't trying to get me to learn my spelling words, and Grandma wasn't trying to teach me table manners—they were simply willing to spend time with me, *on my own terms*.

For some time, I have been interested in the impact that playing with children has in their lives. Have we become so focused on making our children into capable adults that we have robbed them of their childhood? Have we become so intent on making sure that children have all of the advantages of a superior education that we have forgotten what makes them wise?

Could it be that all of the most important skills that we want to bring into our children's lives—social awareness, academic intelligence, appropriate behavior, empathy for others, physical development, and caring family relationships—can all be accomplished almost instinctively through simple play? Is it possible that simply playing with our children is one of the most important things we will ever do for them?

The purpose of this book, then, is fourfold:

1. To help parents, grandparents, and other adults rediscover the value of "simple play" as a method for building the human relationships that help children thrive.
2. To explore briefly (from a research standpoint) the question of how valuable play is to a child's social, emotional, and physical development and to help parents weigh the benefits of "structured" learning versus child-driven, spontaneous playtime.
3. To suggest simple, inexpensive, innovative ways we can play with our children in a variety of different situations.
4. To help parents learn how to evaluate and balance the opportunity costs of the way the family spends its leisure time.

I am not advocating eliminating all of a child's extracurricular experiences. I am advocating a sense of balance. There are opportunity costs to giving our children extracurricular experiences. For example, in my own home I have learned that on the day that I drive my son twenty miles to his trumpet lesson after school, there will be no family dinner, because I am not there to prepare it. On days when there are soccer games (often more than one of them) at opposite ends of town, we give up the evening bedtime story in exchange. When I am away from home helping one child's Technology Club develop a website, the children left behind at home will likely turn to a mindless television program to fill their empty hours.

We are a generation of busy adults with busy children, yet in our effort to provide our children with experiences, education, and social skills, we have inadvertently eliminated the most powerful resource we have for helping our children develop into well-adjusted, responsible adults. We have eliminated *ourselves*.

Chapter 2

Bedtime Is Playtime

I don't remember a single time when I was unwilling to go to bed. It's not that I was an especially cooperative child. It's because I had a playful dad, and he made going to bed fun. Our bedtime ritual was not time-intensive. It wasn't even the same night after night. I was told years later that the ritual developed because my parents got so frustrated about getting everyone in the family tucked in at night. The solution was not obvious at first because it seemed too easy. Mom and Dad had to figure out how to make going to bed more desirable than staying up.

Here's what they did:

After we had said our family prayers together, Dad would give me my choice: "Piggyback, jump, wheelbarrow, or the machine?" he would ask.

If I said "piggyback," I would get a piggyback ride to bed. Dad often made a meandering loop through the house, then down and up the stairs once before he tucked me in. If I said, "Jump me," he would take me by the hands and I would jump my way to bed, but with each jump, he would lift me high into the air and swing me forward in one long-distance leap. It was something like watching astronauts spacewalking on the moon. If I decided I wanted the wheelbarrow, he would hold me by the ankles, and I would push up on my hands and crawl, hand over hand (like a wheelbarrow) to my bed, where he would lift me gently into the air and settle me headfirst onto my pillow.

If I chose "the machine," Dad would sit on the side of the bed and say, "It's the . . . squeezing machine." And he would wrap me up in his arms and give me a bear hug. Then he might say, "Now it's the . . . " (and he would pause to add a little bit of suspense) ". . . washing machine." And holding me with one arm under my neck and another arm under my knees, he would gently whirl my entire body from side to side as if I were in the agitate cycle. Sometimes, he would say, "Now it's the . . . " and pause extra long, which was my cue to shout out the name of the machine I wanted to ride in: the tickling machine . . . the poking machine . . . the pinching machine.

Dad's machine always worked on "gentle" cycle. He was never rough, and poking or tickling never went on long enough to cause discomfort. I looked forward to bedtime because it was a moment of one-on-one time with Dad that I could anticipate nearly every night. My other siblings got the same treatment. Often, after we were tucked in (I shared a room with my younger sister), Dad would stay beside us and read a favorite bedtime story. (Once he had us wound up, he read to us to help us wind back down again). When I visited Boston for the first time as an adult with children of my own, I purposely hunted down a bookstore and bought myself a souvenir copy of Robert McCloskey's *Make Way for Ducklings,* even though I already had a copy at home. It was my childhood bedtime story of choice—a story of two ducks and their search for a safe nesting spot in the heart of Boston. I can still hear Dad's voice in my head when I read it to my own children. Bedtime became a valuable moment to connect with Dad.

Here are a few bedtime games to get you thinking about ways to sneak in a few moments of play as part of your bedtime routine:

Go on a magic carpet ride

Parenting expert Susan Newman, PhD, suggests that you keep a small blanket by your child's bedside, and after she is tucked in for the night, cover her gently with the "magic carpet," tucking it in with a flourish. Once your child is tucked in, you will say, "We're on a magic carpet. Where are we going tonight?" Decide on a destination together and talk about what you will do while you are away. Who will you visit? What will you eat? Where will you sleep? You can even keep a children's atlas by the bedside to inspire you.[1]

Play a favorite card game

Dozens of card games require only a few minutes to play. Once your child is tucked in, play a quick game of War or Go Fish. What other games do you have in your game closet that you can finish in ten minutes or less?

- Read ten questions from the cards of your favorite trivia game and see if you know the answers.
- Play a speed version of Battleship (the first one to sink another player's ship wins).
- Race to complete a Sudoku puzzle.

Have a puppet show

Make simple finger puppets by wrapping the index fingers of both hands with adhesive bandages or masking tape and drawing on a silly face. Make up your own play, or just use the puppets as "narrators" for a favorite bedtime story.

Have a bedtime back rub

With your child resting on his stomach, draw huge block letters on his back and see if he can guess what letter you are writing. Finish with a good bedtime back rub.

Sounds in the dark

Take turns listening for and identifying all of the night sounds you and your child can hear as your child falls asleep. She'll have to be *very* quiet, so this is a fun game for the child who has trouble settling down to rest.

Toe tag

Sitting at opposite ends of the bed, try to catch one of your child's bare feet between your own two bare feet. Then switch and let your child try to catch one of your feet.

Other bedtime rituals

- Have your child "hide" schoolwork under her pillow to show Mom or Dad just before tucking into bed.
- If you play a musical instrument, bedtime is a great time to practice. Play two or three of your child's favorites, and end with a signature lullaby.
- Keep a "thankful journal." Each of you gets to choose one thing you are grateful for and write it in a small notebook kept by the child's bedside. At least once a month, review some of the things you were grateful for the previous month or year.
- Cut out a different paper snowflake every night.

Bedtime games for older children

The best part of my day/The worst part of my day

This simple game only takes moments. Both you and your child will get a chance to tell the other what the best and the worst part of your day were. This could be a great opportunity to give your child a chance to open up and tell you what frustrates him, what makes him upset, what cheers him up, and what motivates him.

Have an indoor campout

Blow up the air mattresses and have a sleepover in the living room (you can involve the whole family if you like). Toast marshmallows in the microwave and tell "I remember when" stories. If it's Christmastime, turn on some soft Christmas carols, and make sure you leave the tree lights on to fall asleep by. During Hanukkah season, watch the candles burn low in the menorah.

Reading aloud

When it comes to bedtime, there's nothing that will help you build bonds of closeness like a good read-aloud or bedtime story. The benefits of reading aloud extend far beyond their value in building relationships. A 1985 statement by the Commission on Reading, included in the document *Becoming a Nation of Readers*, summarizes the value of reading aloud in profound terms: "The single most important activity for building the knowledge required for eventual success in reading is reading aloud to children."

If you've never felt the magic of reading aloud at bedtime, tonight is a good time to start.

Here's the easiest way to begin:

1. Purchase or borrow a copy of Jim Trelease's *Read Aloud Handbook*. (You'll find a representative list of recommend titles at www.trelease-on-reading.com/rah_treasury.html.)
2. Visit the library and check out one or two of the read-aloud books recommended (choose something age-appropriate for your child).
3. Tuck your child in and read.[2]

There is no age limit for reading aloud. Some of my most productive conversations with teenage children happen when I show up at bedtime unannounced and ask if I can read a few pages of a novel or short story I think will interest them. If nothing else, it gives me a good excuse to be in my child's room at a time when we can speak privately without interruptions. Once I've finished a short excerpt of something I think he'll enjoy, I just mark the spot where we stopped and leave the book on a nearby dresser. Sometimes the book will have piqued curiosity enough to get picked up and read later. Sometimes it won't.

Your teenager may not have anything more to say to you, but if you've made yourself available and you've eliminated all of the outside interruptions, your child will at least have an opportunity to open up to you if he needs your listening ear.

If you have not been in the habit of reading or talking with your adolescent child, he'll be immediately suspicious. Ease him into a conversation by giving him a sincere compliment: "I was impressed with how well the defense worked together in your soccer game." Even the surliest teenager can't resist a sincere compliment. And even if the conversation is one-sided, you'll at least have the comfort of knowing that he fell asleep with your heartfelt praise ringing in his ears.

Building family bonds at bedtime

Kim told me of a favorite evening ritual at her house. Often, just before she tucks her children into bed, she will give one of her daughters a lotion foot rub. "One night my girls offered to lotion my feet before bed, as I often do for them," she wrote. "In consequence of some long fingernails, the lotioning tickled me so much that I burst out laughing and started wriggling all over the bed. My girls' faces lit up, and they were laughing as hard as I was. They redoubled their lotioning/tickling efforts until the room resonated with near hysterical laughter from everyone. They couldn't get enough of seeing Mom laugh. I am sure I need to make more room to laugh with them. I suppose it is only because we laugh together in life that we can trust each other with our tears."

Mary O'Neill found out how valuable her favorite bedtime game was when the second adopted child joined the family. Both of her daughters were adopted in China, and the older one, Molly, had a favorite bedtime game known as "adoption." Together, mother and daughter would recount the moments that led up to Molly's adoption. They would act out Mary's packing to go to China, her travel on the airplane, and her first meeting with Molly. Soon after the second daughter, Claire, joined them, Mary overheard a tender exchange between the two little girls. Molly, speaking to her baby sister, said, "You were born in China. Mommy carried you in her heart. We loved you the moment we saw your picture." Mary sums up the anecdote by saying, "Have I mentioned how blessed we are?"[3]

Silly or serious, calming or crazy, bedtime is prime time for building a close relationship with your child. All she needs is five minutes to play with you.

Reader's Homework

Based on what you have read in this chapter, what ONE idea for playing with children appeals to you most as something that you could feasibly do in your own home? (This can be an idea you read about in the book, an idea of your own that came to you as you were reading, or something you remember experiencing as a child).

Write your ONE idea here:

_____

_____

If you'd like, record this idea in the "Gallery of Ideas to Try" at the end of the book.

Notes

1. Newmann, "Bedtime Rituals that Forge Warm Memories."
2. Trelease, *The Read-Aloud Handbook.*
3. O'Neill, "Double the Pleasure, Double the Fun."

Chapter 3

Playing in the Great Outdoors

Hiking, backpacking, beachcombing, and other
"worldly" pursuits

• •

Recently, I rediscovered a photograph of my sister, my dad, and myself on top of Mount Baldie. I remember Dad balancing his 35mm camera on a rock, setting the self-timer, and then running to pose with his two oldest daughters. I believe I was about eleven years old. My sister would have been ten. In the photo I am wearing an apple green polyester pantsuit. Both of us have our hair tied back in straggly ponytails, with wisps of blonde hair curling around our faces. It is a photograph that captures the single most memorable experience I ever had with my dad—a weekend outing with just Dad and my sister. I remember the experience so vividly that I can tell you that we ate scrambled eggs, raw hashbrowns, and burned bacon for breakfast; that we pushed over at least a dozen dead Quaking Aspen as we hiked back down the trail; and that there was a pile of dog food near the base of a tree in the campsite where we stayed. Why have the details of that forty-eight-hour period etched themselves so indelibly in my memory? I am certain that the experience stands out because it was such a glorious weekend. It was the only time in my life I remember my sister and me having Dad entirely to ourselves, on our own terms.

I grew up in a large family with eight siblings. My dad was an educator by profession. Although we had the benefit of a long summer vacation together, the financial situation eliminated many of the opportunities for trips to amusement parks, airplane flights to exotic destinations, and expensive dining. Instead, our family outings included hikes in local canyons, paddling a canoe at a nearby pond, camping, or floating down frigid mountain streams on patched-up inner tubes. Those experiences were powerful bonding opportunities for my parents and their children. Mom and Dad were wise enough to know that they did not need to spend a lot of money to spend time with us. They were also wise enough to know that the trips to the mountains stripped away all of the convenient distractions like television, the telephone, and the computer, giving us space to interact with each other instead. These trips also turned us into a "captive audience" of children who had to leave our friends and our toys and our schoolwork behind. Mom and Dad knew exactly how to fill the void—they filled it with themselves.

I don't believe I could overstate the impact that these frequent outings had on my life. Maybe scrambling around beneath the base of a massive natural arch carved out of the flaming red sandstone gave me a sense of my own place in the world. Maybe the smell of the pine trees helped me notice that I had been breathing all along. All I know is that my parents' efforts to help me experience the world around me helped me value my surroundings and myself. The earthy pleasures I learned about from these vacations refresh and renew me to this day. Moreover, the experiences allowed me to create a relationship with my parents and my siblings that I would not have had otherwise.

There is a lot to be said for any family vacation and its power to bond families, but I think outdoor experiences are unique in that they strip away so many outside distractions; we are left with space to contemplate things we may not have noticed otherwise. Colors are more intense because we see them in natural light; smells are more distinct because they are unfamiliar. Our bodies are subjected to greater alterations in cold and hot than they are accustomed to, so we have a heightened sense of tactile awareness. We exert ourselves physically, so we are hungrier. It is quieter, so we can hear more. I suppose this same sense of heightened sensory aptitude spills over into human relationships as well, and although it is more difficult to document the reasons, I know that I connected with my parents on a different level when we were in a natural environment.

I remember telling my dad an "inappropriate" joke during our trip to Mount Baldie and being surprised to hear him laugh. Normally, I would have expected him to scold me, or at least frown his disapproval. For some reason, he did not. I'm still sorry for telling him the joke, but because of his reaction, I could tell it was somehow safer to talk with him than it would have been if we were home, sitting around the dinner table. I distinctly remember that impression—that this was a trip when I could say just about whatever I wanted to, and my dad would listen.

Of course there were many other great outings, each with a different kind of impact. How did my parents use these diverse opportunities to "play" with me, and how do other parents use similar outdoor opportunities to create moments when family relationships can be strengthened?

My dad is a good photographer. He built a small darkroom under the stairs in our home where he would develop his own black and white photographs. When I was still in elementary school, Mom and Dad gave me a small, inexpensive camera of my own for my birthday. It was a Kodak Instamatic "point and shoot" camera with one-use flashbulbs that would fire only once and then melt into the plastic cube that housed them, leaving a distinct smell of burning plastic every time I took a picture.

One morning, on one of our family campouts, Dad woke me up early and took me on a walk to the lake. The water was smooth, without a ripple, so that the golden autumn trees and the sapphire sky were reflected perfectly in mirror image against themselves. I snapped a picture, and every time we looked at it after that during our Sunday evening slideshows, Mom would comment about what a great photo it was. Dad taught me to see things I would not have noticed otherwise. Over time, as we carried our cameras along on all-day hikes across slick rock trails or on short overnight family backpacking trips, I learned to see what he saw—the contrast in layers of Navajo sandstone, the interesting shape of a wild mushroom, and green moss against a wet stone in a small creek bed. It was a different kind of "play," of course. It wasn't something you might consider to be "play" in the usual sense of the word, but it was a connection I had with him that none of my other siblings ever cared to intrude upon—no one else owned their own camera.

The outdoor game I played with my mom happened much more accidentally. I had a school earth science assignment to collect and identify forty different varieties of wildflowers. It was early spring, and beyond the dandelions growing in the front yard and a few violets along the irrigation ditch bank I passed on the way home from school, I could see that there just weren't that many wildflowers in the world. But Mom knew otherwise, so she took an afternoon and showed me where to find wildflowers. We picked Scarlet Globemallow next to the side of the freeway. There were Desert Primroses in the foothills just outside of town. We found wildflowers growing in the cracks in the gutter in front of the fire station and along the fence line at the city cemetery. Then she took me home and taught me how to press them between layers of newspaper with several encyclopedias stacked on top. I was hooked. I was also the only student in my entire grade to get full credit for the assignment. That summer, after I had saved enough money, I bought my own copy of the *Audobon Society Field Guide to North American Wildflowers*, and from then on, every time Mom or I saw any color by the side of the road in some out-of-the-way place, we'd yell for Dad to stop the car so we could get out for a closer look. It was a game no one else in the family wanted to play, but Mom and I still relish the sight of a meadow full of flowers or a pretty card covered with a few pressed violets.

Since I have become an adult, I have learned the environmentalist creed that wildflowers should be left where they are to re-seed the next generation of wildflowers. I appreciate the concept of "leave no trace." But I also appreciate adults who remember that in order for a child to learn to love nature, he must be allowed to have hands-on experiences, and now and then, that means "controlled destruction"—damming up a river, rolling rocks down a slope, pushing over dead trees, or capturing bugs. Adults can help protect a child's right to play by taking a deep breath and relaxing a little.

On a hike in a national park a few years ago, our family joined a ranger-guided hike into the Fiery Furnace at Arches National Park—an area at risk for overuse that the National Forest Service protects by requiring a permit in order to hike there. Before the hike began, the ranger carefully explained the importance of avoiding stepping off from the path and damaging the cryptobiotic soil. Cryptobiotic soil is a living soil crust that includes soil lichens, mosses, green algae, microfungi, and bacteria. It helps prevent water and wind erosion, unless it is crushed—usually by human footprints or machinery.

At one rest stop along the trail, another hiker, who had been introduced to us as a well-known naturalist, expressed dismay that the ranger allowed some of the children to leave their parents to clamber among the rocks in a large open area. Later, he growled at one of the younger hikers: "I wouldn't mind if you moved your foot." Confused, the twelve-year-old boy stepped to the side. "Off from the plant!" barked the man, motioning to a fragile piece of greenery on the canyon floor. A few minutes later, the ranger who was leading the hike explained to the group that this location was the only known habitat for an endangered plant known as biscuitroot.

I understood that this well-meaning environmentalist was concerned about protecting a fragile area and an endangered plant, but I had to smile at the irony that he would be the one among us most likely to prevent any of the youngsters in the group from developing an interest in becoming future naturalists. Surely he did not learn to love the red rocks of the Southwest Desert merely by gazing at them from the trail. If we are to teach our children to be responsible about the world they live in, we will have to give them opportunities to touch, climb, and bump into things. And sometimes, we will have to be with them to help them understand why climbing, touching, and bumping are not appropriate. In the process, we will develop relationships with them that will foster their healthy growth and the likelihood that our planet will be the same, vast, beautiful wonderland for their grandchildren.

There is an abundance of activities available for parents and children who want to "play together" in the outdoors. Here are just a few you may not have tried yet:

Letterboxing

If you love treasure hunts, don't mind hiking a little, and know the difference between north and south, you'll want to give letterboxing a try. A letterbox is a small, waterproof container that generally contains a rubber stamp and a logbook. Sometimes you'll find small collectible items like postcards or stickers inside the letterbox container. Using treasure hunt clues downloaded from the Internet, letterboxers will seek out a box hidden out of sight somewhere on public property. Once you find the letterbox, you can record your name (and your own personal stamp, if you choose) in the logbook. Many letterboxes are hidden near sites that have historical significance. You'll find letterboxes literally all over the world, and whether you find one on the island of Aruba or inside a small crevice on Independence Rock next to a 150-year-old signature of one of the pioneers who traveled the Oregon Trail, you'll get hooked as soon as you try it. Visit www.letterboxing.org to learn more.

Geo-caching

This is letterboxing for the technologically advanced. Using a GPS (global positioning system) receiver, along with other navigational techniques, you'll search to find hidden containers known as caches. Again, the geocache container generally includes a small reward of some type. You can help yourself to some of the reward, as long as you replace it with something of equal or greater value. Today, you can find geocaches in more than 222 countries around the world. Like letterboxing, certain rules of ethics apply, so learn more from www.geocaching.com or www.terracaching.com.

National Park Service Junior Ranger Program

During a recent visit to a local national park, we were pleasantly surprised when a park ranger offered us a big red backpack full of activities and games for our children to enjoy during our stay at the park. We used star charts to find constellations at bedtime, went on a scavenger hunt to see how many different species of birds we could identify, and carried a small net and ice cube tray to the banks of the river where we fished out polliwogs and rock rollers to study up close.

With attractions as diverse as trains, dinosaurs, star gazing, and animal and plant life you have never studied before, the National Park Service has created dozens of hands-on learning experiences for children and families to enjoy when they visit one of the national parks. Interested students can complete a series of activities during their stay, share their answers with a park ranger, and receive an official junior ranger badge or patch. See how many you can collect.

Take a hike!

One of the simplest ways to hook your kids on the great outdoors is to take them for a short, scenic hike and provide a little trail mix on the way. You can find dozens of Internet resources for great hikes to take with children. Most public libraries will also have publications that will help you choose the best trails, as well as educate you about safety, appropriate gear, and so forth. Check out the Passport to Adventure program sponsored by outdoor retailer REI. You'll find a list of recommended kid-friendly hikes at www.rei.com/store/kids_passport.jsp.

Bike (hike, skate, or ski) a rail trail

Introduce your children to the pleasures of mountain biking by renting or borrowing a good bike and finding a paved biking trail near your home. If you're a real novice, you can send a logistics vehicle to the end of the trail (to pick up bikes and riders after the day's ride is over) and start at a location where you can bike downhill for the bulk of the ride. It's a fair bet you'll be hooked after the first ride. As you improve, you can talk with experts in the area about the best off-trail riding.

Walking and biking trails are becoming popular all over the United States, thanks to groups like the Rails-to-Trails conservancy. Rails-to-Trails is a nonprofit organization working with communities to convert unused rail lines into hiking and biking trails. The conservancy maintains an impressive online catalog of trails at www.traillink.com. Search by region or by activity. You can find great trails for snowmobiling, cross country skiing, and even inline skating.

Find a ghost town

You might find nothing but an old foundation or two and a few toppled gravestones, or you might find a thriving city with a drugstore that sells old-fashioned ice cream sodas. Visit www.ghosttowns.com to learn about once-thriving cities in your own area. Although it is against the law to take anything of archeological value from a ghost town (including rusty nails you find with your metal detector), you can dig up a lot of history instead.

Closing the generation gap

With a little bit of time, one of the outdoor activities mentioned here could become one of your family's most beloved hobbies. With luck, you will still be playing some of these games with your children's children. Sometimes outdoor games are passed down from generation to generation, and sometimes the games link generations backwards. That is what happened to me. My oldest son announced one afternoon that he had joined a rock climbing club and that the first outing was a climbing expedition six hours away from home. There would be an overnight stay involved, and since he had had a driver's license for less than a year, I was not at all excited about the prospect of allowing him to drive 450 miles alone to hang around the campfire with what I assumed would be a group of drunken college students. We eventually struck a compromise: He could go, but I would go along as chauffeur. I understood intuitively that my job was to sleep in the car and stay as invisible as possible so that he couldn't be embarrassed when he was the only one who showed up with his mommy. As we drove that evening, he introduced me to some of his favorite music—a new Broadway musical, *Wicked,* that I had never heard of (but which has since become one of my favorites) and a guitarist by the name of Jack Johnson. Who would have thought I could enjoy his music that much!

We arrived at camp after dark, and I was surprised to discover that all of the college-age students were already sound asleep, since they had been climbing all day. The next morning, we left camp at first light and sat on an outcropping of rock to watch the sunrise and eat oranges and granola bars together. Later, he hitched a ride out of camp, standing on the running board of another climber's four-wheel drive. I watched him drive away with the group, determined to stay out of sight and read a book, but within an hour, my curiosity got the best of me. I walked about a half mile to the climb site and found a shady spot by the side of the road where I could watch. Within minutes, another climber came along and offered me a camp chair and a pair of binoculars. What I saw astounded me. One of the more experienced climbers was headed up one of the most difficult routes. I watched him methodically place each handhold and each foothold in a motion so fluid and so rhythmic that it mesmerized me. If *watching* a climber was this exhilarating, I had little doubt that *being* the climber would be thrilling as well. I could finally stop doubting my son's judgment.

Shortly, my son came down the road, looking for me. "Mom, why don't you come and see what we're doing?" he asked. I told him I was trying to stay out of sight so he wouldn't be embarrassed and he just laughed. "Come on," he said, "I'll teach you to belay." For the rest of the afternoon, I craned my neck backward and watched as climber after climber went up one of the dozens of different routes bolted into the rockface. Their knuckles bled and they grinned. Their foreheads dripped sweat, and they just reached into their chalkbags and climbed higher. As far as I know, there wasn't a lazy drunk among them. And long before the sun started to dip in the sky, my son said, "Let's quit now and go home while we're still having fun." When we got into the car, he pulled *my* mp3 player out of my duffel bag, and we listened together the rest of the way home.

Reader's Homework

Based on what you have read in this chapter, what ONE idea for playing with children appeals to you most as something that you could feasibly do in your own home? (This can be an idea you read about in the book, an idea of your own that came to you as you were reading, or something you remember experiencing as a child).

Write your ONE idea here:

_____

_____

If you'd like, record this idea in the "Gallery of Ideas to Try" at the end of the book.

Chapter 4

Playing with Your Food

How playing at the dinner table builds caring,
responsible, intelligent children

● ●

I arrived a little bit early for dinner. My contribution to the potluck meal was spaghetti sauce, and it looked and smelled wonderful! I had used a special recipe, adding fresh mushrooms and a whole variety of seasonings. When it was time for the meal to start, Pat, our dinner hostess, handed each of us two huge plastic gloves, invited us to sit, and then covered the entire table with a big sheet of sterile plastic sheeting. Next, she proceeded to load our "plates" with spaghetti and sauce, green salad, and garlic bread. Only there were no plates. There were also no forks or knives, and certainly no napkins.

Instead, Pat had painted a plate, a napkin, and a fork at each place on the table. The plates were big swirls of pink and yellow and green paint. The napkins were triangular blue patches painted at the left-hand side of the plate right where you might have expected a real napkin to be. We ate directly from the tabletop, using nothing but our hands. The reaction was mixed. Some of us dove right in, gleefully slurping spaghetti as if we were five again. Others were mortified. We mused about the source for the plastic gloves. "I think they're the big gloves used on the farm during calving season," commented one dinner guest as she sucked ranch dressing off her thumb.

How much silliness can you tolerate at your dinner table? No one will argue the fact that it is important to teach our children appropriate table etiquette, but if we've only seen the dinner table as the location for re-fueling our stomachs and teaching table manners, we've missed half the attraction of the dinner table. Is it time to reinvent the dinner hour in your home? Can you make it a place where hearts and minds are nourished alongside tummies?

Food for thought: Turning Meals into a family priority

Family mealtime is quickly going the way of the dial telephone and the typewriter. We are working parents with deadlines that keep us at the office late. We are soccer moms in the middle of spring season. We are fathers and mothers who need to get to evening meetings. We are youth with track meets to run, vocabulary words to memorize, and quadratic equations to solve. We are children who are missing something really, really important on TV if we stop to eat right now.

If yours is the typical busy American household, it will not be uncommon for you to go days without taking time to put a plate and a meal on the table. Mealtime, if it happens at all, consists of hanging over the breakfast bar with a fast food taco. A fork is optional. Vegetables are nonexistent.

By now, you have probably become aware of all the research surrounding the importance of a consistent family meal. Children who participate in regular family mealtimes are less likely to be obese, commit suicide, drink, smoke, do drugs, or engage in pre-marital sexual relationships. They are more likely to get a well-balanced diet, they do better academically, they are less stressed, they report having better self-esteem, and they are more likely to confide in a parent when they have a problem.

But if, like many parents, you're already suffering from guilt because there aren't enough family meals in your home, relax. My task here is not to convince you of the importance of a meal. You already know that family meals are critical. My only task is to help you see that with a few simple changes, you can do better than you are doing now.

If your family were all gathered around the table doing whatever it is that you do around the table that makes eating together important, what would your family be doing? Picture the scene in your mind. What is happening?

- Who is present?
- What are you eating?
- What are you talking about?

Let's paint the picture of perfection first. Dinner will be in a formal dining room. The table is set with the best china. Mother spent the afternoon preparing the delicious meal, and there are hot, homemade rolls, linen napkins, and candlelight. At precisely 6:00, which is when you agreed dinner would start, the entire family comes to the table. During the meal, the children excitedly volunteer information about what happened to them at school that day. Dad will share an insight from the evening newspaper, and the entire family will have an animated conversation about various current events. The children will have perfect table manners, no one will answer a cell phone call during the meal, and each family member will linger after they have finished eating. When the meal is over, everyone will carry his own dirty dishes to the dishwasher and then remain behind to help clean up the kitchen and the dining room.

Now that we've considered that narrow view of perfection and have realized that this kind of meal is not likely to happen once a year, let alone every night, let's ask the questions again and consider whether some nontraditional meal options are acceptable:

- Who is present? (Is it still a family meal if only part of the family can be there?)
- What are you eating? (Is it still a family meal if we are eating something as simple as a bagel?)
- What are you talking about? (Is it the conversation at mealtime that makes it so valuable, or is it something else?)

I suppose the first hurdle to overcome when you decide you want to have more meals together is to give yourself "credit" for the nontraditional meals in less than ideal settings, when only part of the family is present. Once you've conquered your lack of perfection, you can start looking more closely at ways to make family mealtime happen more consistently.

Eliminating Mealtime Scheduling Conflicts

According to the National Center on Addiction and Substance Abuse at Columbia University, the three most common reasons parents and teens cite for failure to eat together as a family are (1) one or both parents work late,

(2) family members are too busy, and (3) family members have conflicting schedules.[1] Here are a few suggestions to help you see what other families have done to eliminate these conflicts and make family mealtime a priority:

One or both parents work late

- If Mom is working the late shift, Dad can put together a picnic and then take the kids to meet Mom for a quick dinner in the office conference room. A rotisserie chicken, some whole-grain rolls, some baby carrots with dip, and a few fresh strawberries make a quick, nutritious meal you can gather at the grocery store in less time than it takes to go through the drive-thru.
- Evaluate. Do you *really* have to work late, or can you put something in your briefcase or on your flash drive and finish at home? Is it an option for you to commute home long enough to have dinner and return to work later?
- Jill lives and dies by her slow cooker. She has a list of a dozen favorite meals that can all be dumped in the crockpot at 8:00 AM and forgotten until dinnertime. All she has to add is a serving of bread or a vegetable, so dinner can be on the table five minutes after she walks in the door.
- There is no rule that says family mealtime has to fall between 5:00 and 6:00. Provide a light dinner, like a bowl of soup or a grilled cheese sandwich when the children are hungry. Later, when Dad gets home, get together for a late-evening salad or a light dessert.
- There is also no rule that you have to eat when you're at the dinner table. Maybe you'll just want to take ten minutes to gather around the dinner table and share the events of the day even though dinner has been cleaned up and the dishwasher started two hours ago.
- Make yourself a simple chart on an index card or an adhesive note. Stick it to the refrigerator. Make an X in the box every time you have a "family meal"—or any time your family members sit down together and connect with one another. That act alone will increase the number of meals you have together in a week. It will give you a reason to think about doing better.

Monday	Tuesday	Wednesday	Thursday	Friday	Saturday	Sunday

Family members are too busy

- Laurie has a large family with children whose variety of interests often takes them away from the home at mealtime. Each Sunday, the family holds a brief family council. For part of the meeting, they look at the calendar and decide what hour of the day *most* of the family members can meet for a meal. Once mealtime is agreed upon, family members are expected to arrange their schedules and be home for dinner. On Monday nights, there is a "no tolerance policy." Family members are expected to be home. During the rest of the week, Laurie is more lenient. When a teenaged recently son requested permission to stay at a friend's house, Laurie was surprised when he agreed to come home for dinner, as long as he could have permission to return to his friend's house afterward.

- If a consistent mealtime is not possible, use your family planning hour to schedule the time when the most family members can be available, even if it is a different time every day of the week. Next, using printable magnetic sheets purchased at any office supply store, make your own refrigerator magnets with the dinner hour printed in appropriate increments: "Dinner is served at 5:00," "Dinner is served at 5:30," and so forth. Stick the appropriate magnet to the refrigerator every morning so family members will remember the appointed dinner hour.

- Tina meets with a friend once a month, and they work together to prepare at least fifteen freezable meals. On busy afternoons that are filled with volleyball practice, cello lessons, or PTA volunteer projects, Tina can put a hot meal on the table even when she hasn't been home all day.

- Gleneen always doubles a recipe when she's cooking. One dish goes on the table for dinner; the other goes into the freezer for a busy night later in the month.

- Simplify dinner prep time. Try making breakfast for supper. Throw together an omelet topped with sautéed vegetables and melted cheese or a frozen waffle topped with yogurt, fresh fruit, and chopped nuts.
- Create your own "Fabulous Five" meals that can be prepared entirely from ingredients you keep on hand at all times. These are meals that can be prepared with minimum effort. On any given day, when life comes at you so fast you don't have time for the meal you planned, you can choose one of the "Fabulous Five" and put a meal on the table in minutes. Teach your children and spouse to make all five, and you'll have additional "chefs" onhand who can put the meal together in a pinch. (See recipes for my family's "Fabulous Five" at the end of this chapter.)

Family members with conflicting schedules

- Michelle is "religious" about three things: She creates a dinner menu for the week every Sunday afternoon. She does her grocery shopping every Tuesday. She puts place mats and plates on the table every night. She has observed that there's something about the routine of setting the table consistently (even if dinner isn't started) that encourages the family to take dinner seriously. Because her meals are planned in advance and everything she needs to prepare them is in the house, making dinner never takes more than thirty minutes.
- Do some painful evaluation: What is keeping your family away from home at mealtime? Can some of the conflicts be eliminated? Dee and Terri had a young daughter who was developing into a fine competitive swimmer. Unfortunately, practices were scheduled from 5:00 to 7:00 PM daily, which would take both a daughter and a mother out of their home at a crucial time every evening. It became clear that the family would either have to give up its dream of family meals together or its goal of supporting each child's individual talents. In

this case, they chose the family time, while encouraging other rewarding activities for their daughter.

- Make *breakfast* the most important meal of the day. There aren't nearly as many distractions for your family at 6:30 AM as there are at 6:30 PM. Terri offers at least one serving of fresh fruit every morning so that her kids can get a jump start on their daily five servings of fruits and vegetables. "When I take the time to have the fruit prepared and cut up, they always eat it, but I know they would go without otherwise," she says.

- You're late coming home from piano lessons, and everyone is hungry. Is there an alternative to the drive-thru? Here's my family's favorite option: Beginning at the entrance of your favorite grocery store, give each of your children a budget and a five-minute time limit. Assign each child to find something from a specific food group that can be prepared easily at home. One family member could be responsible to select the bread item for the meal. Another could have the responsibility to purchase a vegetable. Mom or Dad can supervise the main dish (something that can be prepared in fifteen minutes or less but that has significant nutritional value). Don't forget to assign someone to find a light dessert.

Playing with your food: Games for the dinner table

Now that you've decided to get serious about having meals together, the second part of the task is to get *less serious* about what you do once you're gathered around the table. Once you've tackled the task of gathering your family for a meal, teach them that the dinner table is a light-hearted, welcoming place. "We work really hard to keep any issues that may be inflammatory or contention-causing away from the table," asserts Terri. Make it a point to reserve arguments, unfriendly debates, and criticism for another forum. Ban cell phones and the newspaper. Turning on the television should not even be a consideration. Turn on the telephone answering machine and ignore the doorbell. This is priceless family time. Learn to eliminate the interruptions.

You can also make the table a fun place to be by looking for games that can be played as the family is gathered. These suggestions are a bonus, of course. The best part of the family meal conversation is that it doesn't have to be structured, but once in a while, a good game might set the tone for a happier meal. Use games as a method for gathering the family and keeping them busy while the cook is putting the finishing touches on meal preparation. Use them to keep children entertained while they're waiting politely at a favorite restaurant, or use them as an excuse to keep everyone together just a little longer at the end of the meal.

Games to encourage conversation

How was your day?

Decide who will go first. Then ask the classic table question, "How was your day?" The first person begins with one sentence about their day. The game moves around the table with each person adding a sentence to the story. How silly will your story get? How many times around the table can you go? Does the ending of your story sound anything like the way the day actually went?

Ylimaf gnilleps

Have a backwards spelling contest. Choose the name of one of the dishes being served and challenge any family member to spell it backwards. Do you prefer SADALIHCNE or FAOLTAEM for dinner? Feel free to make it a rule that you have to ask for any item by its backwards name for the rest of the meal: "Please pass the RETTUB." You can practice spelling words from school the same way.

Under glass

Are you lucky enough to have a tabletop covered with glass? If so, you can put a map of the world under the glass and have some great conversations about places you would like to travel. With a set of dry erase markers near the table, you can play hangman, draw pictures blindfolded, or write scrambled words for your children to unscramble.

Super-charge your dinner conversation

What do you think the answer will be if you ask this question at your dinner table next time Grandma and Grandpa come to visit? "Recall an instance when you have been surprised by the persistence of nature—a sprout of growth after a devastating frost. Share how you have witnessed firsthand the earth's resilience."

Do you feel a story coming on? Inspired by Earth Day and all of the good food that comes to us from the earth, Douglas Love, noted playwright and children's theater aficionado, created dinner table game cards aimed at helping families reinvent dinner table conversation.

"I've designed the cards to spark imagination, memories, and laughter," says Love. "We hope families will incorporate the cards into their meal to inspire connections they might not otherwise have made." This beautiful and economically priced set of cards is available for purchase, or you can download eight sample Earth Dinner™ Creativity Cards at www.earthdinner.org to help inspire you as you create your own questions for dinner table conversation.

"Blue plate special"

Keep a blue plate (or any special plate that is different from those usually used during the meal). Mom or Dad can recognize a child's special achievements by allowing them to eat from the honorary plate.

"Chews" wisely

Have everyone count how many times they chew one bite of food (make sure everyone is chewing the same item—a bite of steak, a morsel of bread, a forkful of salad). Now take turns guessing who chewed the most and who chewed the least. Try a few rounds with different foods on your plate.

Learn table manners from around the world

Etiquette is all about learning to make other people comfortable around you, so the reason you want to teach your children good table manners is not so much a matter of keeping them from embarrassing themselves as it is a matter of helping them understand how to put other people at ease. The rules are different for different parts of the world, of course. Did you know that in some countries, it is proper to burp loudly after the meal; that in Spain, it is appropriate to throw your garbage on the floor after a deli meal; or that in China, it is rude to clean all of the food off your plate? Use the Internet and find out about table manners from around the world. Then serve a meal of Japanese dishes and see who can slurp their noodles the loudest (it's good manners in Japan, honest).

Take a fun online world etiquette course at www.fekids.com/kln/flash/DontGrossOutTheWorld.swf

Table games just for fun

Designer table setting

Does the fork *always* go on the left side of the plate? Have a creative table-setting contest, allowing each family member to set the table exactly as they choose—each on a different night of the week. The winner gets one evening off from helping with the dishes. Set the plates on top of the cups. Fold the napkins into origami shapes. Choose a theme such as football, a foreign country, or a particular color, and create an appropriate centerpiece. During "designer table setting week," there are no rules except that the family must be able to eat in spite of the results. In other words, go ahead and arrange the plates and utensils into an elaborate sculpture of a robot in the center of the table. Just be prepared to see your masterpiece disassembled when it's time to serve the entrée.

Psychic silverware

You'll need a mother (or other dinner guest) who is in on the game for this one. First, tell your children that you have discovered that their mother (or dinner guest) has psychic powers. Ask your cohort to leave the room and then ask one of your children to choose a number between one and ten and whisper it quietly so that everyone at the table (but not the "psychic" who has left the room) can hear. Call your partner back into the room, and then ask everyone in the family to pass you all of their clean silverware. You'll need at least ten knives, forks, or spoons. Proceed to arrange them carefully in any design you choose on top of the table. Then call the psychic back into the room. The psychic will look at the arrangement of the silverware, guess the mystery number, and amaze everyone! You can keep this up for days before your children figure out the trick.

Here's the trick: Imagine your child has chosen the number 7. When your "psychic" re-enters the room, you will briefly rest seven of your fingers on the edge of the table—long enough for the psychic to see but not long enough for your children to notice. (If you have especially observant children, you can also rest your fingers on the table *after* you have arranged the silverware—the careful arrangement of the silverware is only a visual distraction, so make it look like there is some pattern involved by carefully crossing the silverware at a variety of angles and in several different patterns).

Head of the table

Any child who can identify something extraordinary he or she has done that day can appeal for the privilege of sitting at the head of the table. Only the person who normally sits at the head of the table gets to decide if the experience is worthy of special recognition. If it is, the head of the table can pick up his plate and switch places.

Celebrate the occasion

Make any meal special by choosing a theme. Serve fajitas and sangria for Cinco de Mayo (May 5). Serve only green foods for St. Patrick's Day (wait until they see you're serving milk with green food coloring in it!) Celebrate Backwards Day and serve dessert first. Enjoy a special breakfast on the patio for Father's Day. Create a special birthday tradition like stuffed French toast for breakfast every time someone turns one year older (don't forget the candles—stick them right in the French toast).

Three of a kind

The person at the head of the table names a category such as kinds of fruit or wives of Henry VIII or capital cities in Asian countries. He challenges the player to his immediate left to think of three of a kind. Play continues with each player around the table choosing the category for the individual on their left.

Slammers and creepers

Here's a game you can use to pass the time while you're waiting for the rolls to finish browning. Half of the family sits on one side of the table (Team 1), and half on the other side (Team 2). The players on Team 1 pass a nickel secretly beneath the table to any member of their team. The players on Team 2 yell "SLAMMERS!" or "CREEPERS!" If they called "Slammers," members of Team 1 bring their hands up and slam them, palms down, on the table. If they called "Creepers," members of Team 1 place their closed fists palm down on the table and slowly open their hands, trying to keep the nickel out of sight.

Team 2 begins choosing hands that are NOT holding the nickel. These empty hands are eliminated. Team 2 gets one point for each hand they eliminate. When they uncover the nickel, that turn ends, and the nickel goes to the opposite side of the table.

This is a fork, this is a spoon

You probably played this classic at a family reunion sometime in your life. The head of the table hands a fork to the person on his left and says,

Head of the table: This is a fork.
The person on the left (dinner guest #1) responds: A what?
Head of the table: A fork.
Dinner guest #1 (turning to the person on her left): This is a fork.
Dinner guest #2: A what?
Dinner guest #1 (turning to the head of the table): A what?
Head of the table: A fork.
Dinner guest #1 (turning to the person on her left): A fork.
Dinner guest #2 (turning to dinner guest #3): This is a fork.
Dinner guest #3: A what?

Play continues around the table. Once you have that mastered, start a fork moving clockwise around the table and a spoon in the opposite direction.

Games to entertain you while you're waiting at the restaurant

Napkin tearing

Give each family member a paper napkin and have each put their napkins behind their back and tear the napkin into the shape of a Christmas tree (or a rabbit, a flower, or anything else). Display your handiwork for everyone else at the table to see.

Table art

Give everyone a piece of paper and a crayon and challenge them to put their paper on top of their head and while holding the paper there, draw a snowman. (Or choose a subject more suited to the season.) This one is great if you're stuck waiting in a restaurant and you have access to a few paper napkins and some of the crayons they hand out with the kiddie menus.

I went to Zimbabwe

Build your memory skills *and* pass the time by playing "I went to Zimbabwe" while you're waiting for your meal. The first family member says, "I went to Zimbabwe and in my bag I packed a carrot." The next player says, "I went to Zimbabwe and in my bag I packed a carrot and a bicycle tire." Each family member must repeat the entire list from memory (in the correct order) before adding his own item to the list. To simplify the game, you could require that items be listed in alphabetical order (an *a*lligator, a *b*arber pole, a *c*ucumber, and so forth).

Are Meals really that important?

Essayist Bonny Wolf has observed,

> The dinner table is where children are civilized, at least in theory. They learn not to talk with their mouths full, to say "please" and "thank you," and to keep their elbows off the table. A friend says she and her husband have dinner with their two young sons almost every night. When everyone's seated, Will, a second-grader, says, "So how was your day, Mom?" Their dinner conversations have covered everything from what happened on the playground to a discussion on the finer points of Star Wars and the Senate filibuster.
>
> What these kids get (along with their pot roast and mashed potatoes) is a serving of safety, stability and a sense of belonging.[2]

Beyond the nutritional benefits of family meals (and there are many), beyond the preparation for adulthood, the most important purpose for family meals seems to be the opportunity to forge connections.

Recently, my oldest son was preparing to leave home for the first time. His education during this next phase of his life was to take him to a country halfway around the world for an extended period of time. Early in the afternoon, I found a small specialty shop that sold cuisine from the country where he would be living, and for dinner that night, I served some of the unfamiliar vegetables and the aromatic and spicy dishes that we had never tasted but which would become standard fare for him. It was a celebration, but the mood was somber. I think all of us realized that it would be a very long time before we would have the opportunity to gather our entire family together for a meal again. There was something urgent about that last celebration together, and we lingered for a long time after the meal was over. It was one of the great blessings of my tenure as a parent to be able to look across the table with no regrets—to know that each of us will have a few memories of hot dinner rolls, a warm bowl of soup, and conversation with people who cared about us.

That is the essence of family dinner—conversation, warmth, constancy. The rest is gravy.

Reader's Homework

Based on what you have read in this chapter, what ONE idea for playing with children appeals to you most as something that you could feasibly do in your own home? (This can be an idea you read about in the book, an idea of your own that came to you as you were reading, or something you remember experiencing as a child).

Write your ONE idea here:

_____

_____

If you'd like, record this idea in the "Gallery of Ideas to Try" at the end of the book.

Notes

1. The National Center on Addiction and Substance Abuse
2. Wolf, "Commentary: Value of family meals together."

The Fabulous Five
Five simple meals you can keep on hand to prepare in a pinch

Taco Soup

1 pound ground beef (brown and freeze ahead)
1 onion, chopped (or use ¼ cup dried minced)
1 pkg. taco seasoning
1 can stewed tomatoes, undrained
2 cups water
1 can tomato sauce
1 can corn, undrained
1 can kidney beans, undrained
Optional toppings: tortilla chips, sour cream, grated cheddar cheese

1. In large saucepan, cook the ground beef and the onion; then drain off the grease.
2. Stir the taco seasoning into the meat. Mix in the remaining ingredients except the toppings. Bring the soup to a boil, reduce the heat, cover, and simmer for 15 min.
3. Top each serving of soup with tortilla chips, a dollop of sour cream, and grated cheese.

Updated Fetuccini Carbonara

All of the ingredients for this dish are "storable." Just keep some peas, a small container of cream cheese, some ham strips, and a little Parmesan cheese in the freezer and rotate them as often as possible)

8 oz. fettuccini, uncooked
1 cup frozen peas
¼ cup cream cheese
¼ cup light (reduced fat) Caesar dressing
1 Tbsp. flour

1 cup fat free milk
1 pkg. smoked ham, cut into short strips
¼ c. chopped fresh parsley (opt.)
3 Tbsp. 100% grated Parmesan cheese

Cook pasta as directed, adding peas to the water for the last 3 min. of the cooking time. Meanwhile, beat cream cheese, dressing, and flour in a small saucepan with wire whisk until well blended. Gradually add milk, stirring constantly until mixture is well blended. Add ham; simmer until heated through. Drain noodles and peas and toss with sauce. Continue to cook until heated through (2-3 min). Sprinkle with Parmesan cheese and parsley. Makes 4 servings.

Pineapple Chicken

(Serve with a slice of pineapple—fresh or canned.)

1 cup water, include liquid from canned chicken
1 c. ketchup
1/3 c. sugar
¼ t. onion powder
¼ t. garlic powder
½ t. lemon juice
1 Tbsp. soy sauce
¼ c. water
3 Tbsp. cornstarch
1 20-oz. can pineapple chunks, drained (reserve ¾ c. juice)
1 10-oz. can chicken chunks

In medium saucepan, combine first seven ingredients and reserved ¾ cup pineapple juice. Bring to boil. Remove from heat. Stir cornstarch into ¼ c. water until there are no lumps. Stir into hot pineapple sauce. Return to heat and bring to boil, stirring constantly. Stir in pineapple and chicken. Heat to boiling. Reduce heat, cover, and simmer 5 min. Serve over hot cooked rice. Serves 5-6. (Note: Any cut up raw vegetables can be added at the beginning. Simmer sauce and veggies 10–15 min. before thickening.)

Meatball Sandwiches

prepared meatballs (or make and freeze your own)

1 bottle of your favorite spaghetti sauce

shredded mozzarella cheese (shredded cheese keeps well in the
   freezer)

deli buns (keep a package of sturdy, whole-wheat buns in the freezer
   and rotate them regularly)

Heat meatballs and barbecue sauce in slow cooker (low for 2–3 hrs.)
or warm them in a saucepan. Serve over toasted buns, topped with cheese
and any variety of chopped sandwich vegetables (pickles, shredded carrot,
olives, onions, and so forth.)

Navajo Tacos

(Serve with a glass of Orange Julius or a quick fruit smoothie for a
complete meal.)

1 can chili

frozen rolls (2-3 thawed rolls patted together into a round
   disk and fried like a scone are a quick substitute for traditional fry bread)

shredded cheese

salsa

canned olives

any fresh vegetables you happen to have on hand—chopped
   green onion, tomatoes, and lettuce are all good choices

Fry the scones in hot oil. Warm the chili and place ½ cup of chili
on top of each fry bread scone. Top with cheese, chopped olives, and
vegetables.

Quick OraNge Julius

2 cups crushed ice (10–12 ice cubes)
1 cup milk
1 cup water
¼ cup sugar
¼ cup orange flavored powdered drink mix (or substitute 6 oz. frozen
    orange juice concentrate)
1 tsp. vanilla extract

Place ingredients in a blender and blend until smooth. To turn this recipe into a fruit smoothie, substitute 1 cup of any flavor yogurt for the milk. Next, throw in any fresh, frozen, or canned fruit you have on hand and blend until smooth.

Chapter 5

Turning Work into Play

Ideas for having fun while you work together

• •

One of the Jensen family farm's major cash crops during the Depression was several acres of sugar beets, which had to be thinned every spring. Hattie, my great-grandmother, would take a hoe out to the fields, and as she "blocked" the beets, several children would follow behind, thinning unnecessary seedlings out of the row of plants so that the remaining beets would have space to grow. Hattie would tell stories as she worked: how her grandmother dealt with a chicken-stealing Indian; how their father had once encountered a rattlesnake, and being afraid to move, had lain down in the dirt until the snake had crawled across his chest and out of sight; how she had survived a diphtheria epidemic that had taken her sister's life. It was the only "whip" she ever used. If her children wanted to be able to hear the stories, they had to thin their row fast enough to keep within hearing distance.

Hattie knew what wise parents still understand. Working together is a singularly effective way to teach a child much of what he needs to know to succeed in the world, and a parent who is willing to shift the focus of work from "getting the job done" to "building a relationship" can find hundreds of ways to make work enjoyable.

As I have interviewed adults and asked them to recall their most vivid memory of playing with an adult, about 20 percent of the time, I find someone who cannot recall a single moment when they played with a parent. "I only remember working with my parents," they will say. And often, there is consternation in their tone of voice and you can see the wrinkles appear in their foreheads: "Wow! I'd never thought about that before. Didn't we *ever* have fun?" And then after thinking about it for a few minutes, they realize that they did not have deprived childhoods after all. While their parents' struggle to make ends meet meant that parent-child recreational opportunities occurred infrequently, these parents did bless their children with something equally as important: They allowed their children to *work alongside of them.*

Interestingly, the adults who tell me their parents never played with them, but *did* work with them, are some of the most successful, well-adjusted adults I know. As a rule, the children of parents who worked hard to survive are not generally workaholics themselves, but they *are* individuals who have a penchant for playing hard. It is as if they want to squeeze all of their "lost" childhood into the few years they have left. They tax their muscles, their knee joints, and their schedules with a string of canoe trips with their children, water skiing adventures, and hiking in the backcountry. And when they are not playing, they are successful attorneys, writers, business owners, educators, appliance repairmen, and accountants. They are adults I admire, because along with a strong work ethic, they appreciate the value of leisure. They have found the balance that eluded their parents who were struggling to put the next meal on the table. I have yet to find any of them who are not vocally grateful for parents who taught them the value of work. And I have yet to find any of them who do not also appreciate the value of play.

Let me make a clarification. I expect that a workaholic parent who is an absentee parent does not garner the same kind of admiration. The children who valued their parents' work ethic were almost exclusively children who were allowed to work alongside their parents. Somehow, in spite of the long workdays expected of them, these parents were able to demonstrate, by example, the benefits of labor, and by their presence, the fact that a relationship was as important as making a living. They managed to send the message, "You are important to me."

Ours is no longer the agricultural society that lent itself to the probability that children and parents would work shoulder-to-shoulder nearly every day. Many of us are able to provide for our children's needs without the requirement that they share some of the labor burden. Consequently, we fight one of two opposing battles: Either our children are growing up in affluent homes where work is neither needed nor expected, or they are growing up in less-affluent homes where they are unsupervised and spend too much of their time sitting in front of the television or the computer. Many of us are concerned that children of this generation are growing up learning that it is perfectly acceptable to put forth minimal effort. Is it dangerous to focus so heavily on play when so much of what our children do already revolves around entertaining themselves?

While I believe strongly that children need to learn to work, I also believe that work does not always have to be onerous and tedious. It is a lesson I learned slowly. Not more than a year ago, after another evening of listening to me give my children a lecture about "learning to use your time constructively," my husband pulled me aside and shared a simple truth with me: *There is a difference between leisure and laziness.* At first, I could not comprehend what he meant. He referred me to a quote by a university professor by the name of Karen Lynn:

> Idleness puts us in a passive role, whereas leisure usually calls on us to participate mentally or physically or creatively; idleness merely passes time, whereas leisure fills personal needs; idleness occupies us, but leisure renews us; we put the responsibility for filling our idle time on something outside ourselves, whereas we look within ourselves for our leisure. Of course, these distinctions are ultimately private ones; one person may watch football or read novels only in order to numb the mind and extinguish an afternoon, whereas someone else's approach to football-watching or novel-reading may demand such alertness, such appreciation, that it is the highest kind of leisure.[1]

One of our duties as parents is to figure out ways to help our children learn to create opportunities to participate in mentally engaging, physically demanding activities. One way to do this is to help them learn to turn work into a form of recreation—an opportunity to become engrossed in a complicated task. Why is this so important? Because "being absolutely absorbed in a challenging activity" is what makes a human being happiest.[2] For young children, this is simple, because work is not a passive activity to them. It *can be* absorbing and challenging, and therefore, it *can be* fun. Let me explain it another way:

Work can be playful for a child. Can you recall watching an adult perform one of these tasks when you were young and wishing you could be allowed to play too?

- Misting the houseplants with a squirt bottle
- Driving the riding lawnmower
- Playing in the soapsuds in the kitchen sink
- Spraying furniture polish on the piano
- Hosing down the car
- Painting a wall in the basement
- Ironing a shirt
- Picking the strawberries from the garden
- Typing, stapling, licking envelopes, and sticking stamps
- Running junk mail through the paper shredder
- Baking brownies, putting frozen fruit into the blender, or kneading bread dough
- Cleaning windows with a squeegee
- Polishing the silver
- Running a power drill
- Pouring the detergent and fabric softener into the washing machine
- Pruning the rosebushes
- Emptying the lint out of the dryer vent
- Climbing on the roof to hose leaves out of the rain gutters

Adult work is intriguing and interesting to children. Toy manufacturers turn this simple truth into high profits. You can buy everything from miniature ovens powered by light bulbs to lawnmowers that growl and spurt bubbles for exhaust. Children recognize adult work for what it is: an opportunity to have fun.

In his book *The Mystery of Children*, Mike Mason identifies the contrast between working adults and working children: "Adults largely avoid working with children because children have an unnerving habit of turning work into play. This drives adults crazy because we tend to be so goal-oriented." It is irritating to send a child to clean his bedroom only to find him playing with blocks he was supposed to be picking up. If you have ever tried to wash a car with a fourteen-year-old son, you know how infuriating it is when he keeps trying to start a water fight. For adults, work is about results. That is why an adult can shower in four minutes flat and it can take a five-year-old a full hour to finish his bath.

Here's a hint: One of the first rules for turning work into play is to relax about the outcome and enjoy the journey more. That means when you are vacuuming a room, you worry less about whether the vacuum leaves parallel lines in the carpet and more about how to convince your toddler that you are locked in a battle to restrain a howling, gobbling monster that devours interlocking blocks, green army men, and other toys left on the floor in the living room. It means being satisfied that the top half of the full-length mirror is sparkling and leaving the pucker marks on the bottom half where the two-year-old left evidence that she had been kissing her own reflection again. Another delightful way to enjoy the journey more is to be willing to learn from our children, who can show us that work can be accomplished *almost* as efficiently but with a lot less negative mental exertion if you are willing to exercise your imagination.

Work can feel like play if you are willing to use your imagination

I first became acquainted with adults who understand how to turn work into play when I was introduced to Mrs. Piggle Wiggle in the second grade. If you were lucky enough to have a second grade teacher who read aloud in class, you will likely know that Mrs. Piggle Wiggle lives in an upside-down house, and children from all over the neighborhood are encouraged to come and dig in her backyard for buried treasure or bake sugar cookies and spill the crumbs. Mrs. Piggle Wiggle does not do dishes simply to make the cups and saucers clean. Instead, she shows the children who visit her that doing dishes is exciting if you pretend that you have been captured by a witch and the only chance of escaping her clutches is to wash every single dish and have the entire kitchen sparkling before the clock strikes. In addition, beds must be made without a single wrinkle, because if they are not, the Cruel Queen, who inspects the bedding every morning, will have the victim thrown in the dungeon.

I am a poor pretender, so when I was a young mother, my imagination did not extend beyond "I'll race you to see who can pick up all of the yellow blocks faster." I never considered exerting my mental capacities to see if my creativity could extend to something as mundane as loading the dishwasher or getting the lawn mowed. I envy some of the parents I have spoken with who caught on to the idea of playworking soon enough to teach their children that work does not always have to feel like drudgery. Here are some of their ideas:

Feed the animals

For younger kids, it can be fun to mimic an animal (or watch Mom or Dad mimic an animal) as you are cleaning up. Pick up your toys and stuff them into a kangaroo pouch (pull the front of Dad's T-shirt into a pouch and toss the toys in, or tie a pillowcase loosely around your child's neck, fill it with dirty laundry, and then hop to it and put things away). If Mom needs to dust the tops of the doorframes or catch the cobwebs hanging from the ceiling, she can become a giraffe by inviting a dustcloth-wielding child to ride on her shoulders so they can reach the cobwebs together. Legos and small building toys could be sucked up into one of your sleeves if you were an anteater.

Go fishing

Gather up all of the laundry into one huge pile in the middle of the room. Tell your child it is time to "go fishing," and first you are going to fish for dirty sock fish. Once your child has retrieved all of the dirty socks and tossed them in a pile, he can go fishing for all of the dark-colored fish or all of the light-colored fish. Sorting laundry is never more fun.

Stage your own show

Show your teenaged son how to mimic the old furniture polish commercials by spraying just half of the piano bench and polishing it, then comparing the difference between the "just polished" side and the "unpolished" side of the bench for an invisible audience. Older kids might also get a kick out of pretending that they are demonstrating a new line of bathroom chemicals as they show their studio audience how well this product powers through soap scum and that one leaves the faucets sparkling.

Ant hill

Catherine and her children created a game called Ant Hill to help them clean up clutter quickly. They each pretended they were hungry ants gathering food to store inside the ant hill for the winter. Every building block, stuffed animal, and wind-up toy had to be gathered into the toybox before bedtime.

Searchlight

This one is fun right before bedtime. Dad turns out the bedroom lights and then stations himself at the foot of his child's bed. One at a time, he shines a "searchlight" (flashlight) on a grenade that is about to explode (a toy, a dirty article of clothing, and so forth). The bomb squad must race to put the item away before ten seconds tick off the clock and everything goes kablooey!

Maid service

Tell your teenaged daughter that for today, you are running the housekeeping service for a five-star cruise line, so for practice, you are going to trade rooms. While you perform "maid service" in her quarters, she will swap you and clean the master bathroom. Don't forget to leave a mint on the pillow. Pretty soon, she'll catch on and start folding the ends of the toilet tissue into a triangle.

Mom and Dad, you can do this. The next time you come home to soda spilled on the kitchen floor and pizza crusts caught between the couch cushions, how will you solve the problem without making everyone in the house wish you had just stayed at the office?

How would you clean a room if:

- You were a famous detective and your children were bloodhounds?
- You were a street sweeper and your child were a broom?
- Items had to be put away in the order of the colors of the rainbow (red, orange, yellow, and so forth)?

If that isn't working for you, try applying your creativity to a specific task. What is there about the task that you can turn into a recreational activity?

- How would you sweep the garage if two brooms and a hockey puck were involved?
- How much faster would you get the weeds pulled out of the flowerbed if your child earns a nickel for every weed he pulls and then shoots it into a bucket from ten feet away? What if he loses a nickel for every weed *you* shoot in successfully?
- How would you get the interior of the car cleaned and vacuumed if you were mimicking a pit crew at the Indy 500?

- Would making dinner be more fun if everyone was invited into the kitchen to help and you all had to speak in French accents?

The next time you are faced with an onerous task, try applying your imagination before you apply the elbow grease.

Work caN feel like play if there is someone to play with you

Our ancestors understood this concept well. That is why the annals of the Wild West tell of quilting bees, barn raisings, and hunting expeditions. Difficult work is just more fun when there are others to share the task, and usually, it gets done faster. That is why it is almost *always* more effective to say, "If you'll mow the lawn, I'll trim the edges, and then we'll play a game of HORSE," than it is to say, "If the lawn isn't mowed by the time I get home, you'll be grounded."

One of the chores I dread is folding the socks. There are several feet in my household, and washing socks, as my grandmother would say, is like stringing beads without tying a knot in the end of the string. Early on, I learned that one of the reasons sock folding is such a pain is that socks are exponentially unmatchable. The more colors, sizes, and patterns of socks there are in the laundry bin, the more likely it is that the mate will be missing, and therefore, the more tedious it is to match them. I simplified this problem by purchasing predominantly white socks. After a year or two, I got even wiser and started buying each child a specific brand of socks. This way, the socks with the logo on the ankle always belong to one son. The socks with the grey toes always belong to another. But I still hated folding socks. One evening, when all of my family members happened to be gathered together in the family room, I gave each of them a lapful of socks and then told them that on the count of five, they could separate their own socks from the pile and then throw the remaining socks across the room to their rightful owners. The only rule was that you were to avoid throwing a sock at anyone else's head. Within three minutes, and after a lot of giggling, each of us had a lapful of our own stockings, which took less than a minute to match up and put away.

Kitchen work is also a great group activity. One family I heard of instigated the "Ten Minutes." This is much like the ten commandments in that failure to abide by the "Ten Minutes" exacts a serious penalty. The "Ten Minutes" simply mean that every member of the family who gets the privilege of eating dinner also earns the privilege of spending ten minutes to help clean it up. There are no exceptions, and avoiding your "ten minutes" means that you clean the kitchen alone the next night.

The signal to begin work is when Dad steps into the kitchen, and taking a damp washcloth from the sink, yells to one of the children, "High or low, fast or slow." That child knows that it will be his job to catch the dishcloth and wipe the dining room table. He can then decide whether he wants his pitch to come in low and fast or high and fast, or low and slow. This simple game signals to everyone that the "Ten Minutes" are about to begin.

We will not always have time to work side-by-side with our children, but doesn't it make sense to have good experiences when we do? As I interviewed teens about the times they found it easiest to communicate with and connect with their parents, a surprising number of them identified times when they were working together.

Work can become play if you have the right soundtrack in the stereo

Every website and parenting book you read about teaching a child to work recommends putting on some good, fast music while you clean. Polka music is loud and fast, and so is Fatboy Slim, but if you make me listen to Fatboy Slim while I work, I am likely to want to slit my wrists before the dusting is finished. Ditto for any fourteen-year-old and polka music. In order to keep the peace, just look for music that has a BPM (beats per minute) of 120–140. Then create a CD full of favorites both you and your children can agree on. Here are five titles to get you started, but your best bet may be to ask your teenager to plug his personal mp3 device into a set of speakers and share some of his favorites.

- "Zydeco Boogaloo" (Buckwheat Zydeco)
- "Blue Mountain Hop" (Bela Fleck)
- "Symphony No. 40 in G minor, K550: I Molto Allegro" (Mozart)
- "A Little Less Conversation" (Elvis Presley)

- "Orange Blossom Special" (Various artists—try Johnson Mountain Boys)

Leave time for play by giving work a time limit

In the Lee household, the first half of the day on most Saturdays is reserved for deep cleaning. Everyone takes part, and in the event of scheduling conflicts, children are allowed to finish their work in advance *before* Saturday. But it is also understood that as soon as the work is complete, the whole family will take the second half of the day to play together, even if the activity is as simple as going for an afternoon of flying kites. The Lees are satisfied that they are teaching good work ethic by showing their children that work comes before play, but that when you work together, there is always time for both. Here are a few more ideas that demonstrate how to make work "doable" by making it playful and giving it a time limit:

We are going to work for thirty seconds and that is all … (sort of)

Make a list of thirty-second jobs that can be done around the house. Then write each job on a craft stick. Beginning at a central starting point, allow your children to take turns pulling one craft stick from a can and then racing to see if the job can be completed before the thirty-second timer rings. Set a limit for the number of thirty-second jobs each child must complete, or contain your game to a single room, and keep pulling sticks until the room is spotless:

- Clean a mirror.
- Empty one trash can.
- Dust the top of the piano.
- Empty the silverware compartment in the dishwasher.
- Wipe off the front of one appliance.
- Change the towels in the bathroom.
- Put on a new roll of toilet paper.
- Refill the soap dispenser with liquid soap.
- Pick up ten things and throw them in a basket.
- Clean one side of the kitchen sink.

- Wipe up a spill on the counter.
- Shake out a rug.
- Water a plant.
- Clear one place setting from the dining room table.
- Refill the salt or pepper shaker.
- Wipe off the table.
- Dust two picture frames.
- Stack up magazines or newspapers.
- Fold a throw or a blanket.
- Wipe off the piano keys.
- Swab out the inside of a toilet.
- Clean the bathroom sink.
- Put all of the dirty laundry from your bedroom floor into a laundry basket.
- Hang up an outfit.
- Wipe all of the fingerprints off all of the light switches.
- Sweep the porch.
- Clean the inside of the car windshield.
- Dust the dashboard.
- Empty the dryer vent.
- Gather up empty hangers from a closet and take them to the laundry room.
- Wipe down a doorframe.
- Fill a pet's food dish.
- Bring in the mail or the newspaper.

Tack-on chores

When children are learning to be responsible, sometimes it is easier if you break the task into smaller steps. For example, if you want a four-year-old to learn to set the table, begin by showing him how to fold a paper napkin and place it underneath the fork at each plate. The next week, let him be in charge of counting out all of the plates *and* putting a napkin and fork at each place. A week later, he'll be able to learn where to put the cups above the plates. As you break the task into doable steps, you'll give him the confidence he needs to learn to do the job right every time.

Tack-on chores work for more complex tasks as well. If you want a child to learn to do her own laundry, start by expecting her to bring her own clothing to the laundry room and sort it. Do this every week for a month. Provide a bin for dark-colored clothes, one for light-colored clothes, one for jeans and towels (these can be easy to split into separate batches later), and one for dirty socks and things that need to be bleached. The next month, write the laundry instructions for each kind of clothing on a card and attach it to the front of the appropriate bin: "Dark colors: Wash and rinse in cold water with 1 cup detergent. White clothing: Wash in hot water with 1 cup detergent with bleach. Rinse in cold water." Oversee the washing until you are confident she knows how to check labels, close zippers, and empty pockets at the start of a batch.

Once sorting and washing are tackled, you can teach about drying, pre-treating, and folding clothing in easy, one-lesson segments. Before six months are up, both you and your child will be confident about her laundry abilities.

Work and then play

Amy is unswervingly consistent about two things: (1) Your bed must be made before you leave the house in the morning, and (2) you can play with friends as soon as your chores are done. There is no whining about playing before piano practice because her children always know what her answer will be: "After your chores are done." Her consistency makes it easy for her children to follow the rules, because the rules never change.

Since it's clear that sharing in household responsibilities is good for a child, is there a point when our children have to learn that work is sometimes just *work*, and it needs to be done whether it is fun or not? Probably so. I don't make time to turn every responsibility into a game, and I don't think any other parent should be expected to do so. But once in a while, it doesn't hurt to make work fun.

Notes

1. Lynn, *Ensign*, 40.
2. Kindlon, *Too Much of A Good Thing: Raising Children of Character in an Indulgent Age*, 48

Chapter 6

What Does the Research Say?

Helping parents understand why playing is critical to a
child's physical, social, emotional, and mental health

● ●

A child who has some free time to play and engage in child-driven
leisure pursuits with a parent (or other beloved adult) grows up
healthier, happier, and more intelligent than a child whose time
is rigidly scheduled into structured academic and physical activities.

This is not merely my opinion. It is an iron-clad, research-documented
fact. Playing with our children is one of our most powerful tools for helping them develop into healthy, empathetic, successful adults. While most
of us would agree that playing with children is important, we're not quite
as sure that it is vital to a child's social and emotional success. Is playing
with children just a really good idea, or does it somehow produce measur-
able, quantifiable improvements in a child's intellectual abilities, social
skills, or emotional health? Will a child whose parents are too busy to play
really be at a disadvantage? Can spontaneous, child-driven play possibly
teach our children as effectively as more structured learning experiences?

This chapter is for the "driven" father out there who would like to
go sleigh riding with his children but feels obligated to clean the garage
instead. It's for the mother who has become so busy with PTA meetings

and Cub Scout pack meetings and all of the good things that she's trying to accomplish for other people's children that she no longer has free time for her own. It's for the father who goes stir crazy sitting for two hours on a Sunday afternoon playing Monopoly™ with his children when he could be doing something that actually interests him—like reading the stock report. It's for the mother who feels obligated to sign her children up for athletic teams and music lessons and dance class and academic tutoring because failing to do so would deny her children the chance to reach their potential. This chapter is for all of us who shake our heads and say, "Playing is too simple. There has to be more to it than that."

The research on play is voluminous. Thousands of studies and thousands of child development specialists, child psychologists, and educators have been examining the question of the importance of playtime for decades, and as one group of researchers put it, "The data are incontrovertible. When children are in environments where learning is occurring in a meaningful context, where they have choices, and where they are encouraged to follow their interests, learning takes place best."[1]

The fact that a loving, supportive relationship with a parent is a requirement in order for a child to develop in normal, healthy ways is also essentially a given. Eminent psychologist Urie Bronfenbrenner may have said it best: "In order to develop normally, a child requires progressively more complex joint activity with one or more adults who have an irrational emotional relationship with the child. Somebody's got to be crazy about that kid. That's number one. First, last, and always."[2]

Most of our children's teachers understand the importance of playing with a mentoring adult. Our children's pediatricians know how vital it is. Psychologists and childcare professionals have all read the research. They know the consequences of eliminating play from a child's life, particularly child-driven, adult-assisted play. Somehow, though, they have not done a stellar job of getting the message to us—the parents. It would be easy to blame politicians who are driving the current educational system of "teaching to the test," but that would be an oversimplification. Perhaps the problem is that as parents, we have become too attuned to those who want to sell us the answers for making our children successful, and we no longer hear the messages that tell us we were doing just fine on our own.

I was interested when I received a postcard in the mail inviting me to enroll my children in a private school. The literature related a testimonial from a mother who observed that her son had made great progress in his preschool abilities. Looking out the window of their car one day, he noticed the rain outside and said, "Mom, there are lots of puddles of precipitation outside today." The mother concludes by saying how pleased she is that her son has learned about the water cycle. It is a great thing, she asserts, to have a child who not only knows how to use a big word but is also able to apply the concept to what he sees going on around him.

The message is motivating. As a parent, who would not like a child to learn about the water cycle? What parent would not want to raise a four-year-old precocious enough to understand how to accurately use the word *precipitation*?

That bright child, riding in the back of his mother's car, has been able to learn and apply a fact about the name for a puddle. And while this early learning about puddles is commendable, I am prone to ponder another question: *Has he ever been allowed to jump in one?* While he may not have learned to use the word *precipitation* if his mother had taken him puddle-jumping instead of taking him to a class about the water cycle, it is certain that he would have gained some equally valuable information about water: that it splashes, that it can be cold, that it turns dirt into mud, that earthworms drown in it.

It is time to remind parents that their role is vital. Our children need us, and to tell the truth, we can get an awful lot of joy ourselves simply by allowing ourselves the time to unwind and be with them. Play is a learning resource that we are allowing to disappear, to our own and society's detriment. A growing body of research shows us the ramifications of eliminating ourselves from our children's learning environments. These researchers are becoming vocal about reminding us of the importance of simple play. Here are some of the warnings they are beginning to sound:

- Children whose free time is overly structured are more prone to stress and suicidal tendencies. They tend to develop pathological perfectionism and anxiety.[3]
- Children who are prematurely pushed into regimented academic instruction display less creativity and enthusiasm for learning in later years.[4]
- Children whose parents overemphasize academic achievement without allowing a child time to "decompress" inadvertently teach that the goal is to get into the best school or the best job at all costs. Consequently, these children are often prone to cheating in order to receive superior grades.[5]

- Children who do not learn self-control, how to tolerate delay, and how to deal with boredom (all skills that are learned through play) are at greater risk for drug use.[6]

Maybe no one ever told you that when you were playing with Play-Doh, you were developing your fine motor skills. It's doubtful that when you played the board game Candyland for the first time, an adult pointed out that the purpose of the game was to help you develop your ability to distinguish colors and learn the mathematical concept of one-to-one correspondence. When your older brother taught you to build a block tower and then helped you build it again and again until you could make it stand by yourself, he probably made no comment about how well you were developing the quality of persistence. Certainly your favorite uncle never mentioned to you when you were learning to play catch that he was teaching you hand-eye coordination and simultaneously helping you learn to cope with frustration. No mother tucks a child in at night by reading a bedtime story and saying, "Darling, it's time for us to develop your vocabulary." And yet this is exactly what happens. The fact that we do not realize we are teaching our children doesn't change the fact that they are learning. Some of our most powerful teaching opportunities will come to us entirely spontaneously. We may never realize that we are teaching our children at all, and they will not comprehend that they are learning. And that is exactly the way it should be.

The benefits of child-driven play

A recent clinical report published by the American Academy of Pediatrics stresses the benefits of child-driven play:

> Play allows children to use their creativity while developing their imagination, dexterity, and physical, cognitive, and emotional strength. Play is important to healthy brain development.... As they master their world, play helps children develop new competencies that lead to enhanced confidence and the resiliency they will need to face future challenges . . . play allows children to learn how to work in groups, to share, to negotiate, to resolve conflicts, and to learn self-advocacy skills.[7]

The report cites the increasing prevalence of families who have become torn between the competing needs of preparing children academically and giving them ample playtime. Parents are spending more and more time arranging special activities or transporting children between football practice, dance lessons, and Girl Scout meetings. Moreover, marketers and educational specialists do a very good job of convincing us that all of these tools (educational software, specialized toys, private lessons) are just part of what good parents provide. As a result, "we can be certain that in some families, the protective influences of both play and high-quality family time are negatively affected by the current trends toward highly scheduling children."[8]

One of the purposes of this clinical report is to encourage health care providers to teach parents to recognize the importance of *balance*. While involvement in extracurricular activities is still encouraged, researchers want parents to understand that these are not the only ways to help children learn the skills that will help them succeed. Simple at-home opportunities like reading together, playing basketball in the backyard, or enjoying a board game after dinner are all highly effective parenting methods.[9]

A second consideration is that unstructured, free playtime gives children an emotional outlet for the pressures they encounter as part of being children. Playing helps a child develop spontaneity and creativity, along with allowing him an opportunity to unwind and decompress. When we overschedule children, we run the risk of creating pressure in their lives that can be detrimental to their physical and emotional health. Moreover, we eliminate opportunities for them to develop other important characteristics and personality traits—everything from the ability to make choices about how to spend their unstructured time wisely, to the ability to settle an argument.

It is time to develop a new mindset. It is time to begin to re-educate parents about the benefits of the lost art of play and recognize that we help children reach their fullest potential when we remember that for young children, play and learning are the same thing. It is time to help parents see that their adolescents crave and benefit from unstructured free time (play) in the company of the adults who love them. It is time to give renewed attention to the physical, emotional, social, and cognitive benefits of playing.

With this in mind, I'd like to propose four "statements of fact" and then elaborate on each:

1. Children and adolescents who play with their parents are less likely to engage in "risky" behaviors.

2. Children and adolescents who play with their parents develop better physical health.
3. Children and adolescents who play with their parents have emotional and social advantages over those who do not.
4. Children and adolescents who play with their parents can be as well or better prepared academically than their peers whose free time is highly structured.

Let's consider each of these premises in light of what researchers can tell us about our role:

1. Children who play with their parents are less likely to engage in "risky" behaviors.

Our efforts to push our children to achieve are laudable. Our children need encouragement, and some need even more than just a gentle nudge to try new things. Unfortunately, our competitive drive often spills beyond the bounds of common sense, and children are the unfortunate beneficiaries of our parental overzealousness. It is usually the child down the street whose parents "don't get it," not us. Our children are only enrolled in after-school stuff they enjoy. Little Johnny three doors down, on the other hand, has been on Ritalin since he was four (so he could concentrate better at preschool), took human growth hormone at age six because he was a little undersized (and Dad was worried he'd never be able to pitch unless something was done), and had a nose job done when he was twelve (to help improve his self-esteem). Little wonder that Johnny has experimented with drugs since he was a high school freshman.

Martha across the street has swim practice at 5:00 AM every day (she is the state champion in the 200-meter freestyle), takes violin lessons (which means an hour of practice daily), and maintains a 3.9 grade point average. She takes concurrent enrollment classes so she'll graduate from high school with her associate's degree. Martha speaks Mandarin Chinese and helps out at the mission soup kitchen every Saturday morning before she goes to her church's youth choir rehearsal (unless a swim meet conflicts). She is also treasurer of the student council. Her mother dismisses her attempted suicide last spring by reminding us that Martha has always been a little "moody."

We shake our heads and cluck our tongues for poor Johnny and poor Martha. Thank goodness we aren't manic overachievers in our home. Sure, we don't eat together as much as we used to, but soccer season will be over soon. Yes, there is a calendar on the refrigerator with everyone's schedules color-coded, but we *are* better organized than the average family. Yes, Mom and Dad are always tired, and we haven't had a quiet date together for at least six months, but our kids will only be young once. We don't want them to miss out on any opportunities—especially if none of the other kids in the neighborhood are missing out. We *are* spending time with our children, after all—twenty minutes to and from soccer practice three times weekly and fifteen minutes in the waiting room between piano and guitar lessons at the music academy.

Researchers are quick to point out that children are becoming more and more susceptible to "adult" health issues, both physical and mental, due to their frenzied schedules. But children's schedules are not the only concern. When a child is overscheduled, Mom or Dad's day planner takes a hit too. The result is that *everyone* has inadequate opportunities to relax, unwind, and enjoy being together.

In his book, *Too Much of a Good Thing: Raising Children of Character in an Indulgent Age*, Dan Kindlon enumerates the difficulties faced by children whose parents do not have time to spend with them and concludes: "Teenagers are at greater risk for drug use when they have parents, whether rich or poor, who have failed to teach them self-control, the ability to tolerate delay, and how to deal with boredom—parents who have not spent enough time with them and who have not clearly communicated that they don't want their kids to take drugs."[10]

Substance abuse is not the only threat. Research also suggests that children with overscheduled, competitive lifestyles are at increased risk for anxiety and depression.

Wendy Mogel, clinical psychologist, has identified another major health risk. Lack of an available parent means that some of these children lack the supervision they need to make good "adult" decisions in their lives. "Many parents are reluctant to discipline their high-achieving children. They are willing to ignore lack of modesty, lack of dignity, and the presence of danger lest they destroy the equilibrium that is resulting in those high grades." As a result, Mogel notes, teenagers do not appropriately moderate their leisure activities. Because they must take more and more extreme measures to prepare themselves academically, they look for more and more extreme methods to relieve the resulting anxiety. Wild parties and participation in extreme sporting events are just two of the methods teens use in an attempt to cram "refreshment" into the few moments of downtime they manage to squeeze in. Mogel theorizes that this is part of the reason we see more and more teens resorting to partying, drinking, drugs, and sex as stress-relief methods.

What does playing with a parent have to do with it?

When children and their parents play together and spend time together in relaxed ways, two things happen. First, the resulting "unscheduled downtime" gives parents and children time to laugh together, to take in a little fresh air together, to eat a good meal around the same table, even to lie still and talk with one another. Children can unwind; parents can enjoy a few moments of leisure. Everyone needs that kind of emotional release—adults and children alike. We discover that there is an alternative to what psychologist Dan Kindlon calls "pathological perfectionism and anxiety." Playing together has the potential to minimize worry and depression, give us an outlet for aggression, and even decrease sleep problems.[11]

Second, playing together gives children and parents opportunities to connect with one another in meaningful ways, so parents have a better idea what is going on in the lives of their youth. When we give our children opportunities to talk to and confide in us, we are more apt to discover their tendencies toward risky behavior in time to help a child choose a different path. When we have time to do the simple things like play with Play-Doh together and then clean it up together, we teach responsibility. When we play Kick the Can and teach children that there are rules that have to be obeyed if everyone is going to have fun, we give ourselves credibility when we try to set other "loving limits" like how much computer time is acceptable and why they can't have a cell phone at age nine, even when "all" of their friends do. When we help siblings play together and make sure everyone gets their fair share of time on the swing, we help children learn to take turns, and even to show compassion for one another.

In a survey of 639 teens, known as the Parenting Practices at the Millennium Survey (PPM Survey), Dan Kindlon attempted to identify some of the factors that keep kids from being "at risk." About 12 percent (or a total of 81 of the 639 teens surveyed) didn't manifest evidence of any of the problems the survey studied, including drug use, laziness, failing to work to their potential at school, depression, and sexual promiscuity. According to Kindlon, "There were 5 factors that distinguished them from everyone else: their families frequently ate dinner together, their parents weren't divorced, they had to keep their room clean, they weren't allowed to have a phone in their room, and they regularly did community service."[12] In short, a parent who had time to be "connected" with a child, who was willing to set loving limits, and who was working to help that child learn to care about others had children who thrived.

2. Children who play with their parents develop better physical health.

Child development professionals have long understood the importance of physical activity for keeping a child healthy. They also understand the importance of good nutrition, and so do parents. But what is curious is the fact that while so many of us understand the importance of good health practices, so few of us implement what we know. The generation of children we are rearing is set to become the first generation in recent history to have a shorter life expectancy than their parents. Health care specialists are becoming more and more concerned about children's health issues related to inactivity on the one hand and the wrong kind of activity on the other. Here's another place where parents have not made the connection between good physical health and simple play.

Parents who play with their children (particularly the "rough and tumble" kind of play and outdoor play that children need so desperately in order to develop strong muscles and bones) are giving their children advantages that will improve lives both in quality and length. And parents who have time to sit with children at family meals help assure that those children are better nourished and maintain better dietary practices throughout their lives.

Let's look at the problems individually:

Inactivity and sedentary lifestyles

Officials at the Harvard School of Public Health have told us that "if type 2 diabetes was an infectious disease, passed from one person to another, public health officials would say we're in the midst of an epidemic." The National Institutes of Health concur: "The number of children who are overweight has doubled in the last two to three decades, and currently one child in five is overweight. The increase is in both children and adolescents, and in all age, race and gender groups."[13] Others report that among five- to eight-year-olds, significant health risks, including obesity, high blood pressure, and cholesterol, occur in as much as 40 percent of children. And while health care specialists are increasingly alarmed at the lack of activity among children who are spending more and more time in front of a computer or sitting in front of a television, education specialists are compounding the problem by eliminating PE and recess during school hours. National policies that impose school accountability measures have forced educators to hoard every possible moment during the school day to academic instruction.

Physical activity that is developmentally inappropriate

Healthcare specialists are also worried about children at the other end of the spectrum—those who are getting "too much" exposure to physical activity, or at least too much exposure to a single sport. Humorist Christopher Buckley published an insightful essay for *The New Yorker* magazine, entitled "Memo from Coach," which satirizes our overzealous efforts to see our kids perform on the playing field:

> Per my memo last June regarding the summer-training regimen, your nine-year-old daughter should now be able to: (a) run a mile in under five minutes with cinder blocks attached to each ankle (lower body); (b) bench-press the family minivan (upper body); (c) swim a hundred yards in fifty-degree water while holding her breath (wind); (d) remain standing while bowling balls are thrown at her (stamina) . . .
>
> If your daughter has kept up with the summer-training program, there's no reason she shouldn't be able to finish out a game with minor injuries, such as hairline bone fractures or subdural hematomas. (Parental support needed!) Remember the Grasshopper motto: "That which does not kill me makes me a better midfielder!"[14]

Children's bones, muscles tendons, and ligaments are still growing. It's a critical time for avoiding injury. And yet the American Academy of Orthopedic Surgeons reports that serious athletic injuries are occurring more often, and to younger children. Coaches want to win, and parents want children to succeed. Sometimes we all forget to consider the price of glory. "I think kids are being forced to focus on a single sport at an earlier age as competitive intensity has ramped up," says Dr. Mininder S. Kocher, MD, MPH, spokesperson for the American Academy of Orthopaedic Surgeons. "This may actually lead to an overuse injury." Surgeons report that forty percent of all emergency room visits are for sports injuries in children between the ages of five and fourteen.

A majority of children cite "having fun" as the reason they choose to play a sport. Parents, on the other hand, have other motives, and the gap between playing for fun and playing to win forces 70 percent of children to drop out of sports by the time they are fourteen. Doctors are concerned that this group of children is then likely to permanently join their sedentary peers on the couch. Unless parents lighten up, their children may be even less inclined to remain active as adults than they would have been if they had never engaged in recreational athletics at all. Indeed, the American Academy of Pediatrics tells us "when the demands and expectations of organized sports exceed the maturation and readiness of the participant, the positive aspects of participation can be negated."[15]

Damage to bones, muscles, and joints is not the only kind of damage parents perpetuate when we forget that a central purpose for playing sports is to have fun. Almost all of us have watched an overzealous parent criticize his own child's performance in front of a whole audience of spectators. Forgetting that the game is for youth and not for adults, sometimes we expect too much. When adults "play to win," children are less likely to be taught how to resolve conflicts without resorting to hostility or violence. They are less likely to learn that doing their best is more important than winning, and they are less likely to receive praise for competing fairly and trying hard.[16]

How parental involvement helps develop good nutritional habits

While you may not consider eating together and playing together to be in the same category, it is apparent that children take a lot of their eating cues from their parents. If playing together (at least for the purposes of this book) is essentially about spending time together and connecting as family members, then the family meal has to be included as one of our "playing" methods. Parents who have time to spend with their children generally place a high priority on a family meal because they know how profoundly it affects adult-child relationships in a home. For this reason, I count mealtime as playtime, in spite of the fact that it doesn't always meet the clinical definition of play. Family meals can be considered playtime because of all the great opportunities they offer us to do playful things with our children—everything from making fruit smoothies together to racing to clean up the dishes. These meals (or the lack thereof) play a profound role in both the physical and emotional nourishment of our children.

I also believe that the consideration of family mealtime is important because it is such a great measuring stick to help us determine whether or not we are maintaining balance in our homes. If parents are spending too much time at work, there is no family meal. If children are overscheduled and parents are spending too much time traveling between other commitments, there is no family meal. If we are too sedentary and watch too much television, or spend too much time on the computer, there is no family meal. In short, when our lives get out of balance, the family meal is usually the first thing to go.

During the thirty years that have ensued since today's parents were children themselves, the rate of obesity in the United States has "more than doubled for preschoolers and adolescents, and it has more than tripled for children ages 6 to 11."[17] This has become a national healthcare crisis, as children who are obese get a head start on health risks such as diabetes, high blood pressure, and heart disease. These problems continue in adulthood, prompting health officials to warn us that obesity will soon replace smoking as our nation's most preventable cause of death.

Studies confirm that family meals, which are generally prepared and served at home, are far more likely to include healthy choices like fruits, vegetables, and whole grains. They are also more likely to limit fat intake and higher concentrations of processed and refined sugars.

When we are not making time to play with our children, chances are good that we are also having difficulty finding time to eat with them. If you examine your own eating patterns now, as compared with those from your childhood, it's pretty likely that you'll see a contrast. Nutritionists estimate that we've doubled the caloric intake we get from sources outside the home since 1977. We're just eating out a lot more often than we used to. And according to the U.S. Department of Agriculture (USDA), when we eat out, we're almost certainly getting meals that are higher in fat, saturated fat, cholesterol, and sodium. We're also getting meals that are lower in calcium, iron, and fiber.[18]

Sitting down together for a meal at home simply ensures our children better nutrition. One study indicates that teenagers who eat at least six meals per week with a parent are almost 40 percent more likely to eat the recommended amounts of vegetables. They also consume more fruits and dairy products and are less likely to skip breakfast.

Parents pass on other good physical habits when they play with their children more often. One benefit is a reduced incidence of sedentary behaviors. When you're outside playing together, you are not inside in front of the TV or the computer. This is important because if your child is sedentary, she is at higher risk for being overweight. And if you happen to allow your children to eat while they are watching TV, there is a "double whammy" effect. Dr. Jennifer L. Temple and colleagues from the University at Buffalo, New York, have recently studied how television affects the amount of food a child consumes and how long a child eats before recognizing that he is full enough to stop eating. Children in her study were divided into three groups: those who were exposed to a clip from a television program that was played repeatedly, those who watched no television at all, and those who sat and watched a continuous television program. Each of the groups had access to food, but the children in the last group consumed about 500 calories and ate for about twenty-one minutes before they lost interest in the food and stopped eating. That was more calories and more time spent eating than the other two groups *combined*.[19] Apparently, children who are distracted by the television don't notice the "habituation cues" that would normally tell them they are full. The researchers pointed out that since children are often eating high-calorie foods when they are snacking in front of the television, this habit could profoundly affect the number of calories a child consumes in a day.

What does playing with a parent have to do with it?

Parents who play with their children improve children's physical health in at least three ways. First, they teach children that being active can be fun. Contrast the phrase "Let's get some exercise" with the phrase "Let's go outside and shoot some hoops together." Which has more appeal to your child? Which has more appeal to *you?* If you can burn as many calories playing full court basketball as you can burn in thirty minutes slaving away on the elliptical machine in the basement (and you can), if you can burn as many calories sledding or tobogganing as you can burn jogging around the block (and you can), and if you can burn more calories playing a casual game of soccer with your kids than you can burn in an hour on a stationary bike (and you will), why are you wasting so much money on a gym pass? Compare some of your favorite activities with some of the exercising you do out of a sense of duty, and you may be pleasantly surprised.

Second, when you are playing with your children instead of sitting on the sidelines watching them play, you are more likely to be willing to let your son or daughter enjoy sports "just for the fun of it." That is, after all, why recreational sports exist. I am not advocating eliminating competitive sports. My own children have realized dozens of physical and emotional benefits as a result of their involvement in competitive sports—not the least of which is improved physical fitness. My sons and daughters have developed work ethic, teamwork skills, anger management abilities, time management techniques, competitive drive, and even better nutritional habits as a result of the efforts of caring coaches and trainers. Children should be encouraged to improve their athletic abilities—within reason. Just keep the opportunity costs in mind. If your child is going to be primed to be the next Olympic champion, what will she give up in exchange? If she is the one making that decision, it may be just the right thing. If an adult is making that decision for her, the results might not be what everyone intends. The longer you can keep sports involvement "playful," the more likely it is you will make decisions that are in your child's best interests.

The third reason playing with children in active ways is important is that eventually, your children will notice and imitate your good habits. Whether you are teaching them to grab an orange instead of a handful of potato chips, or whether you are teaching them that a quick bike ride around the block is a great stress-reliever, your children will be likely to retain the habits that bring them pleasure, and for most children, *any* playtime spent with a parent is pleasurable.

3. Children who play with their parents have emotional and social advantages over those who do not.

One of the striking benefits of play that is often overlooked by the casual observer is the fact that playing is such a powerful way of helping children develop social and emotional abilities that they will need in adulthood but which can't be taught only through academic instruction. Parents are especially important to social and emotional play because a caring adult can help regulate behavior, suggest other options, and cheer on successes.

Social advantages of play

If we want to consider the importance of play in developing a youngster's social abilities, we need look no further than the animal world. Scientists have often documented the fact that young animals "play" in order to learn the rules of how to survive in the wild. "Through rough-housing, animals form social bonds, acquire different dominance ranks and learn what behaviors are acceptable: how hard they can bite, how roughly they can interact and how to resolve conflicts. They then generalize these codes of conduct to other situations."[20]

Children are no different. Playing helps them begin to develop a sense of morality and to understand the customs of their culture. It helps them learn to compete, to take healthy risks, to consider the perspective of another human being, and even to act out adult roles. "Children's active, spontaneous, exuberant, contrived games represent and yield skills of calculation, strategy, negotiation, contrivance, physical skills, and creation of rules and subordination to those rules. The implications for adaptation to society and preservation of culture are profound," writes Joe L. Frost, Professor Emeritus and past president of the American Association for the Child's Right to Play.[21]

Most of us recognize that our environment is full of social cues that we are expected to know and practice—things like going to the end of a line instead of walking to the front of it, waiting until another person finishes a sentence before adding our own insights, or closing our mouths when we chew. And we don't sit in classes to learn these skills. Instead, we learn and practice them at home, during our childhood as we interact with others in an environment where it is safe to make mistakes. For example, it is common to watch very young children get in front of one another as they wait for their turn on the playground slide. It is far less common to see a teenager walk to the front of the line for movie tickets, oblivious to other customers behind her, because she is excited to see the movie. Learning these social skills takes practice, and because one skill builds upon another, playing is one of the very best ways to learn them. Parents and other loving adults make especially good "coaches" for youngsters who are learning to interpret social cues. Playing is vital because the fun and excitement of the experience inspires us to keep coming back for more social training—usually without realizing we are being trained at all.

Through play, children learn several important interpersonal interactions that researchers identify as input, organization, output, and self-monitoring.

1. **Input**: *I can see that Jacob is frowning and looks like he is about to cry. His fists are also clenched.*

2. **Organization** (being able to read and attend to the cues that are given): *I think Jacob is mad because I grabbed his truck.*

3. **Output** (deciding what the appropriate response is): *I had better give back this truck and go find something else to play with.*

4. **Self-monitoring** (figuring out how the interaction went): *Jacob is not frowning now. He is happy, but I still wish I had the truck. I will wait for Jacob to put it down.*[22]

Children who fail to learn these social skills often experience difficulty interacting with their peers. The rejection that results compounds into other problems associated with low self-esteem, including anxiety, depression, and school avoidance, according to Stephen Rothenberg, PsyD, who specializes in learning and attentional disorders and relationship difficulties. These children are also at risk for "later social and psychological maladjustment, including substance abuse and depressive disorders."[23]

Emotional advantages of play

If learning social skills is an important by-product of playing, learning healthy emotional behaviors is quite possibly one of the most important benefits of all. Children who play often, with adult mentors close by, are most apt to learn some of these emotional skills—how to cope with disappointment, how to evaluate and manage risks to their own safety, how to find a novel solution to a problem, how to manage frustration by trying again, how to release stress, and how to lose with dignity and win without alienating others.

Problem solving and creativity

Some of scientists' most creative studies have centered on learning how children begin to manage their emotions through play. A substantial number of them have focused on the relationship between play and creativity. For example, one study looked at the correlation between a second-grader's ability to pretend and that child's abilities four years later for divergent thinking.[24] The children who were the best at pretending when they were young were the best divergent thinkers when they were tested again as fifth graders, and this was independent of IQ. (Divergent thinking is the ability to come up with many different ideas and solutions to a problem.) A child who can tell you that a kitchen spatula is used for flipping pancakes is a good observer. However, if she can tell you a kitchen spatula can also be used as the throwing arm of a catapult, or can be used to press designs into a slice of cheese, or can become the arm of a robot that picks up toys, the child is a good divergent thinker.

Playing outdoors has been identified as a particularly helpful method for encouraging problem solving and divergent thinking abilities in children, since outdoor spaces are often less structured than indoor spaces, and there are fewer restrictions on what kind of play is allowed. If a child wants to run or yell or hang upside down, he can appropriately do so when he is playing outside. If he chooses to lay in the grass and think or climb a tree and observe insects, that is generally considered acceptable as well. This kind of freedom lends itself to many possibilities that are never considered when the child is constrained within four solid walls.

Coping skills and emotion regulation

As children learn to be divergent thinkers, they get better at brainstorming and thinking of ways to solve a problem. These skills are key components of creativity. But problem-solving abilities have other emotional benefits. Children who have higher quality of fantasy in play have also been shown to be able to employ their problem-solving skills to stressful situations. They learn how to cope better than children who are not encouraged to fantasize and pretend.[25]

Another study found that children who engaged in pretend play more frequently, for a longer duration, and with an adult, showed greater emotion regulation ability.[26] Why is this so? Researchers theorize that when a child is encouraged to pretend about a specific event, he can practice modulating his emotion without actually feeling the emotion. A child can "experiment with expressing several different intensities of fear in a story without experiencing that fear in themselves," writes psychologist Russ M. Moore. For example, in one research project, children who were to experience a medical procedure (a blood draw) had the opportunity to watch a nurse perform the procedure on a doll first and then had a chance to perform the "pretend procedure" on the doll themselves. Researchers also gave the children an opportunity to play freely with the doll and other materials before the blood draw was actually performed. They found that these children exhibited less anxiety and less emotional trauma (body posture, the amount of crying, and radial pulse were also monitored) than children in a control group who did not play with the doll before their blood work was done.[27] Children who have difficult life experiences, emotional problems, developmental delays, and autism may have an even more critical need for mentored play, and promising developments are being made that might assist these children in overcoming their social limitations.[28]

Positive risk-taking

Adult-mentored play is also a powerful way for children to develop their positive risk-taking abilities. Think of the first time you attempted to cross the monkey bars, ride a bike, or slide down a slide. Chances are good that an adult or an older sibling, or a least a trusted friend, was on hand to make sure you accomplished your goal safely. Professor Joe Frost, who has spent a lifetime trying to help playground designers, governments, and educators create safe and developmentally appropriate play spaces for children, reminds us that taking some calculated risks can be a good thing, especially when a loving parent is on hand to coach and monitor, and, if necessary, to offer a bandage or remove a splinter. "The view that children must somehow be sheltered from all risks of injury is a common misconception of adults," writes Dr. Frost. "In the real world, life is filled with risks—financial, physical, emotional, social—and reasonable risks are essential for children's healthy development . . . Helping children handle risk is an essential feature of adult conduct for guiding children in being responsible for themselves and for the consequences of their activity.[29]

Empathy and perspective-taking

Another powerful by-product of play is the fact that it allows children to begin to develop empathy. A very young child does not usually have the developmental capability to see another person's point of view. This is why it is difficult or impossible to teach a young toddler to share. Sharing is not usually a developmentally appropriate expectation for a two-year-old. But with time and enough practice, children develop the ability to make connections between how they feel and how others must feel in the same situation. If you have ever played a board game with a four-year-old, you know that winning is generally the only goal. If the adult wins, chances that the child will be willing to play the game again are slim. But if the child is given enough chances to experience winning and losing, she eventually recognizes that others feel emotions similar to hers. She is able to see the game from someone else's perspective. Recently my seven-year-old resisted a move in a board game that would have caused me to lose. It wasn't about prolonging the game. It was about not wanting Mom to feel bad. It was an emotional milestone in that child's life that I celebrated quietly.

What does playing with a parent have to do with it?

Here's perhaps the best reason of all to play: Because it makes us happy. As adults, we recognize that certain activities—running, biking, reading, painting, taking a hot bath—improve our mood. It is no different for children. Physical activity, and even less physical types of play, provide children with an emotional release. "Although it has been the subject of little scientific inquiry in young children, free play has the potential to improve many aspects of emotional well-being such as minimizing anxiety, depression, aggression, and sleep problems . . . Studies in older children have shown that improved mood and emotional well-being are associated with physical activity."[30] It follows, that if playing improves a child's emotional state, it can improve Mom's or Dad's emotional state as well.

"When mothers and fathers play mutually challenging games like gin rummy, Hangman, or Parcheesi with their children . . . the kids have the chance to observe incredibly important behaviors and attitudes in the people who have the greatest influence over them," writes Dr. Michael K. Meyerhoff, EdD, who serves as executive director of a family advisory and advocacy agency. "Restraint, tenacity, courtesy, cleverness, and determination do not evolve naturally—they are learned by imitating good models."[31]

Physicians Hillary Burdette and Robert Whitaker make a compelling argument for the resurrection of "free play" and its abilities to benefit children socially and emotionally. Because all play involves some social-emotional decision making (what to play, who can play, when to start, when to stop, and the rules of engagement), children, together with their parents, their siblings, and their peers learn to "develop and sustain friendships, to cooperate, to lead and to follow."[32] Playing with your child might possibly be the *single most effective method* for teaching her two indispensable skills: how to develop and maintain relationships with other human beings and how to be at peace with herself. Why would we rob children of the opportunity?

4. Children who play with their parents are as well or better prepared educationally than their peers whose free time is highly academically structured.

Now the argument gets complicated *and* harder to sell. How can a child who is left with free time to play *possibly* learn as well? Children who are enrolled in advanced preschools, for example, are a lot better at learning to use words like *precipitation*, and children who don't learn to use the word *precipitation* at some point will never be Ivy League candidates. What it boils down to is that we want the very best education for our children because we know that a great education will give them the edge they need to succeed in the world. We can't afford to let our children "fall behind." Our nation came to that realization when Sputnik was launched. We realized it again when Japan began to outdistance the United States technologically. And we are being warned about it now through the blogs that we send back and forth to each other as parents: "China has more honors students than we have students!"[33]

Daniel Kindlon's tongue-in-cheek articulation of the problem hits home with most of us:

> There is the crucial choice of college. Start thinking about this early! Admission to a top college gets tougher each year. Applicants are not only expected to have high grades and SAT scores: they should be well rounded. Your kid better excel at some activity, be it playing the cello, designing software, or scoring goals on the field . . . It also won't hurt on your child's college application is she has some fascinating life experiences to write about—community service in Africa, an archaeological dig in England, perhaps a summer studying El Greco at the Prado while brushing up on her Castilian accent.[34]

Kindlon's tongue-in-cheek example strikes a nerve with most of us, however. Our children deserve these advantages, and society expects it of us. Why would we give them anything less if it were within our financial means to give them more? Sensitive adults know that *some* of these experiences bless a child's life, make her better-rounded, help her develop understanding of the world around her, and give her discipline and opportunities to succeed. While I do not advocate eliminating extracurricular activities from a child's life, I do advocate balance. When we add too many of these additional cognitive learning experiences to a child's schedule at the complete expense of time they could spend playing with a parent, our children suffer instead of thriving. An increasingly vocal group of child development specialists agrees. Kathy Hirsch-Pasek is a vocal proponent of play. She writes: "Of the myths we harbor as parents, policy makers and professionals, one of the deepest held is that learning is equivalent to intelligence; that achievement and intelligence are synonymous. This is a dangerous conclusion that can have serious consequences for how we teach our children."[35]

In their book, *Play = Learning*, Golinkoff, Hirsh-Pasek, and Singer offer compelling evidence that parents need to be more cautious about "overeducating" youngsters—at least with respect to formalized classroom learning:

> In preschool, when children are pressured to learn in schools with "academic" as opposed to developmentally appropriate curricula, they report being more anxious and perfectionistic . . . than their more playful peers. They are no more ahead in first grade in academic achievement. Such programs also have the effect of reducing children's motivation and making them have lower expectations for their academic abilities, less pride in their achievements, and more dependency on adults . . . regardless of social class.[36]

These specialists go on to point out that "direct instruction" teaching often has the effect of dampening a love of learning in general. Children exposed to a lot of skill and drill had "higher rates of delinquency, were less willing to help other children, and were more likely to experience emotional problems."[37]

Another group of researchers who examine the benefits of make-believe play in children report similarly distressing findings about children whose early experiences are limited to academic tutoring. This practice, they warn, is "undermining children's self-regulatory capacities."

> When preschoolers and kindergartners spend much time sitting and doing worksheets, as opposed to actively engaging in play-based learning, they become inattentive and restless, express doubt about their abilities, prefer less challenging tasks, and are less advanced in motor, academic, language, and social skills at the end of the school year. Follow-ups through third grade reveal lasting, negative consequences, including

poorer study habits and achievement and a rise in distractibil-
ity, hyperactivity, and peer aggression over time.[38]

And the problem certainly isn't limited to preschoolers. It compounds
itself throughout a child's youth, into adolescence, and even into adulthood.
The admissions office at Harvard College offers this forceful argument:

> Faced with the fast pace of growing up today, some stu-
> dents are clearly distressed, engaging in binge drinking and
> other self-destructive behaviors. Counseling services of second-
> ary schools and colleges have expanded in response to greatly
> increased demand. It is common to encounter even the most
> successful students, who have won all the "prizes," stepping
> back and wondering if it was all worth it. Professionals in their
> thirties and forties—physicians, lawyers, academics, business
> people, and others—sometimes give the impression that they
> are dazed survivors of some bewildering life-long boot-camp.[39]

Critics would be quick to point out that these examples are all based
on the school environment, not the home environment. But whether
we are discussing the distressing trend in academic environments that
is eliminating play because teachers need more time to prepare children for high stakes tests, or whether we are discussing the trend in
American homes to be sure that children cram more and more learning experiences into their after-school hours, the results are the same.
Without balance and equilibrium, without some moment to relax and
unwind, without secure relationships with the adults they love, children do worse, not better.

The question remains, will the child who is allowed to play be behind
when he gets done playing and sits down to take the SAT? It's pretty difficult to prove that children excel when they have had time for free play
and recreation in their lives. After all, there is no test for emotional and
social equilibrium. We don't often attempt to put a score on a child's ability to get along with others or on her creativity, or on her peace of mind.
The best we can do is find examples of school systems that follow a more
"playful" curriculum and compare those with more traditional learning
environments and see which method comes out on top. There is intriguing evidence that "playful learning" is the superior method.

Richard Louv, author of *Last Child in the Woods: Saving Our Children from Nature-Deficit Disorder,* is a vocal proponent of our need

to allow our children to get outside to see what the world has to offer them, and asserts that allowing children to interact with their environment in ways that are natural and logical to them is superior to "drill and skill-based" teaching in the classroom. As evidence, he shows how several schools are accomplishing this. Teachers at a Portland Middle School, for example, "employ a curriculum using local rivers, mountains, and forests; among other activities, they plant native species and study the Willamette River." Louv reports that 96 percent of these students "meet or exceed state standards for math problem-solving—compared to only 65 percent of eighth-graders at comparable middle schools."[40]

Internationally, Finnish schools consistently rank as the world's brightest, based on test scores. "Among several distinctive features of these schools is the requirement of a 15-minute recess with play opportunities every hour.[41]

What does playing with a parent have to do with it?

What it comes right down to is that we would be hard-pressed to prove via test scores that playing with children—giving them lots of enriching experiences stretching their bodies, interacting with people who care about and want to mentor them, and allowing them to explore their world on their own terms—is a superior education. Yet most of us can feel "in our gut" that this is so. There is, in fact, quite a bit of research being done that has shown, convincingly, that playful interactions with a parent are vital to a child's educational success.

Suffice it to say that for a child, there is more to learning than simply being able to rehearse facts and figures. Children who have been exposed to rigorous academic learning *do* get smarter. The question is not so much about what they are learning; the question is about what they are not learning. What is the opportunity cost for children who know how to speak French but have never developed the physical strength necessary to pull themselves across a set of monkey bars? What about the child who has memorized a dozen different violin concertos but is afraid to speak to an adult? The elusive key we are looking for is balance. The American Academy of Pediatrics puts it this way:

> Although very well intentioned, arranging the finest opportunities for their children may not be parents' best opportunity for influence and . . . shuttling their children

between numerous activities may not be the best quality time. Children will be poised for success, basking in the knowledge that their parents absolutely and unconditionally love them. This love and attention is best demonstrated when parents serve as role models and family members make time to cherish one another: time to be together, to listen, and to talk—nothing more and nothing less . . . The most valuable and useful character traits that will prepare . . . children for success arise not from extracurricular or academic commitments, but from a firm grounding in parental love, role modeling, and guidance.[42]

Notes

1. Singer, Golinkoff, and Hirsh-Pasek, *Play=Learning: How play motivates and enhances children's cognitive and social-emotional growth.*

2. Shonkoff et al, www.earlychildhoodnm.com/Documents/Early%20Ed%20Center%20Report.pdf

3. Kindlon, *Too Much of A Good Thing: Raising Children of Character in an Indulgent Age.*

4. Hirch-Pasek and Golinkoff, *Einstein Never Used Flash Cards: How our Children Really Learn—and Why they Need to Play More and Memorize Less.*

5. Ginsburg, www.aap.org/pressrom/playFINAL.pdf.

6. Kindlon, *Too Much of A Good Thing: Raising Children of Character in an Indulgent Age,* 157.

7. Ginsburg, www.aap.org/pressrom/playFINAL.pdf, 3.

8. Ginsburg, www.aap.org/pressrom/playFINAL.pdf, 7.

9. Ginsburg, www.aap.org/pressrom/playFINAL.pdf, 8.

10. Kindlon, *Too Much of A Good Thing: Raising Children of Character in an Indulgent Age,* 157.

11. Burdette, and Whitaker, *Archive of Pediatric Adolescent Medicine.*

12. Kindlon, *Too Much of A Good Thing: Raising Children of Character in an Indulgent Age,* 177.

13. Torgan, *The NIH Word on Health.*

14. Buckley, *The Overscheduled Child.*

15. National Youth Sports Safety Foundation, www.nyssf.org/sportparentcodeofconduct.html.

16. Mayo Clinic Staff, www.mayoclinic.com/health/childhood-obesity/DS00698.

17. Kellner, www.gwu.edu/~uwp/fyw/euonymous/Kellner.pdf.

18. Azar, *Monitor on Psychology.*

19. Frost, "The Dissolution of Children's Outdoor Play: Causes and Consequences."

20. Rothenberg, www.nldline.com/dr.htm.

21. Russ, Robins, and Christiano, *Creativity Research Journal.* Vol 12 no. 2: 129–139.

22. Rothenberg, www.nldline.com/dr.htm, 1.

23. Russ, Robins, and Christiano, *Creativity Research Journal*. Vol 12 no. 2: 129–139.

24. Galyer, *Early Childhood Dev Care,* 166:93-108.

25. Moore and Russ, *Developmental and Behavioral Pediatrics* Vol 27:237–48.

26. Singer, Golinkoff, and Hirsh-Pasek, *Play=Learning: How play motivates and enhances children's cognitive and social-emotional growth,* 7.

27. Frost, "The Dissolution of Children's Outdoor Play: Causes and Consequences," 8

28. Meyerhoff, www.findarticles.com/p/articles/mi_m0816/is_10_19/ai_82470764.

29. Burdette, and Whitaker, *Archive of Pediatric Adolescent Medicine.*

30. Zabel, www.chrisknudsen.biz/?p=147.

31. Kindlon, *Too Much of A Good Thing: Raising Children of Character in an Indulgent Age,* 37.

32. Hirch-Pasek and Golinkoff, *Einstein Never Used Flash Cards: How our Children Really Learn—and Why they Need to Play More and Memorize Less.*

33. Hirch-Pasek and Golinkoff, *Einstein Never Used Flash Cards: How our Children Really Learn—and Why they Need to Play More and Memorize Less,* 9.

34. Hirch-Pasek and Golinkoff, *Einstein Never Used Flash Cards: How our Children Really Learn—and Why they Need to Play More and Memorize Less,* 9.

35. Berk, Mann, and Ogan, *Play = Learning,* 74–100.

36. Fitzsimmons, "Time Out or Burn Out for the Next Generation."

37. Louv, *Last Child in the Woods.*

38. Singer, "Epilogue: Learning to Play and Learning Through Play." in *Play = Learning,* 74–100.

39. Ginsburg, www.aap.org/pressroom/playFINAL.pdf, 16.

Online calorie estimator:

(Visit http://www.healthstatus.com/cgi-bin/calc/reload.pl for one example of a "calories burned estimator.")

Chapter 7

IMaginative Play

How pretending helps preschoolers learn and why
children need more of it

• •

*Children learn best not when they are told, but when they can act upon
their environments and construct knowledge for themselves.*
—"Dramatic Play in Outdoor Play Environments," *PTO Today*

My oldest son was a great pretender. Like many firstborn children, he developed an entourage of imaginary friends who entertained him when I could not, kept him company when he was fearful, and had interests that were similar to his. "Big Leon" loved leftover broccoli and could climb to the top of the apple tree without being afraid of falling. Mac was an invisible firefighter, and Detmer loved backyard football games. Rico, however, was our four-year-old's truest friend. Sometimes he was invisible, and sometimes he was a stuffed rabbit who stayed close by at bedtime. We have a beloved videotape of our son at age four, filmed well past his bedtime, on the day when he announced, with tear-filled eyes, that Rico had up and moved to Florida "without even saying good-bye." Rico never returned, but his legacy is rich. If only I had known . . .

If I had known at the time what I know now, I would have been more grateful for the presence of Rico, Big Leon, and others. I would have watched more closely when they were present. I would have been more tolerant of the fact that we had to leave certain doors open so they would not be afraid, that we had to save extra broccoli instead of eating what was on our plates, and that it was okay when a new pair of socks turned up with holes cut in them to make stirrup socks for an invisible baseball game. I could have been more patient if I had known that these peculiar friends were helping my son learn some of the emotional and social skills that would make him a better student, a kinder friend, and a more useful member of society. Had I known then what I know now, I would have been more careful to create opportunities for imaginative play. I would have saved oatmeal canisters, broken telephones, and useless kitchen gadgets more often. I would have read more fairy tales. I might even have allowed more naps underneath the dining room table or in a box in the basement. Here's why:

A child's ability to use his imagination to pretend and to make-believe is a significant predictor of a child's future success. Pretending is what helps him learn the rules of society—rules that enable him to develop complex social skills like taking turns and controlling his temper. Pretend play is the catalyst that will help him develop the ability to think creatively, to speak and write well, to calm himself when he is afraid, to pay attention in school, and to be persistent. A tall order? Maybe so, but scientists have documented again and again that make-believe play fosters all of these abilities and more.

Now for the good news: children who aren't good at pretending can be taught how, and parents are the very best teachers. And the news gets better. Helping children engage in make-believe play is fun, and it only takes moments of an adult's time and a few inexpensive tools. Every parent can do this!

What is pretend or make-believe play?

If you are like me, the phrase *make-believe* probably conjures up images of King Friday and Daniel the Striped Tiger playing with a human troll in a neighborhood you could only get to on a miniature trolley driven by a "grown-up" wearing a green sweater and sneakers. By the time I hit first grade, Fred Rogers's magical neighborhood was considered dorky. Even adults said so. They lampooned his costume and his methods on television shows like *Saturday Night Live* and *The Simpsons*. Consequently, some of us are a little gun-shy of the word *make-believe*. We don't want *our* children to grow up dorky, do we? Perhaps if we comprehend all of the benefits of pretending, it will be easier to understand why Fred Rogers went to such great lengths to teach us how to do it.

Make-believe, also known as fantasy play, dramatic play, representational play, socio-dramatic play, or imaginary play, is early childhood's most fundamental method, even ahead of printed literature, for passing academic, social, and emotional skills to the next generation. Imaginative play is unlimited in variety. Some methods of make-believe include turning an upside-down box into a spaceship, dressing up like a football player, or building a tower out of blocks and pretending that your Spider-man action figure is saving the world. Imaginative play includes singing a song with made-up words as you fall asleep at naptime. It includes moving sand with a toy dump truck, feeding a doll a bottle, or putting on Mom's high-heeled shoes and clomping around the kitchen. Imaginative play can be as simple as drinking invisible water out of a cup and as complex as creating your own version of the lunar surface out of boxes, pillows, chairs, and couch cushions. Whatever form it takes, make-believe play is essential to a child's healthy development, and unfortunately, it is disappearing from our society.

Our children spend so much time with toys that talk, computer screens that teach, and television shows that entertain that they are seldom compelled to learn to entertain themselves. An electronic gadget that will keep a child occupied is almost always available, and when one is not, young children are not learning how to compensate for the lack of one. Instead, they are simply bored. Parents need to be educated if we are to reverse the trend.

How do children learn to pretend?

Social scientists are not certain why children are so naturally prone to pretending. What we do know, as a result of decades of careful research, is that pretending promotes some very desirable developmental characteristics:

1. Children use imaginary play to learn society's **rules.**
2. Make-believe play helps children learn to regulate their **emotions.**
3. Children use dramatic playtime to develop their **literacy and numeracy skills**.
4. Pretending helps children learn **problem-solving skills** and **creativity.**

These have been explored briefly in the previous chapter. But let's take a closer look at each of these skills and consider how pretending helps ensure that they will develop.

Children use imaginary play to learn society's rules

Wendy is sitting at a small table, and her mother is seated opposite her, with her tall knees sticking sideways. "You be the little girl and I will be the mommy," says Wendy (a reversal of roles that is common in pretend play with an adult). Wendy carefully arranges a pile of orange modeling clay on a plate and hands it to her mother. "You already washed your hands, didn't you?" she asks. After being assured that her mother's hands are clean, Wendy remarks, "Well, you can go ahead and eat your pasghetti. But be sure you don't burp." After Wendy's mother finishes slurping up her pretend spaghetti (using a pretend knife and fork), she asks Wendy if there will be salad and french bread to go with the meal. Wendy didn't think of that. Nonplussed, she adds a bright blue interlocking bead to her mother's plate. "Yes, and here are some carrots too."

"Do I have to eat all of my carrots, Mommy?" Wendy's mother turns the tables and asks the question she has heard from Wendy so many times before. Wendy assures her mother that she cannot leave the table until she has eaten everything on her plate. Next, Mother reaches for a nearby box of tissue and says, "Is this the napkin I use to wipe my mouth when I'm finished eating?" Smiling, Wendy nods in the affirmative. Their pretend dinner lasts less than five minutes, and soon, Wendy's mother thanks her child for the wonderful dinner and goes back to the pile of laundry she had been folding before she was invited to dinner. Wendy's play continues with a stuffed bear to replace her mother as a guest for the dessert course.

Wendy is using her playtime to practice some of society's deeply held rules of conduct: washing before meals, eating politely, and being a gracious hostess. Wendy's mother has unwittingly added to Wendy's store of knowledge by teaching her about using a napkin—a skill Wendy has seldom used at her own dinner table. What looks to an outsider as "free play" is not really free play at all. Along with practicing social rules she has already learned, Wendy has had an opportunity to test the limits of the rules. When asked whether or not her guest has to finish all of her vegetables, Wendy answers in the affirmative. According to the book

Play = Learning, "Drawing on experiences in their families and communities, children continuously devise and follow social rules in pretense. In doing so, they strive to bring their behavior in line with social expectations, thereby strengthening their sensitivity to *external pressures* to act in socially desirable ways."[1]

Wendy could as easily have told her mother that she did not have to finish her vegetables and that in fact, she could have two helpings of dessert, but she did not, and most children won't. When faced with an opportunity to be a nonconformist during pretend play, children usually opt to follow the route of social responsibility instead. As a result, Wendy has strengthened her ability to show restraint, to follow the rules, and to be civilized and polite. The self-regulatory abilities she is learning will make it easier for her to meet the academic and social requirements of school later on. Researchers have documented the connection between make-believe play and higher social functioning. Children who engage in lots of complex fantasy play are more "socially competent than those who play less frequently," and as a result, they are more popular with other children and have more positive social activity.[2]

Make-believe play helps children learn to regulate their emotions

It is a beautiful spring day outside, and Jordan and Alesa both want to be the first to use the tire swing. Alesa is older, so she successfully climbs in first. "I am going to take this rocket ship to the moon!" Jordan is immediately upset and begins to protest loudly. Their mother, who is on hand to supervise and do the pushing, says, "Jordan, I'm sure Alesa is going to let you have a turn, aren't you, Alesa."

"I can let him have a turn in a minute."

True to her word, Alesa relinquishes the swing without a murmur when Mom says it is time to trade. Jordan swings for a few minutes, and then Alesa is ready for another turn. Jordan, who is two years younger than Alesa, does not yet recognize the social benefits of sharing and taking turns, so his loud protests begin again when Alesa reaches out and stops the swing so he can get out. The "fair" solution, according to Alesa, would be that they both get to ride in the swing. This presents a problem since the swing is really built for only one small body, but in order to preserve peace, Mom is willing to give it a try.

Alesa gets in the swing, and Mom helps Jordan climb in and settle on her lap.

"Are you ready?" asks Mom. She gives the swing a gentle push. "Look at that!"

Here's how the rest of the conversation went:

Jordan: Too high!
Mom: Is it too high already?
Jordan (a little breathless): Yeah.
Alesa: No. Go way up. Go to the moon.
Mom: You're going to go to the moon? What will we go past
    when we go to the moon?
Jordan looks frightened but remains still.
Alesa: We will go past Missouri.
Mom: You go past Missouri on the way to the moon?
Alesa (squirming underneath her brother's weight): Yup. But
    I think I'm all done with Jordan.
Mom (laughing): Is it Jordan's turn?
Alesa: No!
Mom: Well, I'm going to guess that if Jordan gets off, he's going
    to want to swing again. How are we going to do that?
Alesa (grimacing): Owww! My legs are hurting.

Mom immediately reaches into the swing and lifts Jordan out, putting him a few feet behind where she was standing. He rushes forward to get back in, but the tire swing, which is still moving slightly, bumps into him and knocks him down. There is a fresh round of tears. After Jordan has been comforted, Mom asks Alesa if she's ready now to let her brother have a turn.

Alesa: I will be ready after one more push.
Mom: One more push? Do you think that's okay, Jordan?
Jordan (waiting well away from the swing this time): Yeah.

Soon, Jordan gets another turn in the swing, and Alesa turns her attention to playing with some riding toys that are in the yard.

Without observing closely, it is easy to miss the importance of what just happened. With what began as a playing/pretending scenario, two children have had an opportunity to practice some important skills related to emotion regulation. The scenario went much better than it could have because of the presence of a loving parent. Had she not been on hand, Jordan and Alesa might never have gotten past their initial battle of wills to see who would swing first. Instead, Mom has been able to guide them effortlessly as they've worked on managing their emotions in several ways:

First, based on previous experiences, Jordan knows that Mom has more "authority" than he does and that he can trust her to make sure he gets a turn to swing, so he is willing to control his impulse and wait his turn. Alesa, who is a kind child by nature, does not even have to be encouraged at first to let her brother have a turn. She is thinking about how Jordan feels and, knowing how she would feel in his place, generously allows him to have a turn.

Soon it is time to switch places again, but because Jordan lacks the developmental maturity to be willing to share, Mom steps in and allows them to come up with an alternative. Alesa suggests that they have their turns simultaneously. Mom, with her adult perspective, immediately recognizes that this may not be the ideal solution, but she allows the experiment to continue and helps Jordan climb inside so that Alesa's theory can be tested.

Now, there is a new problem. Jordan's comfort level for swing height does not match Alesa's. For him, they are swinging too high. Alesa, on the other hand, is ready to go "to the moon." At this point, Mom can choose to slow the swing down or to keep it going. Without even realizing she is doing it, she assesses the risks and decides that Jordan is not in immediate danger, and without even responding to him, she allows him to test the limits of his comfort zone. Instead, she instinctively helps Alesa stretch the limits of her imagination. "What will we go past when we go to the moon?" When it is clear that Alesa's legs are being pinched and that the ride is no longer fun, Mom stops the swing immediately.

Now Jordan has an opportunity to learn about the laws of physics. Even though Mom set him down outside the "danger zone," he moves forward and gets knocked over. He is not badly hurt, so it only takes a few minutes to comfort him and offer an insight. "You have to be careful when you are walking in front of the swing, don't you?" To prove that, Jordan understands what he was just taught, he stands well away from the swing the second time, and yet again, he gets an opportunity to exercise his patience.

Within this brief (and very common) five-minute play scenario, these two children have had an opportunity to practice some important emotional skills. Impulse control, regulation of anger, perspective-taking, sharing, problem-solving, risk-taking, creativity, patience, and avoiding danger were all practiced without anyone realizing that learning was taking place. Mom is probably aware of the role she is playing in teaching her children. She made several decisions, albeit unconsciously, that allowed her children to get the full benefit of the learning experience. Given enough of these opportunities, it is easy to see why these children will arrive at school better behaved, more self-regulated, and better able to control their emotions than will children who spent the bulk of their time in front of a television or sitting in a classroom doing worksheets.

Lev Vygotsky, a Russian psychologist who died in 1934, proposed several intriguing theories about children's play that were so profound they are still being explored today. Vygotsky described how children use imaginative play to develop into wiser and more knowledgeable human beings. "In play," Vygotsky wrote, "the child is always behaving beyond his age, above his usual everyday behavior; in play he is, as it were, a head above himself." We saw this in the preceeding scenario in several ways:

- Alesa got an opportunity to show her generosity—something she was not willing to do at first.
- Jordan had a chance to regulate his emotion of fear and kept swinging even though he was afraid at first.
- Alesa got an opportunity to explore her imagination—what *would* I pass if I were on my way to the moon?

Vygotsky suggested that as a child plays, particularly with parents and others who are more knowledgeable about the world, they can stretch themselves beyond the limits of their own understanding. Vygotsky referred to this as a "zone of proximal development" and suggested that children can accomplish more challenging tasks when an adult is nearby to offer social support.

When Annie gets frustrated because she cannot fit a shaped block into the colored cube, Mother turns the cube so that the side with the correct hole is facing up, and *then* Annie can find the right hole. Dominic does not have enough coordination to climb up the rope net at the playground, so his father supports his feet from below until Dominic learns how to place his feet safely. In the same way, adults also help children develop important emotional skills. They teach children how to share, how to understand when they have done something unfair, how to be patient, and how to manage their impulsive tendencies to grab a toy another child is already holding.

Playing is important because children have a much longer attention span for an activity that is engaging and interesting to them. One group of researchers explained it this way: "Consider 5-year-old David, who cannot sit still and pay attention during circle time in kindergarten for more than 2 minutes. Yet when pretending to be a cooperative member of the class while playing school with his friends, David can sit and attend for as long as 10 minutes. Play provides the roles, rules, and scenarios that enable David to focus and sustain interest at a higher level than he does in nonpretend activities."[3]

Because it provides an opportunity for children to attend to an activity for a longer period of time, playing is an especially important way to learn to manage emotion. For this reason, many opportunities for socio-dramatic play and conflict-resolution themes during playtime help children develop better self-regulation abilities. Play, according to Vygotsky, gives a child many opportunities to practice scenarios she encounters every day but in a less threatening environment. For example, the use of procedure dolls was mentioned previously. Procedure dolls allow children to work through the fears they have about surgery, a shot, or a blood draw. Children who are experiencing trauma (such as a medical procedure) cope better with the trauma when they are allowed to act it out beforehand and think through their own reactions and fears.

Dealing with negative emotions is not the only benefit. Lucia can "act out" an argument between two of her dolls and help them come to a resolution. In doing so, she'll develop emotional skills that will help her resolve differences with her own friends. Marcus can pretend he is being pushed from the top of the slide by a monster. He can then assess what it might feel like to his younger brother if Marcus were to push him off from a stool in the kitchen. Marty can lie in his bed at night and vocalize a pretend conversation between two of his stuffed animals about "there is no such thing as giant spiders under the bed." He can use this technique to help conquer his own fears about what is crawling around underneath him. It is not difficult to understand why these techniques are more effective than sitting in a chair and listening to an adult explain that "arguing won't solve anything," or "you must not push other children," or even "you are safe at night even if it is dark in your bedroom." As Vygotsky told us, children "learn best not when they are told, but when they can act upon their environments and construct knowledge for themselves."[4]

Parents can and should give the "lectures," but they should also understand that children are most likely to internalize the rules they are taught when they are given opportunities to "play them out." This is why we so often find children repeating the themes of their own daily conflicts in their playtime. A child might put her doll in the same time-out chair she had to sit in yesterday or bake a pretend cookie for a younger sibling and remind her "not to eat it until it cools down" only hours after she burned her own tongue eating hot soup at lunchtime.

Children who have many opportunities for make-believe play are simply better at resolving conflicts, managing their emotions, and getting along with others in real-life scenarios. This benefit carries beyond the preschool classroom. Children who show good self-regulation as preschoolers will continue to get along better with others throughout their lives.

Children use dramatic playtime to develop their literacy and numeracy skills

Now let's look in again on Alesa and Jordan.

Jordan is still swinging in the tire swing, but Alesa has turned her attention to some riding toys that are in the yard. There are six or seven different ones, and Alesa is carrying them from the side of the yard to the driveway. When she is finished, she counts them. "One, two, three, four," she says to no one in particular and then begins moving each toy to another spot. She has captured her mother's attention.

Mom: What are you up to, Alesa?

Alesa: I am putting them in order—in lines.

Mom: Looks pretty cool.

Alesa: So you can pick out whichever bike you want to.

Alesa continues counting where she left of a few seconds ago: "Five bikes, six bikes, seven bikes."

Alesa (waving her arms in the air ecstatically): I have seven bikes!

Mom: What are you going to do with them?

Alesa (pausing and turning back toward her lineup of bikes): Well . . . everybody's going to come pick a bike out, so . . .

Mom: They can see them all. They're all organized.

Alesa: I cleaned 'em all off, so everybody can ride one if they
want.

Alesa has taken a play opportunity and developed it into a math
lesson. Only she doesn't know it. She has shown her natural tendency to
prefer order to chaos, but this isn't why she lined up the bikes. She has
something else in mind all together. After organizing the bikes, she counts
them for reasons no one quite understands. But it is important to Alesa
to know how many there are, and her ability to stop at four, pause for a
distraction, and then continue counting forward again without starting
from the beginning shows she is developing some mathematical abilities
that will be important later on when she is learning to add. At age four,
she's never done a single math worksheet, but she has been allowed to
pretend as often as she chooses.

Pretend play has many different applications that help children
develop literacy and numeracy skills, and when a child lacks the opportunity to play in this very natural, uninhibited way, the results can be far-
reaching. A recent survey, given to teachers in Great Britain, underscores
another consequence of the absence of make-believe play. The survey,
entitled *Young Children's Skills on Entry to Education*, was given to more
than 700 teachers. "Teachers claim that half of all children now start
school at four or five unable to speak audibly, be understood by others,
respond to simple instructions, recognize their own names, or even count
to five." The researcher who produced the data suggested that lack of adult
participation and playful learning is robbing our children of the opportunity to learn to communicate well.[5]

"Pretending is a form of thinking and learning as well as a form
of play. Although pretending may seem effortless, it is an intellectu-
ally demanding activity," write Marilyn Segal and Don Adcock in their
book *Just Pretending*. One of the intellectual skills developed is the use
of vocabulary. "The real purpose in building a vocabulary of words is
to communicate longer and more complicated thoughts by combining
the words . . . The two-year-old who says, 'Juice all gone,' is using a
combination of words to make a stereotypical remark. Within a short
time, though, the sentences of children can impress us with their creativity, as in the case of a preschool child who looks at the moon passing
behind a cloud and says, 'It looks like the moon is melting.'"[6] That child
has learned to take a concrete object (the moon) and apply an abstract

thought (melting) to it. This is an indication that his vocabulary *and* his ability to think abstractly are maturing. That is one of the benefits of imaginative play.

Here's another way of putting it: Very young toddlers have difficulty using any object for play in any manner other than the way the object was intended to be used. A ball is for rolling, a cup is for drinking, and a telephone is for talking into. Later on, with help from an adult to show them how, they will develop the ability to use these objects in nonliteral ways. A cup might become a hat or a crown. A ball can substitute as a pillow for a teddy bear. A telephone can be used to squash a lump of clay. Once a child can detach a toy from its usual meaning, opportunities flourish for developing new words, new skills, and new applications for using things. An infant can go from holding a block and mouthing it—learning about its texture and weight—to building a stack of blocks one on top of another, to building a small castle out of blocks, with blue ones for the base and yellow ones for the shingles, with square ones to make up the walls, and cylinders and triangles to become the towers. Along the way, she'll learn dozens of new words (square, tower, cylinder, castle, blue) and practice dozens of mathematical processes (sort by color, stack smaller ones on top of larger ones to make a sturdier base, count towers on this side and build the same number symmetrically on the other side). Given enough of these opportunities, she'll be superbly prepared to excel when it is time to take advantage of opportunities for formal learning.

Pretending helps children learn problem-solving skills and creativity

Dr. Jerome Bruner is an internationally recognized psychologist whose research and observations have influenced education worldwide. Bruner tells of an experiment he and his colleagues, Kathy Silva and Paul Genova, once performed in an effort to understand how play influences a child's problem-solving capabilities. The task the children were to perform was to get a piece of colored chalk out of a transparent box. The box had been placed outside of the child's reach, and each child was told that they could use any of the tools at hand, but they must not get out of their chair in order to reach the box. Bruner and his colleagues provided sticks, clamps, string, and other materials. The solution to the problem was to connect shorter sticks together using string and clamps and then reach the box using the stick.

If a child did not succeed immediately in finding a solution to the problem, researchers would assist by giving hints, and if that wasn't enough, they eventually suggested the solution: "Have you thought about the possibility of clamping together two sticks?" Ultimately, all of the children were successfully performing the task, but the researchers were really interested in knowing how children get to the point where they are able to solve problems efficiently. Before the experiment began, the children had been divided into three groups. The first group was given a period of play, and according to Bruner, "in the course of that play they had an opportunity to fool around with the sticks, with the clamp and a string, however they might desire." A second group got "a little pedagogical demonstration explaining how you could join together two strings with a clamp, etc." The third group was simply shown examples of sticks, strings, and clamps and was given a demonstration of what strings and clamps are like. Bruner writes:

> Now let me tell you what happened to the children in those three different groups.
>
> The children in that first group who had a chance to play with the materials in advance solved the problem better than the children in the other two groups. Let me call these children in the first group the "true players." Not only did they solve the problem more often, but they seemed to make better use of the suggestive hints we gave them than the other children. Besides, the "true players" had far less tendency to abandon the task enroute when they ran into trouble. They were more frustration proof. They seemed altogether better at the way in which they went about things, those "true players." They knew how to begin simply; they had far less tendency to try out complicated hypotheses; and so forth.[7]

When given access to playthings, and time to use them, children can create endless play scenarios. They can use leaves, rocks, sticks, blocks, pillows, empty boxes, and a host of other items to build everything from twig huts for fairies or a pool and high-dive for a bumblebee. The more experience they have creating unusual uses for common items, the better they get at being creative. As a result, they are better prepared to apply that creativity and their problem-solving skills later in life. These skills are in high demand in the workforce today.

Older children use these skills as well. One benefit of developing creativity and problem-solving skills is that children are better prepared to succeed academically because they can think their way through problems and come up with solutions that aren't spelled out in a textbook. One student put it this way: "A lot of kids are really stumped if the teacher doesn't explain a math problem well. They will just sit there and stare at the page and get frustrated. But I've learned that if I think about it for a while, there are lots of different ways to solve a math problem. Once, I was taking a test for a state math competition, and I couldn't remember the formula I needed. I had to draw out a picture on the back of my paper and think it through until I could figure out a logical solution. It wasn't the way I had been taught to solve the problem, but I got the right answer."

Why parents are important to make-believe play

While it would seem that make-believe play is simply an instinctive ability for most children, child development specialists have identified one factor that increases the likelihood that a child will become a good pretender with a rich background of symbolic play. Bruner writes:

> [One answer we discovered through our research] about what produced prolonged concentration and rich elaboration in play rather took us aback. *It was the presence of an adult.* I do not mean an adult "over the shoulder" of the child, trying to direct his activity, but one in the neighborhood who gave some assurance that the environment would be stable and continuous, but would also give the child reassurance and information as, if, and when the child needed it."[8]

If parents want to facilitate imaginative play, they need to learn how to encourage a child's thinking without imposing our own agenda. Well-meaning adults who try to turn make-believe play into an academic experience sometimes inadvertently short-circuit the learning process. For example, we spoke earlier of Alesa's efforts to line up and organize several riding toys she was playing with. At first blush, it appeared that Alesa's purpose was purely mathematical. She told her mother, after all, that she was "lining all of the bikes up—organizing them." For most of us, that would be an immediate cue to jump in and impose a learning opportunity. Just think of the possibilities:

- Can you line them up tallest to shortest?
- Can you put all of the bikes with yellow handlebars in one group and all of the bikes with red handlebars in another group?
- Can you put them in a circle instead of in a line?

In order to please that parent, Alesa would have gone about the task of sorting the bicycles by color, and, once she was successful, that would likely have been the end of the activity.

But because Alesa's mother was patient, she soon saw that although Alesa was applying her counting and organizing skills, developing math skills was not at all what she had in mind. Instead, Alesa was lining the bikes up so she could play "bike store"—an all together different proposition than counting, sorting, and identifying. Because Alesa's mother resisted imposing her own agenda (I want to find out if Alesa can sort these bikes based on the color of their handlebars), Alesa had the opportunity to develop her idea into something wonderful—a learning activity that had unlimited potential. In the course of playing "bike store," Alesa could develop her social skills (practice greeting customers), her literacy skills (making signs indicating the different prices of the bikes), her problem-solving skills (how to keep her brother from riding away on one of the tricycles), and even her role-playing skills ("I will be the seller, Mommy, and you be the buyer"). The learning could go on for the rest of the afternoon instead of ending with successful completion of the adult-assigned sorting task.

There are dozens of theories about how children learn, but one metaphor, proposed by Swiss philosopher and scientist Jean Piaget, is especially helpful for parents who are trying to understand their role in encouraging pretending. Piaget used the word *scaffolding* to describe how parents, teachers, and peers help a child learn. When scaffolding is set up on the outside of an office building, those who pass by understand that the scaffolding is not actually supporting the weight of the building, but it is essentially put in place as a support system while the building is being constructed or repaired.

Scaffolding is also an effective method for teaching children. The first time your child tries to roll a piece of clay into a worm, you might first model the technique by making a clay worm yourself while she watches. Next, you might hold your child's hands in your own and help her roll the clay back and forth against the table. Finally, you would encourage her while she tries herself. As a child learns, the "scaffolding" (adult intervention) can be removed a piece at a time until the child is able to accomplish a task on her own.

Modeling (showing a child exactly how to accomplish a task) is necessary and appropriate for very young children. But as children mature, wise parents learn when to back off and let a child progress at his own pace. A loving, supportive adult is crucial to supporting play, but too much adult direction constricts a child's play and, by extension, limits his learning potential. Barbara H. Fiese, in her exploration of interactions between toddlers and their mothers, discovered that toddlers engage in more complex forms of play with their mothers than when they play by themselves. By contrast, "maternal intrusions and questioning" resulted in a child's play being restricted mainly to simple forms of play (mouthing an object, looking at a toy), rather than blossoming into richer symbolic play (using a round block as a wheel, pretending to drink from an empty cup, pretending to shop at the store with a doll). When children initiated the activity and mothers followed that pattern of play, expanding and elaborating on the child's play, more complex play resulted. On the other hand, when mothers "intruded" into their child's play by re-directing the child's attention or initiating a new activity before the child had finished an activity he had started, the amount of symbolic play decreased.[9]

What this research seems to tell us is that children are well equipped to play on their own, and the presence of a supportive adult helps assure that their play continues and expands. Bruno Bettelheim cautions us, "The need, nowadays to systematize children's play—to organize and supervise it in order to give it what we adults view as purpose—stems from the fact that the adult world has become separated from the world of children." The message seems to be, "Just play." Don't worry about the outcome. Just Play. Educational opportunities will create themselves. Just play. Your presence and your attention will be enough to assure that your child develops into a successful, happy adult. Just play!

Facilitating Imaginative play

Once you have bought into the idea that your presence alone is critical to richer play, the next question is to decide exactly what you and your child will do together. If we have grown up in an environment where our own play experiences were restricted, we may not have a good idea where to begin. In fact, social workers have discovered that children from low-income families sometimes lack play opportunities simply because it never occurred to the parents that playing was an option. If you're not good at pretend playing, how can you learn? If you are already pretty good at providing make-believe play opportunities for your children, how can you get better?

Jerome Bruner reassures us: "Let me note first that to play implies a reduction in the seriousness of the consequences of errors and of setbacks." In a profound way, play is an activity that is without frustrating consequences for the child even though it is a serious activity . . . . There is everything to be said, indeed, for letting the child loose in a decent setting with rich materials and some good cultural models to follow."[10]

So take a deep breath and relax. Providing the decent settings, rich materials, and cultural models is not complicated. It is easy to help your child's imagination run wild.

Cultural Models (whom to pretend with)

This means you. "While the capacity for fantasy or pretending is inherent in all reasonably normal human beings, the degree to which it is used by children depends to a large extent on whether parents or other adults have fostered it."[11]

A parent is the most important ingredient to rich, dramatic play opportunities. Grandparents, a beloved aunt, a great babysitter, or a fun-loving sibling make great cultural models as well.

Very young children seem to derive particular benefit from the presence of their mothers. Drawing on information gathered during a longitudinal study of nine children as they grew from infancy to age four, researchers Haight and Miller (1993) showed that the mothers are the major source of pretend play for a youngster.[12] Other researchers concur with this conclusion. Pretend play begins when children are barely old enough to communicate. "While children's play skills are limited, adult scaffolding makes make-believe more interesting, surprising, and absorbing—undoubtedly among the reasons 1- to 3-year-olds prefer to play with their mothers, even when peers and siblings are available."[14] But while mothers are especially important, the presence of any adult seems to have beneficial effects. According to Dorothy and Jerome Singer, who have made children's play a major focus of their professional research, a great adult model can participate in three ways:

Adult role 1: Onlooker

The Singers assure us that "watching children is an art in itself." One of our generation's great "onlookers" was Ruth Weir, who discovered that her child's quiet conversations with himself after he had been tucked in at night were a rich source of information about his worries, his joys, and his concerns. Eventually, she used her recordings of his bedtime narratives to help her understand how children's verbal abilities develop. She learned volumes about her child simply by being where she could hear what he was saying.

Darren's grandfather was able to help a grandson elaborate and extend a pretend activity by observing and then asking a simple question:

Grandpa: What's that you're holding?

Darren (holding a large black squirt gun): It's my fire squirt-out thing.

Grandpa: What are you going to do with that?

Darren: I use it to put out fires and stuff. And this (pointing to his hat) is my fire hat. This is my fire coat, these are my fire boots, and these are my fire pants. I have on fire underwear too.

Grandpa: Fire underwear! Does it have burn holes in it?

Darren gives Grandpa a disgusted look.

Grandpa: So, if I have a fire in my house, you will come and put it out?

Darren: Yes, but you have to call me on the phone at the fire department and I will hurry up and come.

Grandpa: What is your phone number?

Darren: One-one-one-one-nine.

Grandpa: And will you answer the phone?

Darren: Yes, but I will say, "Fire Department. Fireman Joe speaking." Only I will say it real loud.

Grandpa: Your name is Fireman Joe?

Darren: Yes. That is my name now. But someday I will probably be Darren again.

Adult role 2: Participant

It can be delightful to be lured into the pretending game. Your task, once you are called upon as an active participant, is to keep enough distance that you don't become the one who controls the pace of playtime. You can even set a time limit in advance so your child knows that you will play for five minutes and then you need to go back to your own work. Jessica's mother was supremely successful at this kind of participation. Now a mother herself, Jessica writes: "When I was quite young, my mom used to turn the entire house into obstacle courses, puppet shows, music rooms, and anything you can think of. We used to play with those obstacle courses on rainy days for hours and she would simply come in every seven to eight minutes and change it up slightly and we were off competing again." Jessica's mother was a master at participating, and to this day, her daughter remembers how fun Mom's playtimes were.

Sometimes, the participant's role is to be a supporter—helping to find props (do you want me to get your baseball cap so you can be the pitcher?), helping your child choose a play theme (we could pretend like this hut is where the witch lives), or just asking an interested question (do you want to pretend that the bubbles in the bathtub are for making wigs?). Other times, you'll be there just for the conversation.

One of the important contributions a parent makes to pretending is that we are generally willing to go along with whatever the child imagines. When children play with their peers, this is not always the case. There will be a constant battle-of-wills to see whose idea prevails:

"Let's pretend I am the mom and you are the baby."

"No, let's pretend we are going to the store and I am the big sister and you want me to buy you ice cream, but I didn't bring any money."

"But I want to be the mom."

An adult is generally much more willing to be compliant, so ideas don't get bogged down in a lot of negotiation. This is one of the important distinctions between playing with a parent and playing with a peer. A child will have an opportunity for richer symbolic play because of the combination of adult support and the child's freedom to choose.

If you are a reluctant pretender, start by choosing an activity that is enjoyable to you. In *Just Pretending*, Segal and Adcock identified four "sure-fire" playing themes a reluctant parent could begin with:

1. Seeing the doctor: Stretch out on the couch and be the "patient" while your child examines you. "Erik, for example, examined his father and declared that he had grass in his ear. This condition, Erik explained, came from eating a mud pie which had traveled up a little tube from his father's mouth to his ear. Erik administered three shots and a gumdrop pill—and his father was cured on the spot. Such medical magic appeals to the adult imagination as much as to the child's."[14]

2. Imagining a new routine: Pretend to get away from the daily habits. Where will you go? Will you imagine a vacation to a faraway place, or just a trip to a favorite restaurant? One adult remembers daydreaming with his mother this way:

"One thing I *do* remember that had an obvious effect on me was when my mom would spend time with me 'dreaming' about how she wanted to remodel the homes we lived in. She would sit with me and draw floor plans, sketch 3-D images of remodeled rooms, and describe in words how she wanted Dad to build the spaces being remodeled. It was easy for me to visualize her descriptions, and I always loved to listen and think about designing and building with her."

Dave attributes his decision to pursue an education in interior design directly to these early childhood pretending experiences with his mother. "I now work as a project manager overseeing building design and construction. I don't know if I'd have followed this path if it weren't for her," he concludes. Our willingness to daydream with our children can have far-reaching beneficial consequences.

3. Going on a shopping spree: Imagine buying all of the candy in the world. Or go to the zoo and buy an animal to bring home for a pet. Take your child to your own closet, supply them with a wallet or a purse, and allow them to try on and buy anything they want.

4. Being the bad guy: Preschool children play "by the rules," but adults have no qualms about breaking the law, according to Segal and Adcock. That's why dads and moms make such delightfully frightening monsters and evil witches. "After stealing some toys and hiding them, the adult returns to his secret hideout (a favorite chair), where he is captured by the children. They put him in jail and search for the stolen toys, only to find that the robber has escaped from jail and is busy stealing something else."[15] A favorite game with children is the "child sandwich." A wicked witch can capture her child and put him between two couch cushions as if he were a sandwich. The wicked witch cackles and says, "I think I am going to eat this 'Drew sandwich.' What should I put on it?"

"Mayonnaise!" responds Drew. "Pickles and a banana! Marshmallows!"

Imagine being tucked in every night after a wicked witch had turned you into a Drew and marshmallow sandwich with mayonnaise.

5. Make a simple puppet: Here's another simple activity for parents who believe they are pretending novices: Take a plain old sock (any color will do) and put your hand inside. Tuck a fold of cloth between your thumb and the four fingers of your hand. Your thumb is the lower jaw of your new playmate, and your fingers will form the head. At about your wrist, fold an inch-wide tuck in the fabric of the sock. This will form the forehead of your puppet. Now look around the house for a great pair of eyes. You can stick a couple of marbles or playing dice underneath the fold (with the "ones" side facing forward like pupils). Eyeballs can be made of ping pong balls, small stones, or a couple of firm grapes out of the refrigerator. Add a tuft of yarn, some curling ribbon, or some fake fur for hair.

Next, practice your proper puppet technique. Your thumb should move up and down while your fingers (the upper jaw) remain still. See if you can make your puppet purse his lips, ready for a kiss. Can you make your puppet look angry? Sad? If you want a longer nose, just leave extra room in the toe of the sock rather than pulling it tight against your fingers.

Once you have practiced a little, you are ready to launch your pretending session. Begin with something simple. Use your puppet as the narrator for your child's favorite bedtime story. Hide your arm under a pillow and leave only the puppet sticking out. Experiment with strange voices as you tell the story. You don't have to be a fine actor or even a naturally funny person to pull this game off. Your child's delight will be the motivation you need to look forward to your next pretend participation role.

Adult role 3: Stimulator of imaginative play

Children who do not have a lot of world experience may need your stimulation to help them understand how to invent the plot or the story line for their pretend play. Children's books can be a good starting place.

Make sure you read lots of fairy tales and adventure books to your child. Choose a favorite story and then try to imitate something that the characters in the book did. As the stimulator of symbolic play, your adult responsibilities essentially involve helping your children take their own ideas and extend them. Don't worry. This will probably come naturally to you. You'll recall that in an earlier scenario, Wendy's mother helped Wendy extend the menu for her pretend spaghetti meal simply by asking if there would be salad and French bread to go with the meal. I mentioned Fred Rogers and his neighborhood of make-believe earlier. Mr. Rogers was a master at stimulating imaginative play. Something as simple as a cardboard paper towel tube could become anything from a telescope to a track for a marble to roll through to a funnel for sand at the sand table. Mr. Rogers simply provided us with a place to begin.

Another alteration you may have to make to your lifestyle if you want to encourage lots of pretend play is to lighten up once in a while. I remember sitting on top of the kitchen table while my mother mopped the kitchen floor. She would stack the chairs upside-down on the table, and the legs of the chairs would extend upward. On the bottom of each of these chair legs was a pivoting metal piece that served as the base of the chair leg. As I pressed down on one side of the pivot, I could pretend that I was spraying the aliens in the room with an alien-freezing substance that kept them from capturing me and taking me to a foreign planet. I remember always being surprised that Mom would allow this game. Normally, I would not have been allowed to sit on top of the kitchen table. Maybe Mom let me stay there because it kept me off from her freshly waxed floor, but I suspect it also had something to do with the fact that she enjoyed watching me play. A good pretender is likely to get muddy, wet, and sticky at some time in his life. He may jump from tree branches, race his bike wildly down the sidewalk, or hide in a dirty, cramped, spider-infested corner of the basement. As long as you are on hand to keep him safe, you might consider allowing your child to get a few splinters or make a few messy, sloppy, dirty mistakes. Skinned knees and "owies" are an inevitable outcome of a robust childhood.

Rich Materials (what to pretend with)

"When I was little, I loved to practice doing what you really do in life," one nine-year-old told me. "Once, I played 'shoe store' with a shoe rack with all kinds of different shoes—purple high heels, slippers that looked like puppies, and work boots and stuff. We had a cash register, and I remember how much fun it was to pretend I was shopping for the shoes. I would try on lots of them, and then when it was time to pay, another friend would write out a receipt. We didn't even know how to write numbers yet. We just liked writing receipts."

For some children, simply providing a box full of miscellaneous recyclables is a great starting place. Children can glue and paste and staple to their heart's content as they create juice box aliens. I watched recently as one young child took a box and pasted on colored feathers until she had created a fabulously colorful rendition of an autumn tree. There is no right or wrong thing to build, and at home, neatness can be purely optional. Bruner reminds us, "It is characteristic of play that children are not excessively attached to results. They vary what they are up to and allow their fantasies to make substitutions for them. If this variation is not possible, the child very quickly becomes bored with his activity. Watch an infant piling wood bricks and you will be struck by the diversity and the combinatorial richness of how he plays" (Bruner, 61).

With young preschoolers, one fun way to start is to think of your own adult responsibilities and provide your children with some tools they can use to mimic the grown-up world they see all around them. Think about things you have laying around the house that could be pressed into service as "really useful pretending junk." As we have seen, becoming a postal worker, a waitress, or a shoe salesman is intensely interesting for a young child. Here are some of the favorite pretend supplies we gathered up in my home:

Office

Is there a broken keyboard or mouse, an empty stapler, a stack of sticky notes, and a pretend telephone somewhere in your house? Five minutes of cooperative play with you will be enough to give your four-year-old a good idea about how an office is run and keep him busy for the rest of the morning. An office ten-key with a roll of receipt tape will attract even the most reluctant pretender.

Post office

Save some of the empty billing envelopes, unwanted address labels, and adhesive seals that usually end up in your shredder. Salvage your empty shoe boxes and cut a slot in the lid to create your own mailboxes. You can stay in the bathroom and clean the mirror, scrub the shower, and mop the floor, and still extend your child's play by taking time to push an envelope under the door now and then.

Grocery store

Gather some cans and unbreakable bottles from your pantry (or recycle, clean, and save empty cans, boxes, and bottles) and provide a few grocery sacks and a grocery basket or cart (you can use an umbrella stroller in a pinch). A walkie talkie or telephone is useful in case someone needs a "cleanup on aisle five." A toy cash register is a great toy investment since it has so much pretend potential. Your child can use it for everything from running a bakery to running a used car lot.

Car wash

Start with a bucket, an old towel, a spray bottle filled with water tinted with a little blue food coloring to make it look like window cleaner, and a few assorted tricycles and riding toys. Provide a scrub brush and an old toothbrush for "detailing."

Now that you have the idea, what other options do you have for sociodramatic play? Let your child be a doctor, a nurse, a laundromat owner, a librarian, or a waiter. There are dozens of possibilities.

Encourage pretend play with "true toys"

While toy manufacturers are great at making colorful gadgets with all the bells and whistles, I was always intrigued to notice which toys my children used again and again and which toys were "played out" after only a few minutes of use. If I were starting over, I'd be more careful about the toys I chose, and some of these would be on my list:

Blocks: By far, the single-most versatile toy I had in my home was a box full of colored wooden blocks of different shapes and sizes. Their potential uses were unlimited: They could be stacked into simple towers, they could become freeways for miniature cars, they could become a castle for a Barbie doll, or a playhouse for a family of walnut fairies. One son even created an experiment to illustrate liquefaction of soil during an earthquake using a cake pan full of wet sand, a tower of blocks, and a sander to provide the vibration. Every child needs a few good blocks.

Dolls: You can't play house without a doll, can you? If your child owns only collectible dolls—the beautiful, expensive kind with silken hair and a wardrobe that cost more than your daughter's did—consider purchasing one or two dolls that can get "messed up" without anyone being overly concerned. You want the kind of doll that loves to have her hair combed, doesn't mind getting her clothes washed out in the bathroom sink, and can take a bath herself without staying soggy for days. Doll accessories are great, and they don't have to be expensive. Assemble a diaper bag with a doll bottle, a blanket, a change of clothing, and some newborn-sized disposable diapers. Buy a bag of the cheapest diapers you can find with closures that can be used again and again. Miniature people and action figures are fun for some children, and so are stuffed animals, but I found that the more my children owned, the less they played with them.

Dress-up box: Scarves, shoes, outrageous hats, old jewelry, and one or two of the "fancy" dresses or old suit coats you would otherwise send to the neighborhood thrift store all make great dress-up items. In fact, a thrift store might be a great place to find some of the silky, sparkly dress-up items a little girl would love. If your budget allows, add some sturdy costume jewelry. It will last much longer than the plastic stuff you'll purchase at a children's toy store. On the other hand, a shimmering tiara and a feather boa are great toy-store purchases. Watch for after-season sales on Halloween costumes as well. A clown wig, a fireman's helmet, a policeman's badge and handcuffs, or a cowboy hat and bandanna would make fun additions to your dress-up box. Even used sports equipment like an old football helmet and pads or a catcher's mitt will inspire moments of make-believe your child might not have thought of otherwise. Over the years, you could accumulate a good variety of great junk, so consider purchasing a large, sturdy dress-up box for storage, and "rotate" the contents. Put just a few costumes in at a time, and exchange them for others later on.

Art supplies: If you have space in your home to accommodate one, this tool will be used again and again. Choose a bottom drawer in the kitchen you can devote to kids' art supplies. Washable paint with brushes, crayons, a supply of recycled or leftover paper, blunt-nosed scissors, some modeling clay, some good-quality watercolor paints or pastel chalks, fine and broad-tipped washable markers, and some decent drawing paper will make a good basic supply. Keep a painting shirt or apron handy as well. You'll want to keep your supply simple so it's easy to keep the drawer organized. I've bought the fancy magic paper, the glitter glue pens, the colored stickers, and the pre-cut foam shapes before too, but I found that they have very limited appeal after the first use. The basic supplies get used again and again simply because they can be used in such a variety of ways. We've always owned an easel and made the art supplies and paper accessible, and I like to think that is one reason I've never had a child who drew on the walls.

A cash register and a play telephone: As mentioned before, the cash register is a great tool if you want to run a boat store or sell plastic animals in your own zoo gift shop. A sturdy telephone also has dozens of uses. If you have a choice, opt for a battery-operated phone that can actually ring.

Child-sized housewares: There are an infinite variety of child-sized household appliances and kitchen gadgets available. If you choose yours carefully, they'll last long enough for your grandchildren to use. A toy cupboard and sink, a few plates and cups, some plastic fruits and vegetables, and a pretend iron or blender are all examples of some of the items we have in our home. We store our play kitchen gadgets together in a sturdy bin for easy cleanup. Now and then, I'll carry the whole bin to the kitchen and put the contents into my dishwasher for cleaning and disinfecting, so I purposely choose toys that don't have labels that will wash off or flimsy plastic that will melt during the drying cycle (or after the first use at the Pizza and Pasghetti Restaurant).

A collection container and a magnifying glass: For days when a child wants to make a rock collection or press flowers from the backyard, a box to hold the collection and a decent-quality magnifying glass will come in handy more than once. Children who love to observe nature will also appreciate a safe place (a designated shelf or box in the bedroom) to store their found treasures.

A chalkboard or a whiteboard: Very young children will need supervision, but older preschoolers will have hours of fun with an erasable chalkboard or whiteboard with fume-free markers.

Cars and trucks: From the simple Matchbox car to a ride-on, battery-operated Jeep, cars and trucks can be a great source of pleasure for the child who likes to pretend. Smaller cars can be double-the-fun if there are cardboard tubes for tunnels, strips of plastic track for building gargantuan over-the-headboard-and-down-the-bedspread racing tracks, and cardboard boxes for building pretend car washes.

Interlocking blocks: After my oldest son's imaginary friends all moved to Florida, his supply of interlocking blocks saved his sanity (and mine). Legos, Tinker Toys, Duplo blocks, Lincoln Logs, and Knex (to name some of the trademarked brands) are just a few of the toys that have fascinated my preschoolers and kept my school-aged children occupied until way past bedtime. These toys are valuable both by themselves and as props for other kinds of pretend play. A Tinker Toy can become a lollipop. A fort made of Lincoln Logs is a great hiding place for a pile of green army men. Kinex can be formed into flowers that adorn the windowsill of the playhouse. Be sure to save the boxes they come in, or plan to provide storage bins that will keep interlocking blocks organized. A sturdy plastic file folder will help your child keep track of building instructions so that models can be built again and again.

Decent settings (where to pretend)

A small table and chairs: One of the delightful gifts given to my children by their grandparents was a child-sized table and chairs. The table is strong enough to support a child's weight, which is important if you're using it as a doctor's examination table. The chairs are sturdy enough for an adult to sit in, and I've used one myself dozens of times on days when I was invited to sit down and help color, watch a puppet show, or have tea.

A puppet theater: A simple tri-fold puppet theater Grandpa built using heavy cardboard, scrap lumber, and a few hinges has been a beloved play toy at our house. Although you can make your own from sturdy cardboard, this toy has seen enough use that I'd rank it as another of those "you get what you pay for" purchases. A good quality tri-fold with a window cut in the center panel can be a puppet theater or double as a lemonade stand, a dentist's reception area, a bank teller's booth, or a carnival fishpond game. Look for a screen that can't be knocked over easily but *can* be folded up and stored under the bed or in the garage.

A hideout: Find a spot in your home or your yard that can be converted into a secret hiding spot. Cover the dining room table with two large tablecloths and let the sides hang to the floor. Cover the piano bench with a large blanket, make a fort out of chairs and sheets held up with a mop handle, or create a green secret space by hollowing out an area outdoors underneath a large bush or pine tree.

A big, paintable cardboard box: No appliance or super-sized box of toilet tissue should ever find its way to the recycling bin without a tour of duty as a plaything. A box can be everything from a playhouse to a police station. Mom and Dad can cut windows, doors that open and close, and even mailbox slots. With a smaller box, cut a circular hole in the top of the box, attach some shoulder straps, and then step inside. Your box can become a car, a bus, or a locomotive (tape on a flashlight or two for the searchlight or the headlights).

A bathtub: Here's a great spot for pretending, provided you have the right "tools" on hand. If you don't have a bathtub in your home or apartment, a big tub of water on the porch or deck or a full kitchen sink will work almost as well. A few pieces of craft foam cut into shapes stick to the walls of a tub or shower beautifully. A child can play for an extended period with a cup, a funnel, and a sieve (a butter tub with a few holes punched in the bottom is an inexpensive alternative to purchased tub toys). A turkey-baster that has been retired from kitchen use, a medicine dropper, or a sponge will all make fun tub toys as well. Just be sure the shower curtain is closed, or be prepared to mop up after bathtime ends, and keep a container in the bathroom so toys can be stashed under the sink when you are finished using them. Float Styrofoam bowl UFOs, launch a boat made of aluminum foil, or put on a pair of swim goggles and pretend you're in the Olympics. Outside, you can use also use your tub of water for painting the side of the house or designing artwork on the sidewalk and watching it evaporate. Wear clothes you can get wet in, or take a towel outside with you so you can lay on your back and look for shapes in the clouds while your shirt dries.

Outdoor play areas: Playing outside will be discussed more extensively in chapter 8, but it is important to remember how vital outdoor environments are to pretend play. Here are a few outdoor tools recommended by play specialists that will help your child create the backdrop for a plethora of make-believe and fantasy play:

- A swing or swingset
- A sand table or sandbox with tools for digging
- A playhouse
- Loose equipment such as innertubes, clotheslines and clothespins, a two-step ladder, empty cardboard carpet tubes for tunnels, unused plastic lawn edging for ramps for small cars and vehicles

- A small garden area, grow box, or planter for a child-sized garden
- Wagons, dump trucks, bicycles, and tricycles
- Water and dirt
- Nature itself (leaves, sticks, twigs, rocks)

Writer and doll creator Karen Neuschutz recalled a day when her children were having a difficult time getting along together and she decided to take them outside to help her pick raspberries and get some fresh air. Once the raspberries were picked and the children had time to rest, their natural tendency to make-believe set in. Her children created a "raspberry juice factory" out of a tree branch they found in the ditch, some stones they used for trucks, and a few twigs to serve as factory workers. She writes: "The children laughed and showed me the remarkable factory; they were as proud as if they had made a revolutionary invention. Well, hadn't they?"[16]

Neuschutz goes on to point out that the child who finds a stick of wood, names it "Harvey," and carries it around in a blanket for days, and the child who ties a string around a piece of crumpled newspaper and drags it around like a dog are preparing themselves for their adult roles. Parents who are willing to set aside a few precious moments of their own time to direct and inspire children in their pretend play will find that they are uniquely qualified to help a child expand and develop his or her enormously important make-believe play skills.

Children are imaginative by nature, but imagine how much of their development a parent is responsible for. Will a child who likes to play with toy cars instinctively build a tunnel out of a discarded gift-wrap tube? Probably not until he has seen it demonstrated. Will a little girl think of creating an imaginary "bike store" without a tricycle leaning against the garage to inspire her? It is not likely. Will children develop the emotional skills necessary to learn to share if they never have an opportunity to play with another child and covet the toy that child is holding? Only by a miracle. Make-believe playtime is critical to the well-being of a preschool-aged child, and a parent plays *the most critical* role in making sure a child learns to pretend. Whether by providing the model, providing the toys and tools, or providing the opportunity for play, a loving parent is the catalyst a child needs to best develop this crucial life skill.

We've spent an entire chapter talking about the benefits of pretend play in the life of a child. We have yet to address the benefits to the parent who is helping with the pretending. If we were speaking strictly in terms of the good relationship you will develop with your preschooler, then pretending together would be worth it. But there are many significant personal benefits as well. Playing is just plain fun. It can be exhilarating to be the monster chasing children around the family room when you return home after work. It can be a great source of stress-relief to imagine yourself on a cruise to Greece or swimming in a quiet lake. It can be uplifting to recall and re-create wonderful experiences from your own childhood.

If you pay attention, you'll realize how often you use your own "pretending" abilities to help you cope. You use your own imagination every day. You imagine what you will wear and what you will say during your next presentation to the sales committee. You plan out a conversation with your husband over what you would like to do for family vacation. You daydream about how peaceful your life will be someday when your children are raised and you can get the whole house cleaned at the same time. The problem-solving skills you use to help your son build a gargantuan marble maze in his bedroom also help you engineer solutions to personality conflicts among co-workers at the office. You extend the same kind of creativity in garnishing a platter of appetizers before your dinner party that you used when you were showing your daughter how to decorate a mudpie. Pretending skills have all kinds of everyday adult applications that make our lives richer, fuller, and more enjoyable. Pretending with your child is a great way to get more out of your own life.

Notes

1. Berk, Mann, and Ogan, in *Play = Learning*, 10.
2. Brown, Sutterby, and Thornton, *PTO Today*, 3.
3. Berk, Mann, and Ogan, in *Play = Learning*, 9.
4. Brown, Sutterby, and Thornton, *PTO Today*, 1.
5. Singer, Golinkoff, and Hirsh-Pasek. 2006. *Play=Learning*, 5.
6. Segal and Adcock, *Just Pretending*, 30.
7. Bruner, *Peabody Journal of Education*, 64.
8. Bruner, *Peabody Journal of Education*, 67; emphasis added.
9. Fiese, *Child Development*, 1648–1656.
10. Bruner, *Peabody Journal of Education*, 60–62.
11. Singer and Singer, *Make Believe*, 13.
12. Haight and Miller, *Pretending at Home*.

13. Berk, Mann, and Ogan, in *Play = Learning*, 25.
14. Segal and Adcock, *Just Pretending*, 145.
15. Segal and Adcock, *Just Pretending*, 146.
16. Neuschütz, The Doll Book: Soft Dolls and Creative Free Play.

Chapter 8

Right iN Your OwN Backyard

Outdoor play adventures

• •

My grandmother had a grove of small plum trees in her backyard. Early in the spring, a scattering of purple phlox nested between the spindly trunks of the close-growing trees. As far as I am aware, the plums were never pruned or sprayed, and the fruit was rarely harvested. Grandma's plum tree grove, it seems, existed purely because of its natural hide-out capabilities. In the summer, we could slip into a small opening in the circle of trees and find our way into a small clearing underneath the overhanging canopy of green that was the perfect shelter from the hot summer sun. Depending upon who had played there last, there could be an assortment of tin cans and old pickle bottles we had used to gather a collection of water skeeters and moss from the artesian well-fed irrigation ditch in front of Grandma's house, or there might be an old iron skunk trap and a few empty electrical wire spools. The largest spool, when turned on its end, was big enough to become a small table. The smaller ones were just right for child-sized stools. In the center of the spool-table you might find empty paper cups left over from Grandma's last batch of homemade gelatin popsicles, or a collection of shining horse chestnuts and locust tree pods gathered from the sidewalks along the tree-lined street where she lived. Almost always, you could find a pile of "play money" left over from a day of playing house. This currency was really the coin-shaped, paper-thin, and nearly transparent seedpods of the matured phlox plants.

One of the blessings of my childhood was that I was born long before personal computers were a household item. Our black and white television got only average reception, so its entertainment value was restricted both by a lack of programming (we only had access to five channels) and by Mom's insistence that we limit our viewing to an hour or less each day. As a result, many of my out-of-school hours were spent outdoors. I had the advantage of living in a neighborhood where it was safe to play hopscotch in the front yard with friends or walk to a neighbor's house to play Kick the Can in the evening. We lived within biking distance of a branch of the public library and a decent park. Our own backyard had a lawn big enough for a game of croquet and trees tall enough to climb. There was a sandbox under the Box Elder tree, a rabbit hutch, and nearby, a patch of earth Mom had intended for a small garden. There was too much shade for a prosperous garden, but at least once a summer, we dug a gigantic hole in the dirt—just because we could. Think back to your beloved childhood play space. Were you blessed to have a patch of earth somewhere where you could sit and think and breathe?

Why is it that nostalgic memories of our own childhood play spaces engender the desire to reproduce the same good experiences for our children? When we are asked what developmental or cognitive benefits there were, we don't have clear answers. We're sure outdoor play was good for us, but outside of the murky assumption that there was some physical activity involved, we can't put our finger on a reason outdoor play might be important.

Just for fun, let's compare outdoor play with vitamin D intake. If you think back to your junior high health class, you might remember that vitamin D deficiency in infants causes rickets and osteomalacia. Rickets is a disease that causes soft bones and skeletal deformities, and osteomalacia results in muscle weakness and weak bones. Osteomalacia is particularly difficult to diagnose because the symptoms are subtle and often go undetected, especially in the early stages of the disease. Unless treated, a vitamin D deficiency results in an increased risk for adult health risks like osteoporosis. Lack of vitamin D has the potential to affect a child's quality of life *forever*.

I think outdoor play for children is a little bit like vitamin D. We know that it's good for us, even though we don't know what it does. We're pretty sure our kids are getting enough of it, even though we don't monitor their intake very closely. But because citizens of our country have been able to take its availability for granted for so long, we do not recognize the severe symptoms that indicate when a child's intake is inadequate. As a result, much of the impact of a deficiency is not noticeable until later in life, when it is difficult or impossible to reverse the damage—damage that has gone undetected but has quietly and cruelly impaired the individual for most of his lifetime.

So what does vitamin D have to do with outdoor play? As it turns out, lots, since exposure to sunlight is one of our most important sources of vitamin D. But that's not the real point here. The real point is that getting enough outdoor play is a lot like getting enough vitamin D. We have taken it for granted for so long that we don't even recognize the "symptoms" that are cropping up in our children because their generation isn't getting enough of it. Children get benefits from outdoor play that we do not normally quantify. We do not comprehend the critical need for outdoor play, and we certainly don't appreciate enough what its value was in our own lives. Only now, after a generation of raising children who aren't getting enough outdoor time, are we beginning to recognize that there are undetected consequences.

The adults who insisted that I needed to "go out and get a little fresh air" probably didn't ever think too hard about why it was important. They just knew it was. Today, however, things are different. As parents, we have gotten to the point that some of us are actually avoiding sending our children outside to play, either as a method of keeping them safe or because it's just easier for us that way. The persistent lack of outdoor free play that characterizes the lifestyles of today's youth is impacting them in ways we have only begun to understand.

Ecologist Tim Gill has observed, "Children are disappearing from the outdoors at a rate that would make the top of any conservationist's list of endangered species if they were any other member of the animal kingdom."[1] Our children's detachment from nature and natural surroundings will be a detriment to them unless, as caring adults, we can help reverse the trend.

There are many reasons we have let our society get to the point where we are willing to rob our children of their childhood right to play outside. Access is the first issue, and safety is a close second. Our urbanized society does not seem to value wild spaces, and where they are available, they are difficult to get to. As land prices increase, the average size of a building lot shrinks, and backyards, if they exist at all, are manicured and sterile. Our streets and neighborhoods are also considered less safe than they were a generation ago. If you are like me, no child leaves the house unless I have some assurance that they will be safe from pedophiles lurking in the shadows, bullies roaming the alleys, and cell-phone wielding drivers who distractedly swerve into the bike lane and drive 45 mph in 25 mph zones.

Landowner liability issues prevent children from roaming undeveloped land at will, so sandlot baseball games on the vacant lot on the corner are a thing of the past. Instead, free play is replaced by organized sports. Even outside recess time is being restricted and eliminated in many schools, or at least "organized" into structured play, due to more stringent academic requirements. But the biggest culprit of all is certainly the prevalence of electronic entertainment media, which provide us with hours of uninterrupted babysitting for only a nominal fee.

Other authors have argued the critical need for outdoor play more eloquently than I can. Richard Louv's *Last Child in the Woods: Saving Our Children from Nature-Deficit Disorder* is a notable example.[2] But it is worthwhile for parents to consider some of the recent research and why experts are telling us outdoor play might be more critical than we have previously realized.

Benefits of outdoor play

1. Outdoor play enhances gross motor activity in children. Because of this, outdoor play is probably the single most effective method of childhood obesity prevention available to us.
2. Outdoor play facilitates friendships and promotes cooperative social behaviors and attitudes. Ironically, the more dangerous our neighborhoods become, the less we allow our children to play together, so children in high-crime neighborhoods, who stand to benefit most from outdoor play, tend to get less and less of it.
3. Children who play outdoors have more opportunities

to develop social coping skills. Research indicates that over-protected children are bullied more often because they have not had the opportunity to develop some of the self-confidence and interpersonal skills they need to thwart bullying.

4. Frequent breaks from active classroom work (especially breaks that allow children to burn off stored energy) help most children concentrate better when they return to a classroom setting.

5. Researchers at the University of Illinois have discovered that some children who suffer from Attention-Deficit-Hyperactivity Disorder (ADHD) find relief from the symptoms of the disorder through contact with the green outdoor spaces.

6. Children who have outdoor experiences have important opportunities to conquer their fears of the unknown— everything from "stranger danger" to a dark forest.

7. Children who are allowed to have hands-on experience with nature tend to value it more. Because they have opportunities to develop appreciation for their natural world, they become wiser "consumers." They make more responsible environmental choices and are better able to understand the environmental consequences of their decisions.

Why are parents important to outdoor play?

As with other types of play, outdoor play has dozens of hidden benefits, and children need adults to help them get the most from their outdoor play. As a parent, you are the one who facilitates outdoor play by making the appropriate spaces and equipment available. You are the adult mentor who makes outdoor play look fun and keeps it safe. You are the one who controls outside distractions that encroach upon the time needed for outdoor play, and you are the teacher who makes the great outdoors come alive.

How will you promote outside play when both you and your child would quite honestly prefer to stay indoors and play Nintendo? Don't worry. It just takes a little thought, a little space, and a little time.

Create spaces for thought

Many of us can remember a "hidden" corner of the world where we preferred to spend time alone. It may have been a grove of plum trees in Grandma's backyard, or it may have been at the edge of a wash where there was a trickle of water and a little good dirt to play in. Perhaps your hidden corner of the world was in a leaf-sheltered treehouse, inside a backyard playhouse, under the stars on the roof of the apartment house, beneath the outstretched limbs of a big pine tree, under the boardwalk at the beach, or nestled behind the shrubs near the back porch. Many of us had a quiet corner where we could sit and daydream and decompress.

Winnie the Pooh referred to his quiet corner as his "thoughtful spot." Children need these spaces today as well but are perhaps less likely to find them unless adults help to create and preserve them. With a little ingenuity, you can help your child choose or create a "thoughtful spot" in even the most urban environment, and with luck, you'll find (and begin to use) a place of your own for pondering and reflection. Here are a couple of ideas to get you thinking. Once you start dreaming of the possibilities, you'll find that your options for a protected, quiet place are only limited by your imagination.

- Find a piece of shade in your yard (or create one by planting a tree or fast-growing shrub) and make a small hammock or a comfortable seat available.
- Author Richard Louv recommends creating an 8 x 8-foot space in your garden, surrounded by a small furrow. Plant sunflowers (both 8-foot and 4-foot varieties) in the furrow and lay down a carpet of groundcover plants inside.
- Create at least one green wall as a shelter from the sun. Plant ivy along the side of a shed, or hang strings from the balcony of a deck and at ground level below, plant pots of scarlet runner beans, or another climbing plant that will curl its way up the strings, providing a living sunshade.
- When you are choosing a backyard play structure, look for one that has a balcony level with an open area underneath. Plant tall shrubs or blooming hibiscus that will shade the lower area for most of the summer, or hang a simple shower curtain rod on one side of your play structure and tie up a big piece of heavy fabric with a natural motif in the design.

- Purchase a good quality "puppet theater" that can be carried outdoors on a good day to provide a quiet corner of the world even when landscaping at your new home isn't matured enough to provide shade.
- Make a "garden playhouse" for about fifty dollars by creating a tunnel of PVC pipe and chicken wire. Then plant a few vines to climb over the top of the tunnel. Find instructions at www.familyfun.go.com (search for "garden playhouse").
- Find a space at a nearby park where your child can scratch in the dirt or build fairy huts out of sticks and twigs within sight of a watchful adult.
- Take your child hiking, camping, picnicking, or beachcombing more often.
- Look for "thoughtful spot" options indoors if outdoor play isn't an option. The nook underneath the stairs or even just a corner of the bedroom with a comfortable seat and a basketful of books will do just fine. This is one of the best reasons to avoid putting a television in a child's bedroom. Leave them some space where they can be absolutely alone if they choose to be.
- Go for a nighttime pajama ride (just tuck the kids into their seat belts after they are all ready for bed). Enjoy an evening driving in the darkness listening to quiet music, or find a spot far away from the city lights where you can get out and do a little stargazing.

There's task #1: Provide a place where your child can simply sit and think, and then help her clear her schedule so that she has time to use her "thoughtful spot" as often as she chooses.

Provide the necessary "spare parts"

Task #2 is to help your child turn off the TV or the computer more often and get outdoors. Just getting him outside may not solve the problem, however. An adult has other responsibilities if a child is to benefit from outdoor play. Picture this: Your mother sends you outside to play in the backyard. You are fortunate that you have some green grass and a swing structure outside. You stand in the back door and contemplate the possibilities: "I could swing for a while." So, you swing for a few minutes.

Now what? Should you roll around in the grass? Should you look for four-leaf clovers? Should you jump up and down a little?

The point is that even a nice, green outdoor space has limited possibilities without some "spare parts." And often, even when the "spare parts" are available, some children lack the ingenuity to know how to use them immediately. That is where a playful parent comes in. As the provider of parts and the playtime facilitator, you can change the picture of this scene with just a few moments of your time and with minimal expense.

Take your nice green lawn and your swing set, and add a ball. What about some sand and a pail full of water? How about some rope and a few pulleys for lifting the bucket up and down? Now what if you add an old sheet, some clothespins, a pool noodle, a tennis racket, a tricycle, and a jump rope? With just a few additional tools, the possibilities have expanded immensely. Now your child can bounce a ball against the wall, build a sand castle, put on a play with shadow puppets, jump rope, build a fort, have a carwash, fight an imaginary war, or swat at butterflies. Add Mom or Dad as a playmate (or even have Mom or Dad invite a friend from down the street to play), and the possibilities could keep a child busy all week!

In European countries, the "adventure playground" is a popular alternative to the American playground (the ones we see in our public parks that are limited to a colored plastic and steel structure with a few bark chips underneath). Adventure playgrounds are unique in that they are purposely designed to enhance a child's gross motor and imaginative play. Adventure playgrounds will include old tires, running water, ponds full of frogs, mud to play in, rope bridges, rafts made of lashed-together logs, open camp-fires, or a small garden spot. Generally, these playgrounds will employ the services of a "play worker" or "play ranger"—an adult attendant who has been trained to help children dream up all sorts of interesting, open-ended play scenarios without imposing an adult play agenda. They also provide the necessary supervision that helps children have fun building campfires and pounding nails without getting hurt. We are starting to see adventure playgrounds in larger urban areas in the United States, but liability issues will likely prevent large-scale implementation in the United States without grassroots intervention by well-informed parents. Meanwhile, as a parent, you have the privilege of assuming "play ranger" status for your own child, and you can probably make a pretty good effort at providing an adventure playground right in your own backyard. If you lack a backyard, don't despair. Most of these adventures can be played out elsewhere. You'll just have to be a little bit more creative than the average parent. Consider some of the following additions to your own backyard adventure playground.

A swing set or play structure

If you have the space and the means, a swing set or playground structure can be a lot of fun. But because a play structure constitutes a substantial financial investment, do a little homework before making a purchase. Once you've chosen the playset you think you would like to purchase, sit down and brainstorm about all of the ways your set can be used by a three-year-old. Can she swing if there is no one around to help her? Can she play safely with a dump truck on the platform of your play structure? Is there a slide she can reach without assistance?

Now think of at least ten different ways your play structure can be used by a ten-year-old. Is there a bar if she wants to hang upside-down from her knees? Could she enclose the structure in cardboard or old blankets and make her own fort? Will her ankles drag if she wants to swing? If you are going to invest hard-earned cash in a play structure for your child, do your best to make sure its design enhances play, rather than hindering it. Otherwise, go with an inexpensive version that will last for a few years until you can afford to upgrade, and use the cash you save to invest in some "really good junk."

"Really good junk"

If you can't afford the play structure of your dreams, smile and think of all of the great "spare parts" you can accumulate instead—things that don't look nearly as glamorous to the untrained eye but that give a child even more pleasure.

- A sand box or sand table, with tools for digging and scraping
- Wagons, dump trucks, riding toys, tricycles, roller blades
- A basketball hoop, a badminton net with rackets, a soccer goal
- Loose equipment such as plastic rain gutters for water play, carpet tubes for tunnels, empty boxes, buckets, pool noodles, hula hoops, clothesline, and clothespins
- Trees, bushes, shrubs, leaves, grass, dirt, sticks, twigs, mud

- A permanent playhouse or a temporary one made of old sheets hung over the swing set, a big appliance box, or blankets supported by clothesline
- A shovel and a patch of dirt for digging in
- Basketballs, tennis balls, baseballs, beach balls, and so forth
- Sidewalk chalk, a kite, bubbles and bubble wands, a plastic wading pool
- Old fence boards, nails, screws, hammers, and screwdrivers
- A picnic table
- A sled, tools for molding blocks of snow for a snow fort, parts for outfitting a snowman
- A small ladder or stepstool
- A couple of big storage bins for cleanup

A playful adult

Once your supply of really good junk starts to accumulate, you may need to invest twenty minutes now and then to teach your child what to do with it. Aside from the fact that you make a good trainer, a willing mom or dad is also just a lot of fun to play with. This doesn't have to be a daily commitment, but think of all of the ways you can enhance and expand your child's play by mentoring and showing them how to have fun, how to build a better sandcastle, or how to really sink a good hook shot.

If you're truly stumped about how to play with a child outdoors, visit your public library and check out a few books that will give you some ideas. You'll find everything from books that include a play idea for every day of the year (*365 Unplugged Family Fun Activities* by Steve and Ruth Bennet) to books that will help you learn to do some of the things you always wanted to learn how to do as a child but did not. *Catch a Fish, Throw a Ball, Fly a Kite* by Jeffrey Lee gives step-by-step instructions for teaching twenty-one time-less skills like how to skip a stone, how to throw a Frisbee, and how to find constellations at night. If you already know how to do all of that stuff, thank your lucky stars for an adult who took time to play with you.

I've included a few ideas to get you thinking about the possibilities for outdoor fun. Most of these activities can be carried out at a public park or other open area if you don't have access to a yard of your own:

Learning to play again: Get your hands dirty

Make mudpies

Dump a little water in some dirt and squish it around with your toes. P.S. Mom, this will make your feet dirty. This is not a crime. Pat some of the mud into a miniature pie tin salvaged from a frozen pot pie or a plastic tray you rescued from the recycling box. This is known as a mud pie. Now, scavenge some garnishes from around the yard. Twigs, spent flower blossoms, seed pods, and bunches of green grass are all acceptable decorations.

Make monster bubbles

Make "monster bubbles." Mix a solution of six cups of water, two cups of Joy dishwashing liquid, and three-fourths cup corn syrup. Next, thread two drinking straws onto a three-foot piece of yarn and tie the ends of the yarn together (this will be your monster bubble wand). Pour the monster bubble solution into a deep cookie sheet, and holding one drinking straw in each hand, immerse the bubble wand into the bubble solution and lift it out. Start running. On a good, warm, moist day, you'll get huge bubbles perfect for chasing. (You'll have to teach younger children how to pop the bubbles with a stick or another drinking straw to help prevent bubbles from getting in the eyes.)

Lie in the grass and whistle

Make a grass whistle. Hold a fat blade of grass between your two thumbs, with both thumbnails pointing toward you. Blow through the little oval hole below your thumb knuckles to make the grass whistle.

Plant something

If you have space, children get a lot of pleasure out of planting and tending a small garden spot of their own. If you are not a gardener yet, or the available space is limited, start by allowing your child to plant a miniature flower garden or a favorite berry or vegetable all in one contained pot. You will need:

- A basket or pot for planting
- Potting soil mix
- Slow release fertilizer, such as Osmocote
- Water absorbent, such as Suber Sorb C or Soil Moist

(this will help the soil maintain moisture and is critical if you are using a small container).

• Your choice of plants (select sun or shade plants, depending on where your pot will be located). Brightly colored flowers that bloom all season long (nasturtiums and marigolds grow quickly), strawberries, fast-growing radishes, and cherry tomatoes are a few of the plants that children enjoy tending.

1. Fill the container with professional potting soil. Make sure the container has drainage holes. You can put in rocks or shards of broken pots at the bottom of your container to improve drainage. Make sure there is a hole at the base of the container for excess water to leak out.
2. Sprinkle some slow-release fertilizer into the soil and work it in.
3. Mix a water absorbent into the soil. (This keeps the soil moist so you don't have to remember to water as often.)
4. Transplant your pre-purchased bedding plant into the soil, or plant seeds according to package directions.
5. Water the plant well and keep it moist

When the soil becomes dry to the touch, your child can water the plant and squirt the foliage with a water bottle with a spray attachment. Help him clip off spent blooms from any flowers.

Learning to play again: Invent something

Discover ropes and pulleys

Using a rope and a few purchased awning pulleys (available at any hardware store), show your child how to rig up a pulley system to lift supplies from ground level up into a tree. If you don't have a tree, throw the rope over the top spar of a swing set. If you don't have a swing set, screw an eyebolt into some inconspicuous corner of the roof of your house, or hang the pulley from another rope suspended between the fence and the basketball standard. If you don't have a house, the same rigging system will work between two sturdy trees at the park or between the fence and the play structure at a favorite playground. Use your imagination.

A rope and pulley can lift a bucket full of supplies into the treehouse, lift a peanut butter sandwich from ground level to the top of the backyard deck for a picnic, or even become a "go fish" game if you attach a hook at the end of the rope and station a wading pool full of toys underneath. Once you have the hang of playing with a rope and pulley, you can turn your swingset and an old sheet (which becomes a stage curtain) into an outdoor theater venue, create a sail and rigging for your cardboard box pirate ship, or suspend a hula hoop in the air for football quarterback target practice.

Design your own miniature golf course

Make a set of croquet wickets out of old wire hangers and use any round object as a ball. You "score" when your ball goes through the wicket. You can build a simple course with a series of wickets, or ramp up the "difficulty level" by creating obstacles to go around, under, and through.

Create your own masterpiece

Tape a sheet of butcher paper to the garage door, gather a few washable tempera paints, and create your own mural. Take a pad of drawing paper to the park, the beach, or the most colorful spot you can think of, and paint what you see. Or, put colorful flowers on a piece of fabric, cover them with a sheet of tissue, and pound them with a wooden mallet until the color transfers to the cloth.

Learning to play again: Get your heart thumping

Researchers who study children's play have noticed an interesting phenomenon. When children are deprived of the opportunity for physical activity for an extended period of time, "they will, when given the opportunity to play, engage in more intense and sustained bouts of physical activity play than they would have done if not so deprived. This generalization, in turn, suggests that physical activity play is serving some developmental function(s) such that a lack of it leads to compensation."[3] In other words, children cooped up without the opportunity to play will compensate for their lost playtime by playing harder (and perhaps more roughly) when they are let loose. This suggests that physically active play is not just a bonus, but that it is in fact *critical* to a child's development. Outdoor play, which is usually more physical in nature, may be particularly beneficial to children who express a need for physical activity through aggression and other undesirable behaviors.

I was interested, as part of my research for this book, to learn about the benefits of occupational therapy for children who suffer from sensory integration disorders. A child whose nervous system does not adequately process sensory information may have hypersensitivity to stimuli like light, touch, or sound. These children benefit from therapy that helps them find the "just right" level of sensory input. A child who suffers from a sensory integration disorder might bang into furniture, push other children, or crash into walls in an attempt to fill his need for sensory stimulation. Therapy can give him many opportunities to bump and crash in a safe environment so that he can function better outside of therapy as he goes about his day-to-day tasks. I wonder if this isn't some of the reason children exhibit the need to play—all of them are developing their ability to monitor and control sensory information.

Whatever the reason, it is clear that children get very real benefits from outdoor physical play. That is one of the reasons that of the play experiences we recall as adults, a large percentage of them involve outdoor play with our parents. Kim shared a typical example with me:

> When I was about five, we moved to a house with a huge, undeveloped backyard. The yard was full of hills, trees, vines, and dirt. Soon after we moved in, my dad decided to construct a swing in the backyard for us to play on. I remember the day the swing went up. It was a grand affair. Dad, Mom, my three brothers, and I descended the steep backyard and picked out the perfect tree to hang a swing in. Its trunk was too fat for any of us to wrap our arms around, and its limbs reached high into the sky. With my dad's help, my oldest brother went scurrying up its trunk with a yellow rope over his shoulder and eventually secured it over a sturdy branch. I remember thinking, "They're risking their lives to help us have a swing to play on!"
>
> My dad had bought a round swing seat with a hole in the middle, so he slipped the hanging end of the rope through the seat and tied a knot under it. Voila! We had a swing! Dad helped me onto the swing the first few times, and we took ride after ride on that marvelous swing. We soon realized (much to my mom's chagrin and Dad's delight) that if we climbed a nearby tree, stood out on one of its limbs, and had someone throw the swing up to us, we could jump off the limb onto the swing and enjoy an absolutely amazing, high-flying ride. I spent the next five years of my life playing on that swing. The

building of the swing was a great family event all by itself, but the labors and the feelings of that day lived on every time I jumped on that swing. Every time I flew through the air and swooped up high enough to touch the dangling branches of tree above, I knew I had a dad who loved me.

Douglas also singled out swinging as one of his favorite childhood memories, but for a different reason. By the time he turned ten, he still had not learned to swing. His parents took him to the park over and over again until he learned to control his leg muscles and his movements became coordinated enough to allow him to pump his legs and swing without assistance.

Douglas remembers the experience as one that helped him connect with his parents—one that helped him develop appreciation for the way they felt about him, and undoubtedly, one that increased his confidence and self-esteem. Active play has a unique ability to help parents and children relate to one another better.

It isn't even the activity that seems to matter. It's just the time spent enjoying it. While it is tempting to promote active play as a method for improving children's physical health, it also seems important to emphasize that this is not the only reason, nor even the *best reason* for active play. Physicians Hillary Burdette and Robert Whitaker put it best when they said, "Play has the potential to improve all aspects of children's well-being: physical, emotional, social and cognitive. We argue that the current emphasis on increasing physical activity in young children to address the problem of obesity, while an important public health agenda, might be more successful in the exposure (physical activity or exercise) were promoted with different language (play) and if a different set of outcomes were emphasized (aspects of child well-being other than physical health)."[4]

With that caution in mind, think of all of the ways to get your heart pumping just because it is fun:

- Play hopscotch.
- Grab a basketball and challenge your child to a game of HORSE.
- Find an empty parking lot and get up a game of broom hockey.
- Play Indian Ball, a baseball game you can play without fielders, because scoring depends on how far you hit the

ball. Ball stops in the infield=foul. Ball gets through the infield but is not stopped by an outfielder=single. Ball travels past outfielder=double. Ball dropped by an outfielder=triple. Ball that goes over the outfielder's head=homerun.

- Set up an inline skating obstacle course.
- Have a bike rodeo to see who can travel a certain distance the fastest, then who can travel the same distance the slowest, without stopping or letting his feet touch the ground.
- Jump rope.

Make trampoline ice cream

This recipe is well known to families who like to make ice cream by putting the ingredients inside a can (which is inside a larger can) and kicking it around the yard for a while. Another method is to use the same procedure, but to mix the ice cream while jumping on a trampoline together. You'll need:

- A can that holds about a gallon of liquid, with a tight-fitting lid (a coffee can will work fine). Use a metal can, if possible. Plastic buckets will not conduct the cold adequately.
- Another can that will hold the smaller can. We use a 3-gallon storage bucket with a lid
- 2 quarts whole milk
- 2 cans sweetened condensed milk
- 1 4-oz. package instant pudding (any flavor)
- 1 cup sugar
- 3 cups rock salt
- 10 pounds crushed ice

(You can use smaller 1-pound and 3-pound coffee cans if you want to divide the mixture up into three batches)

Stir the pudding mix into the sugar, and then mix in the milk. Add sweetened condensed milk. Place ingredients inside of the smaller can, and seal it tightly. (A strip of duct tape or packaging tape will help hold the lid down). Place the smaller can inside the larger can and begin layering the ice alternately with the rock salt until the small can is surrounded by ice and salt. Place a second lid tightly on the larger can or bucket.

For added safety, wrap the larger bucket in a towel. Then take the whole contraption outside to the trampoline and take turns jumping for about twenty minutes. You can take the lid off and check the ice cream to see if it is hard enough. If not, replace the lid, add some fresh ice and a little more salt, and burn off some more calories (don't worry, you'll be putting them back on soon).

Go snowshoeing in the dark

One of the best dates I ever went on with my spouse was an after-dark guided snowshoeing trek at a local state park. We worked up a good sweat, only to cool off immediately when we stopped to admire the stars. Since then, my sons and their father have gone on similar trips both on snowshoes and on cross country skis. If there is a full moon, you won't even need a flashlight. Stop now and then to listen for owls or other night creatures. We recommend carrying a battery-operated headlamp for emergency use (keep your hands free) and sticking to groomed snowshoeing trails with beginners. Be sure to check with an expert about avalanche danger before you head out on your own.

Hike to your favorite star gazing spot

Many of us remember a magical night in August watching the Perseid meteor shower. You'll find information on meteor showers you can see from your own hometown at stardate.org/nightsky/meteors. Be sure to take along bug spray and a comfy blanket. The experts say that if it is dark enough for you to see each star in the Big Dipper, your eyes are adjusted to the dark well enough to see meteors.

If you don't want to wait for a meteor shower, borrow a star chart from your local library, purchase one online, or even print one from your favorite Internet site. Familiarize yourself with the major constellations before you even step outside. If possible, choose a clear, moonless night so you can see more stars.

Learning to play again: Become a Neighborhood

Here's another way active outdoor play can benefit a child. Help your child get to know his or her neighbors. Clinical psychologist Lynn Henderson has said that when we shelter our children from interaction with the outside world—when we keep them locked up safely indoors where we believe they will be safe, we inadvertently deprive them of opportunities to become "self-confident and discerning, to interact with neighbors, or to learn how to build real community—which is one defense against sociopaths."[5] So another form of play that I favor, partly because I loved it so much when I was a child, is the opportunity to be outside at night playing in the dark. I learned to be less afraid, and the opportunity helped me develop relationships with the extended community that lived close by. Wise parents will join their children in this play, and while promoting their safety is a primary reason, your child never needs to know that is why you are there.

Shake up your evening routine at home and go outside to get to know your neighbors on a cool evening instead of lounging in front of the television. Start with a round of good, old-fashioned night games. Invite everyone on the block, or just start playing and see who joins you. Just in case you've never played some of these tried-and-true favorites, I've included the rules for a few of them below. Parents can and *should* play along. If your neighborhood isn't a safe place to play at night, take a group to a park or a school playground. There is safety in numbers, especially if parents are along to have fun too. Many of these games can be adapted for indoor play in case of bad weather.

Kick the Can

STEP 1: Select an object to serve as the "can"—an actual can, a ball, or a small, taped-up box. Select someone to be "It," and set the can in a clear, open area. Choose an area to serve as the "jail." This should be within sight of the can, but not blocking it.

STEP 2: The player who is "It" stands by while another player kicks the can as far away from its original resting place as possible. Once the can is kicked, all of the players run and look for a good hiding place. "It" retrieves the can and puts it back where it was and then goes out to look for players.

Instructions for "It"

- If you find a player, you "capture" him by calling out his name and calling out the location of his hiding place while you are stepping on the can.
- If you are correct, that player is "captured" and has to go and sit in the "jail."

- You may need to wander away from the can to look for hiders, and when you do, the uncaptured players will try to sneak back to the can and kick it before you can put your foot on the can and call out their name.
- If the can is kicked, run after the can and put it back again (all of the players in jail will go free).
- If you succeed in capturing all of the players, the first one you caught becomes "It" for the next round of play.

Instructions for remaining players

- After the first player kicks the can away and you hide, your job is to try to sneak back to the can and kick it before "It" sees you.
- If you are captured, you will have to wait in jail until another player rescues you by kicking the can while "It" is away.
- If a player successfully kicks the can, everyone in jail escapes to hide again before "It" puts the can back in place.
- Players can move around at will, but if they get caught, they must go immediately to jail.

Flashlight Tag

This is a fun night game, especially for younger children. It is simply a combination of hide and seek and tag. The person who is "It" waits at the jail and counts to 100 while everyone else hides. Then, taking her flashlight with her, "It" searches for the hidden players. When someone is caught ("It" shines the beam of the flashlight on the person captured and calls out his name), that person has to go and wait in the jail. The first person caught will become the new "It" once everyone is found.

As a variation, the person who is "It" can simply hand off the flashlight to the player she caught, and that player becomes the new "It." If you have lots of players, you can have more than one flashlight-wielding "It." Players may change hiding places any time.

Run Sheep Run

Choose a "home base," and then divide into a red team and a blue team with a captain for each. The red team will stay at "home base" while the blue team hides. After they are hidden, the captain of the blue team (the hiding team) returns to home base. He will join the members of the red (searching) team as they go out to look for the other players. Any member of the searching team who finds a member of the hiding team will notify the captain, who will yell, "Run sheep, Run!" At this signal, all players should run to home base. If the last player back to home base is a member of the red team, the blue team hides again. Otherwise, the teams will switch places.

But hold everything! The blue team (the hiding team) can create a strategy. They can decide on code words in advance that their captain can shout out to warn them. *Cucumber* might mean "they are getting far enough away that we can make it back to the goal first, so get ready to run." *Pineapple* could mean "danger, they are getting close to you, so stop moving around." Once the blue team's captain thinks the red team is far enough away from home base that the blue team can make it back sooner, he can also call out "Run Sheep, Run!" and both teams will have to race back to home base.

Sardines

This game can be played indoors as well as outdoors, although it must be played in the dark. It is the backwards version of hide-and-seek. The person who is "It" hides, and everyone else goes out to search for him. If you find "It," you simply crawl into his hiding place with him and wait for everyone else to discover you, one at a time. The last person to find the pack of "sardines" is "It" for the next round.

Hug a Tree

Here's a fun night game for your next campout or evening picnic at the park. Choose an area with a lot of trees. Players pair off, and one acts as the guide who takes his partner on a trek to find a tree to hug. For safety purposes, it is best not to use blindfolds. Just encourage each of the "tree-hugging" players to keep his or her eyes tightly closed. The guide will lead the hugger to a tree, and the hugger will have two minutes to hug the tree, feel the tree, smell the tree, and so forth. Then they will be led back to the waiting area. Once everyone has had a chance to hug a tree and has returned to the waiting area, the huggers should try to find their way back to "their" tree (this time they can keep their eyes open). Even in a thickly forested area, it is possible to learn a lot about an individual tree—enough to know it when you meet it again. You might have to pay attention to whether you walked through gravel or leaves to get to your tree. You'll have to remember how thick the trunk was and whether the bark was rough or smooth. If you have paid attention, you should be able to find your tree quite easily. The guides can make this easy or more difficult by leading the players around in circles and over and under obstacles. Once huggers find their trees, they can switch places with the guides and play again.

Fireflies

Players are divided into two teams, and boundaries are set for the game. Each member of the first team is given a flashlight. They are the fireflies, and they will be given time to hide. The second team will count to 200 before going out to look for the fireflies. Every few minutes, the leader of the second team will blow a whistle or yell "lights on," and the fireflies must switch on their flashlights for three seconds. Fireflies can be captured if someone on the opposite team calls their name. (As a variation, you can thread a strip of colored fabric through a belt loop for the opposing team to try to grab.) Change sides after ten minutes if all of the fireflies are not captured.

Check the Internet or your local library to find rules for playing dozens of other nighttime neighborhood games. One of our favorites is to get everyone a glow-in-the dark light-stick necklace (available at party stores) and play Capture the Flag on the local high school football field on a dark and moonless night. Teenagers can gather friends or even play these games on a group date, or they're fun for family reunions.

See if you can resurrect some of these favorites in your neighborhood (you'll find rules posted on the Internet):

- Capture the Flag
- Fox and Geese (a game to play in the snow)
- Fox and Chickens
- Red Light, Green Light
- Pom Pom Pull Away
- Ghosts in the Graveyard

Control the TV and the computer

I have screen-addicted children in my own home, so I know how difficult it can be to get children to turn off the computer or the TV and get out of the house. If you've expressed a willingness to turn off your own computer and play along, and your kids *still* aren't willing to join you, you might have to get mean and nasty. Or at least exercise some parental control.

An Internet search under "parental control" will help you learn some of the tricks of the trade for controlling electronic equipment in your home. This goes beyond being able to filter Internet sites or block inappropriate television shows. If you have control issues that can't be managed by simply setting limits (and even the best parents struggle with enforcing limits when they aren't in the home to see that the rules are followed), there are a few tools available, although I hasten to add that even the best of these features are not infallible. For that reason, I'll refrain from making recommendations, since what works for me may not work for you, and technological innovations are always improving. But knowing these tools exist may help you teach your children better viewing habits:

- **PC control software:** You can purchase and download software that will give your children access to the computer for a pre-determined amount of time each day, and program the computer to turn itself off when the time limit is reached, or "playtime with Dad hour" approaches, whichever comes first.
- **Television control tools:** Along with a V-chip that comes pre-installed in most televisions manufactured since July 1999, parents can control television watching by making use of built-in timers that will turn a television off at a pre-determined hour. Check your owner's manual for more information. If that fails, there are dozens of additional tools you can purchase and connect to your television—everything from a token system that only turns the TV on after a token is earned and deposited, to locking outlets that make it impossible to plug an electronic device in without parent approval. The following sites are only a beginning. Type "parental control + TV" or "parental control + computer" into your Internet browser window for more ideas.
- Try some of these safe media websites:

  www.familysafemedia.com: a resource for learning about controlling media use in your home

www.controlyourtv.org: a site that educates parents about television use in the home, recommends some great programming, and offers suggestions for monitoring television use

www.tvguidelines.org: a site produced by the TV Parental Guidelines Monitoring Board that educates parents about use of V-chip technology in the home

www.akrontech.com: a site that includes downloadable software to help control computer and television use

www.pcmag.com: one of several online pc computing magazines that rate the effectiveness of parental control software; find recommendations for the best parental controls currently available

Curtail some of your adult-organized activities

One of the most significant hindrances to relaxed, leisurely outdoors play in my home is our participation in adult-organized, highly scheduled, recreational, and competitive sporting activities. When they were young, it seemed important to let my children "taste" everything, and all of our friends and extended family members seemed to follow a similar pattern. It was our notion that these were opportunities that good parents just provided for their kids. Baseball ran from April until July, and soccer from August through October. Or was that gymnastics from September to November and swimming lessons from May through August. No, I forgot. It was ski lessons on Saturdays from January through March and basketball on weeknights. Then when the oldest got old enough to play flag football, it was soccer on one end of town with one son and football at the other end. When my daughters got into the act, we had to add softball and volleyball.

I did this to myself, of course. I wanted my children to have fun, exercise their bodies, develop friendships, and learn responsibility. I didn't consider the fact that it would decimate our family mealtimes and run up my gas bill. It wasn't until the soccer coaches proposed that we join a "super-league" that would play games in other states and require twice-weekly attendance at practice in a city that was an hour away that I gathered the courage to say "enough." I remember sitting at the parent's meeting, feeling my blood pressure rise. When it was my turn to comment, I could only say, "I think these boys deserve a childhood, and I have to consider the sacrifices I will be expecting from the rest of my family." My observation was met with icy stares from some and nods of agreement from others, but my son did not join the super-league after all.

I am not trying to be self-congratulatory. It was not an easy decision at the time, and there's always the lingering possibility that I made the wrong choice. Hindsight has given me the comfort of knowing that of the dozen or so young men who played advanced-league soccer with that first team, none of them (to my knowledge) was offered a scholarship or played competitively beyond high school. One is studying pre-med at a private university, one is pursuing a career in graphic arts, one works on his grandfather's farm during the summer and attends the university in the fall. Another is serving a proselyting mission for his church in a third-world country. We still suffer some angst about whether our sons might have had better coaching, won more games, and learned better technique if we'd been willing to make the sacrifices to put them in a tougher league, but there's also the question of what they might have given up in exchange.

I should be clear about the fact that I am not trying to discourage organized sports programs all together. I have just learned that the benefits come with balance, and when we allow the pace of our lives to become frenetic because we are trying to manage too many organized activities (whether it be sports or piano lessons or any other worthy activity), the benefits diminish.

Experts worry as well, since our children are exposed to more and more of these kinds of activities at younger and younger ages. "Basic motor skills, such as throwing, catching, kicking and hitting a ball do not develop sooner simply as a result of introducing them to children at an earlier age," warns the American Academy of Pediatrics. "Teaching or expecting these skills to develop before children are developmentally ready is more likely to cause frustration than long-term success in the sport."[6] The committee responsible for this policy statement also reminds parents that it is important to identify "reasonable goals" for participation in sports. Write them down. Once those goals are established, it is easier to notice when playing organized sports doesn't meet the original intentions. Here are some possible "child-friendly" goals:

- Acquisition of motor skills
- Increasing physical activity levels
- Learning teamwork and social skills
- Learning good sportsmanship
- Having fun

Without these benefits squarely in our sights as the real reason to have our children participate in organized sports, we risk letting adult-oriented goals (like winning at all costs or becoming the next Tiger Woods) take too much precedence.

It should be pointed out that informal family sports activities have some of the same teaching benefits of organized sports. Maybe the stuff you hoped they would learn in organized sports can be learned better in the backyard. Pay close attention to what happens the next time your children get into an argument over an infraction of the rules during a family wiffle ball game, and you'll see what I mean.

"Unlike formal sports activities, where responsibilities for oversight are vested in designated officials who follow codified rules, informal sports place family members in direct positions to decide rules, award penalties, challenge player actions and extensively justify their reasoning." Because of this, even a backyard game of tag can be a powerful way for parents to explain, justify, and teach rules of appropriate social behavior, including the "rights and wrongs of certain actions."[7] The informal sporting events we engage in with our children give us a prime opportunity to help our children eliminate undesirable behaviors and attitudes like whining, cheating, displaying un-sportsmanlike behavior, or lacking loyalty.

As it is, to this day, I fight a battle between giving my children an opportunity to develop their physical fitness and keeping them home to develop relationships with their siblings. Sometimes, I'm not sure whether family vacation is more important, or whether staying in town to support the team in a weekend tournament is more important. Sometimes we have to decide whether to support one son from the sidelines at his first home game of the season, or whether to be in attendance for our daughter's piano recital. But I am certain that we probably do not cause our children irreparable harm if we refuse to enroll them in every single opportunity. They will be better served if we can balance organized sports involvement so that time remains for some outdoor free play. We generally try to let our children choose involvement in one athletic pursuit and one fine arts pursuit. Additional commitments, if they choose them, are made on their own time and their own dime, which means they pay dues themselves and are responsible to walk or ride a bike to practice. That balance works pretty well in our family. It leaves time for family vacations in the off-season and a reasonable number of evenings per week that are free from outside commitments. The balance you strike in your own family may be different, but it is important to find a balance. If you are too busy for a pick-up basketball game in the driveway now and then, you are *too busy*.

Discover the great outdoors for yourself (agaiN)

One of the reasons children don't get out-of-doors is that adults are so sluggish about leaving the safety of an air-conditioned living room to show them how. Take three minutes and write down all of the green spaces within a fifteen-minute walk of your home. Is there a park, a nature preserve, a stream, a school playground, a soccer field, a wooded area, a hiking trail, or a bike path anywhere nearby? Think of at least five places you can get to, and then make a check mark next to any of those places you have visited within the last six months. Embarrassing?

1. _____

2. _____

3. _____

4. _____

5. _____

If you are raising your children like hothouse plants, it is time to turn off the TV, put on a little sunscreen, and give your legs a stretch. If you can honestly say, when you return, that an hour in front of the screen would have been more refreshing, you can go back to eating your potato chips and surfing for videos of people feeding broccoli to their pet hamsters on YouTube. Resign yourself to the fact that your children will never develop the dexterity to climb a tree, experience the exhilaration of holding a kite string in a breeze, or find a shell half-buried in the sand on the beach. Now if that's enough guilt, let me show you why you will enjoy this as much as your child will.

On a cool summer morning just a few years ago, I had an assignment to choose a good hiking spot for a group of young Boy Scouts. A recommendation from a more experienced leader led me to a great hike within twenty minutes of my own home, so I loaded up my children to go with me to check it out. I carried a daypack, a few water bottles, and the Audubon Society's *Field Guide to North American Wildflowers*. I had also borrowed a copy of a tree field guide from the library, and not know-ing how good my kids were going to be at hiking, I tossed in ten zip-top bags full of some of my children's favorite finger foods: marshmallows, peanuts, whole-grain crackers, and pretzels. What followed counts as one of the ten most memorable summer mornings I have ever had in my life. But I'll let my son and daughter tell the story:

> Mom had to figure out how to help the Boy Scouts find ten signs of plant life and ten signs of animal life, so we decided to look for plants as we hiked up and then look for animals when we came back down. It had rained the night before, leaving everything fresh and beautiful, and the hike wasn't very hard. We followed a little path by the side of a stream.
>
> Mom had to point out the first wildflower to us, and then she showed us how to find it in the field guide so we would know its name. We found Philadelphia Fleabane first and learned that it is called Fleabane because it was once thought that the fra-grance would repel fleas. We also learned that the big fat burrs that stuck to our socks were from a plant called burdock. In oriental countries, the roots of burdock are called *gobo*, and they are a delicacy. We found wild geraniums and yarrow and sky-rockets and these really bright flowers called fireweed. We also started to look at all of the different leaves on the trees.
>
> We weren't just on some "forced march" up the hill. We could walk as slowly as we wanted, and we really started to see things we would have missed. Mom got a few yards ahead of us and then brought back these little bluish-gray berries and asked if we wanted to see if we could find some. We had to really look until we saw a juniper tree away from the trail and up a little hill. Now that we were good at looking closely, it started to get really fun.
>
> After a while, we decided we had gone far enough, and Mom gave us a different bag of treats for every plant we had been able to identify. We found maples and oak leaves and juniper, and a whole bunch of others, so we took our marsh-mallows and our M&Ms and our crackers and dumped them all into one big bag and shook it up to make our own trail mix. We sat there on a fallen log and ate it together.
>
> When it was time to hike down, we started looking for evi-dence of wild animals. We found stumps that had been chewed by beavers. We saw three different kinds of butterflies. We

could hear the birds. We saw deer tracks in the mud. Someone found a skin from some kind of an insect on the trail. It was like the exoskeleton of a bug without any insides. Some bug had simply walked out of his skin! We learned later from a television program that it was probably the skin of a cicada.

We found dozens of little white shells from some kind of snail. But the most amazing thing was when we walked past a tree and there were all of these things fluttering to the ground. It was a dead tree. And when we looked at the things that were fluttering down, they were ants with wings, and when they got to the ground, they shed their wings and they just crawled away. It was so cool! We wouldn't have noticed them if we weren't looking.

Purely by accident, we had learned the value of looking closely. With that experience, the forest came alive, and since then, nothing has ever been quite the same. It only took a morning to make a memory that has changed how each one of us views the world. It was so easy! It was so refreshing! It was so fun! It would be one thing if it only affected me (the parent) in a positive way. But what has intrigued me is the fact that my children were just as fascinated as I was, and to this day, they recall the experience with the same delight that I feel. Something happened on that morning that none of us can explain. We came away from the experience changed, somehow. We were better people, more alert, and more alive.

Richard Louv said, "Let me say something about the pressures that parents endure. Simply put, many of us must overcome the belief that something isn't worth doing with our kids unless we do it right. If getting our kids out into nature is a search for perfection, or is one more chore, then the belief in perfection and the chore defeats the joy. It's a good thing to learn more about nature in order to share this knowledge with children; it's even better if the adult and the child learn about nature together. And it's a lot more fun."[8]

Becoming an advocate for play

Child-safe outdoor spaces are harder and harder to find. But as adults, we wield a lot of clout that we can use to protect both our children and their playtime. We can be vocal about opposing the elimination of school recess time. We can meet with city planners to be certain that those who design parks and play areas consider child development when they plan playgrounds, not just limitation of legal liability. As one play advocate has said, designers usually don't know much about child development, and child development specialists don't usually know much about design, but as parents, we can be certain that committees who plan parks and playgrounds include *all* the right experts.

Where playgrounds already exist, parents must lobby for safe, well-maintained parks that provide lots of "rough spaces around the edges"—natural spots for exploring, watching bugs, and digging in the dirt, and not *just* manicured playing fields.

President Theodore Roosevelt said, "Since play is a fundamental need, playgrounds should be . . . within walking distance of every boy and girl." Estimates indicate that only half of the U.S. population currently has access to that privilege. Where playgrounds do not exist, parents can work with local authorities, corporations, and even children's charities to help create them (see www.kaboom.org as an example).

We can resist inappropriate adult intrusion in child's play by insisting that organized sports for younger children focus on developmentally appropriate goals. This may include lobbying for training for coaches. City recreation departments should provide clear expectations for adult behavior from the sidelines, and help coaches understand that in leagues for younger children, *every* child deserves the right to equal participation, not just the five who can score the most points.

Tim Gill advocates that many of us need to relax and not be quite so paranoid. Pointing out that fewer than one child in a million is actually killed by a stranger each year, Gill says:

> We parents also have the power to resist the seductions of consumerism and play our part in restoring to children some of the freedoms we took for granted when we were young. We can say no a little more, switch off the screens and direct our children's curious eyes to some altogether more expansive vistas. In doing so, we need to face up to our fears and chip away at the free-floating anxiety that can so easily beset us. Some threats—traffic, for instance—are real, and can ultimately only be tackled by governments in response to political pressure. But others need to be seen for what they are: a social neurosis stemming from a collective loss of nerve . . . What would most help parents cure themselves of risk anxiety

is more of these reassuring, supportive messages: more voices that say: "You can be a good parent and still give your children a taste of freedom."[9]

Most of us who fear for our children's safety can eliminate virtually all life-threatening danger simply by being there to play with them.

Above all, we can modify our own behavior and make ourselves available to our children for regular, relaxed, fun outdoor playtime. Sit back and close your eyes and remember your fondest outdoor play experience. Now open your eyes and take your child there. Kim had a mom who did:

> My mom's hobby was driving, especially in beautiful places, so I spent much of my childhood and teenage years driving and playing with her in the mountains. One of my very favorite things to do was to play on the bank of a river and make elaborate "houses" out of the wet sand. We also caught frogs, had stick sword fights, scaled ravines, collected rocks, chased birds, climbed trees—and always, we had a picnic. When I think back on my childhood, when were we *not* playing? Playing is what made us a family. And it was all absolutely free, other than the gas to get there, the tuna sandwiches in the picnic basket, and the time that passed while we drove and played and talked.
>
> One summer day in my teens we got the idea to go blueberry hunting. Our plan was to drive through all the beautiful countryside we could find, with the goal of finding a blueberry patch, picking a basket full of berries, and returning home to make a batch of warm blueberry muffins out of them. We did just that. It is one of my favorite memories to this day. My mom was always full of such ideas, which made me feel like I had the best mom in the world and that our family was the center of a continuing adventure.

Reader's Homework

Based on what you have read in this chapter, what ONE idea for playing with children appeals to you most as something that you could feasibly do in your own home? (This can be an idea you read about in the book, an idea of your own that came to you as you were reading, or something you remember experiencing as a child).

Write your ONE idea here:

_____

_____

If you'd like, record this idea in the "Gallery of Ideas to Try" at the end of the book.

Notes

1. Gill, *Ecologist Online*.
2. Louv, *Last Child in the Woods*.
3. Pellegrini and Smith, *Child Development*, 582.
4. Burdette, and Whitaker, *Archive of Pediatric Adolescent Medicine*, 2.
5. Louv, *Last Child in the Woods*, 127.
6. American Academy of Pediatrics, aappolicy.aappublications.org/cgi/content/full/pediatrics;107/6/1459, 2.
7. Kremer-Sadlik and Kim, *Discourse & Society*, 40.
8. Louv, *Last Child in the Woods*, 162.
9. Gill, *Ecologist Online*.

Chapter 9

Playing with Dad

How great dads use playtime to build strong bodies,
healthy minds, and emotional bonds

. . . .

One of Heidi's earliest memories is of the moment when her father
would come in the door after work in the evening:

> My dad was in the U.S. military and he would come
> home from work in his uniform, sit down on the couch, and
> call me over to help him. I would then help him undo his
> boots . . . and my siblings and I would all crowd around for
> some romping time with dad. He would swing us around,
> give us rides on his back, and roughhouse with us until he was
> too tired to play any more.

Some of the fondest memories of childhood can involve happy times
with fathers—biological fathers, non-custodial fathers, and stepfathers
included. In spite of all of the research that focuses on mothers and their
impact on a child's development, I think it is telling that when I ask children
and young adults to remember their happiest times playing with a parent,
they overwhelmingly choose memories of moments with their fathers.

Researchers have discovered the same phenomenon. One study com-
piled research from several different sources and made the following
observations:

- Fathers engage in vigorous physical play . . . more frequently than mothers.
- Children—especially boys—prefer physical play with either parent to any other form of play, but their pleasure seems to be more intense during physical play with their fathers.
- Mothers are perceived by children primarily as a source of well-being and security, while fathers are the preferred playmates, particularly for boys.
- Fathers tend to excite their children whereas mothers tend to contain them.[1]

While fathers are generally less involved in child rearing than mothers, there is one child-rearing domain where Dad is king: playtime. It is one area where his impact can equal or even exceed a mother's. And whether playing with fathers is so memorable because it happens infrequently, or simply because it is so much fun, fathers can take great comfort in knowing that their willingness to be playful with their children creates fond memories that will be drawn upon long after that child reaches adulthood. That fact alone ought to motivate fathers to fit more playing into their busy schedules.

"As a little kid, my dad was the most handsome, kind man in the whole world in my eyes," writes Eun-Jin. Whenever he came home from work, he would throw me up in the air and catch me while I laughed with joy. When I was six, I remember running around playing tag with my sister and my dad . . . Because we lived in Seoul, Korea, in the middle of the city, houses with backyards were very hard to spot if they existed at all."

She remembers a particular day when she and her father were playing tag in the parking lot of a local fast-food restaurant. "On this particular day, we were having a lot of fun running around until my dad fell as he tried to catch me. He sprained his ankle so badly that he could not use his leg for a couple of weeks. . . . He was also the one who taught me how to ride a bike, helped me roller skate, and took me to fly a kite," she recalls.

Let's look briefly at some of developmental milestones for children and why playful fathers have a special role in helping a child get the most out of each stage of development.

Father play encourages physical development

Even with young infants, fathers demonstrate innate child-rearing abilities that rival any good mother's. Studies that compare mothers and fathers in playful situations with their children show that like mothers, fathers are very good at adjusting their level of play to a child's abilities. They know when to encourage exploration. They instinctively know when to speak more slowly and use shorter phrases. They respond just as willingly to smiles and cries. They have an innate sense of what is too easy or too difficult for a child to do, and they adjust their expectations accordingly.[2] In other words, playing with a child comes quite naturally for most fathers.

Infants who are developing their motor skills participate in a lot of repetitive physical motion. It is not uncommon to see an infant rock back and forth in a seated position, bounce up and down while being held, bang a toy on a tray again and again, or flail their arms up and down. Child development specialists theorize that since it is difficult to ascribe any purpose to these rhythmic motions, the real function must be to help an infant develop control over his muscles. Fathers are great at extending and complementing this muscle development with many of their play-time games. Bouncing a child gently on a knee, holding a baby's hands or feet and clapping them together gently, or sticking a tongue in and out while your infant watches intently and then tries to mimic are all examples of repetitive father-child play that enhance a baby's development. Playful fathers help infants learn all kinds of important motor and coordination skills, and while their play will also build a child's cognitive and verbal abilities, one of their vital contributions to their child's development is their willingness to act as the "human jungle gym." Children relish climbing on, bouncing on, and rolling with a willing father.

I was enchanted recently to observe one father who was holding an active nine-month-old on his lap. Sitting and facing his dad, the little boy took great delight in pressing his feet against his father's torso and pushing himself backward until his head and neck hung upsidedown over the tops of his dad's knees. Eventually, dad would gently lift his son upright, only to have the action repeated over and over again.

When that game got boring, Dad handed his son a sippy cup full of water. There was a small leak in the cup's lid, and when the baby discovered that water would drip out of the cup, he sat mesmerized for a full five minutes, turning the cup upside down over and over again and watching, fascinated, as the water dripped down the front of his dad's silk tie. I was delighted to see that the father allowed this game to continue uninterrupted for several minutes—much longer than a well-dressed mother would likely have tolerated it. Dad was not oblivious to the fact that he was getting soaked. It's just that letting his son have a learning experience mattered more than a damp shirt. I am certain that this lucky baby is going to have a great childhood.

Father play encourages academic development

One of the singular differences between father and mother play is that fathers are far more likely to play games just for fun. While mothers create games because they teach academic concepts, fathers create games purely for their entertainment value. And because the games are fun, children probably learn more from their fathers than they realize. "My dad taught me how to count by using cards, and we would always play games together," writes JoLynne. "He also used to play games with me with the change he would carry in his pocket. I would guess how much he would have in his hand."

You would be hard-pressed to find a child who would willingly sit down for a three-hour geography lesson with his mother. But three-hour tournaments with the board game *Risk* are common at my house. My sons and their dad think they're just having fun. The fact that they can identify major coastal seaports and name several mountain ranges on continents halfway around the world is a purely incidental bonus. Children know and trust that Dad's motive for playing is to have fun. And that's exactly the way it should be.

Father play encourages social development

Every night, Hal and Kya share a special dance. Kya's mother, Jessica, writes, "It is truly the highlight of Kya's night, and she will giddily run and put on 'dance pants' which are also her pajama pants. We use the dance to bribe her into anything because she loves it—('eat your dinner and you can have three minutes of dance time with Daddy!'). Their favorite song is 'Shooby-dooby,' known to the rest of us as 'Pennies from Heaven,' and she'll run and giggle so hard! Any time she creatively concocts a new dance move (usually quite contemporary) we'll applaud and she'll close with a dramatic bow. Sometimes at night when she says her bedtime prayers, she'll express thanks for 'fun dancing with Daddy.' "

Jessica expresses the belief that this playtime builds Kya's self-worth and ingenuity, ends even the roughest day on a positive note, and gives little Kya a sense of her special place in the world.

Dads are especially good about giving children a sense of their place in the world. My sister remembers going to a restaurant with our dad for her eighth birthday. On our family budget, nights out at a restaurant were rare. Nights out at a restaurant with Dad all to yourself were rarer still. Dayna remembers Dad making sure the waiter brought a miniature strawberry cake just for her.

She also remembers his dog piles and tickle fights on Sunday nights. He'd build a fire in the fireplace, Mom would pop some popcorn, and then Dad would sit down and read the Sunday comics to us. Sometimes we would sit in a semi-circle near him and hold our fists out while he chanted, "One potato, two potato, three potato four . . ." (hitting one of our fists with his each time he counted). "Five potato, six potato, seven potato, MORE." And if your fist was the last one he touched, you had to pull it out of the ring. When the last fist was gone from the circle, it was time for wrestling, and one of us would take his glasses for safekeeping, and another would retrieve his wallet and car keys. He could hold three or four of us down at once—two in his arms and two more underneath his long, lanky legs.

Rough and tumble play encourages healthy competition and relieves stress

One important contribution of a playful father is his strong role in helping school-aged children learn to control their aggressive emotions through rough and tumble play.

Kyle remembers roughhousing with his own dad in a game they affectionately called "Steamroller," which involved trying to run and jump over his dad, who was trying to rest on the floor. Now and then, Kyle's father would grab one of the children as they attempted to keep over him, and a wild game of tickling, taunting, and giggling ensued.

A father who knows how to "play rough" with children without overstepping the bounds of playfulness (in other words, without reducing a child to tears or a fit of temper) helps a child learn the competitive skills he or she will need in the adult world. A father's willingness to help his children compete and struggle physically seems to help children learn the following:

- To defend themselves
- To face adversity
- To deal with environmental threats
- To confront others and if necessary, defend their own rights
- To deal with conflicts without becoming combative or aggressive
- To avoid problematic situations all together[3]

While these "competition skills" might not be as important in some cultures, children from Western societies seem to derive special benefit, since the ability to be competitive is well regarded.

But fathers have to use some caution, since there is a fine line between playfulness and abusiveness. A child might not always appreciate rough-housing that might seem merely playful to a father. In this case, the rule of thumb seems to be the child's countenance. As long as your child is still smiling, she is probably still having fun.

Ashley has had experience with this. Her relationship with her mother has been tenuous at times, but her dad has managed to maintain a friendship in an unorthodox way. "My mom gets mad when Dad wrestles with me," she says. "We wrestle and push all the time. I think both of us take out our frustrations a little, but that's not the main thing. The main thing is giving each other attention. I can only think of one time when my dad got so rough with me that I cried." I asked Ashley if she actually enjoyed this kind of play, or if it was something she merely puts up with. Her response was intriguing.

"I really like roughhousing with my dad. It's pretty addictive. Rough play is sometimes the only way dads have to show their love. They're too tough to give hugs and write affectionate notes and stuff. There are times when I think I wrestle with my dad almost daily. I like the fact that he's paying attention to me, so I'm willing to put up with the pain. I kind of have to live up to his expectations and show that I'm as tough as the boys, since I am the second oldest, and my dad didn't get any sons." When asked if there were any secondary benefits of playfighting with her dad, Ashley grinned and said, "If someone was trying to kidnap me, I'm pretty sure I could give them a battle."

Ashley's favorite memory of playing with her dad, however, was a water fight that started accidentally. "That was really fun because we would put each other in a headlock and throw water on each other's face.

It went on for like four hours until my mom got mad. We finally sprayed her with the hose too. She had fun too once she got into it."

Children who live in homes where there is a high incidence of stress seem to particularly benefit from physical play with their fathers. The emotional release is good therapy. David's parents were both athletes. His father played professional football, and his mother loved tennis and volleyball. Playing at the park was a favorite release from the stresses of family life and a struggling marriage. "It was our way of having fun together," writes David. "It must have been a way to relieve a lot of stress that my parents were going through. I just remember always having fun whenever we would to go the park. There were never fights or anything of that sort, just smiles and laughter."

Matt has similar fond memories of playing that gave his family an emotional release from a different kind of stress:

> A few months before my eleventh birthday, I got my dad to take my brothers and me to the local middle school basketball gym. This was a big deal to me for two reasons: First, I thought my dad had the best running hook shot I had ever seen and played better in cowboy boots than all of my friends could play in their Jordans. Second, my dad had cancer at the time, and playing basketball was something he rarely did when he wasn't sick. In retrospect, maybe that's why he took us.
>
> We didn't play long; he was too out-of-breath for much serious competition. We mostly just shot baskets, listened to my little brother tell random stories, tried to show off our incredible athletic ability, and beamed every time we got to watch Dad take a shot. Other than just spending time together, there really wasn't anything that noteworthy about the experience.
>
> A few months later, my dad passed away, and life became a lot more serious. I haven't forgotten that day, or the many other good days my brothers and I spent working and playing with my dad, and I haven't forgotten the things he taught us about being a father [because he was willing to spend time with us].

Matt's father found a way to create an experience that gave his sons some respite from the pain and anxiety they must have felt about his condition. The resulting memory still gives his son peace today.

Father play encourages healthy risk-taking

Another physical benefit for school-aged children is a father's willingness to allow a child to take risks that mothers sometimes hesitate about. "Play itself enhances risk, and the more active and adventuresome the child, the more risk she may assume or be prepared to safely assume," writes Dr. Joe Frost. A thoughtful father will find many opportunities to safely push the limits of his child's abilities. I remember the way I felt as I rode my two-wheeled bike around the block again and again with my father jogging along beside me, keys jangling in his pockets, holding on to the back of my bike and giving me the assurance that he would not let go until I was ready to ride on my own. This went on for weeks until one day, I felt enough courage to try riding on my own and went outside while he was at work to see if I could ride all the way around the block unassisted. I remember clearly gathering my courage because I wanted so badly to surprise my dad by showing him I had conquered this new hurdle. The exhilaration I felt that morning as I coasted back into the driveway, my legs shivering like Jell-O after my first successful solo trip, is one of the most vivid memories I have of personal accomplishment. Dad's bike was a big orange klunker with a fender big enough for one child to ride on the back of his bike while he held another of us side-saddle in front of him. (This was long before the days of safety seats and bike helmets.) From that day forward, I relinquished riding on dad's bike with him, but I took extra pleasure coasting down the big hill between our house and the grocery store about a mile away, where we would ride to buy Monday night ice cream cones.

Many of us can remember our first trip down the slippery slide, the first dive off the diving board, the first trip across the monkey bars unassisted, or the first ascent to the top of a rock wall. Playful fathers can be a great source of encouragement and reassurance to children who are hesitant to stretch to overcome the next obstacle.

Father play encourages fitness

Family recreation is another important form of play, and dads create great memories as they provide families with opportunities to play hard.

Linda writes:

My dad taught us to water ski at an early age. He was an avid skier and enjoyed playing in the water with us. Mom was afraid of the water, but she would ride in the boat as the designated "observer," which Michigan law required when pulling a skier. We went to the lake almost every Saturday in the summer. In the winter, my dad used the tractor to plow the snow from the yard and roads in our rural neighborhood. He often gave us rides in the loader of the tractor (I shudder to think how dangerous that was) or behind the tractor on the toboggan. I often wondered why my mom didn't watch us much. Some things are better not knowing. Amazingly, none of us ever got hurt . . . . Occasionally, when there was nothing pressing to do in the fields or it was getting dark, we got up a softball game. We usually played "Three Bucks and Up" since there were only us three girls and my little brother and my parents. Mom even played sometimes."

Playing hard—really exerting ourselves physically—is an important aspect of developing physical fitness, and fewer and fewer children experience its benefits. The reasons for sedentary lifestyles of today's children are varied. Some children stay inside because it is the only place they are safe. Others have many electronic gadgets to entertain them without moving a single major muscle group. Still others fail to develop physical abilities simply because they are afraid of failing. Psychologist Dan Kindlon laments that our culture tends to discourage children from trying too hard. "We fear that unless we are very good at something and look like winners, we will be marginalized, left behind. This can make it hard for kids to become absorbed in an activity. Failure is defined as not being the best, and we tend to define all activities on a continuum or winning and losing."

For this reason, a father's willingness to engage his children in physical pursuits simply "for the fun of it" gives them many experiences of playing for pleasure instead of playing to win at all costs. Fathers do well to remember that playful behavior is characterized by flexibility, self-motivation, and positive emotion. In other words, play, in order to be play, should be fun and not particularly goal-oriented. Fathers who love to see their children develop athletically, culturally, or academically must exercise some restraint to be certain that their expectations to see children succeed don't eliminate the pleasure of the activity—at least not on a regular basis.

Dustin's comparison between playing with his dad "just for fun" and playing on an organized sports team is a good illustration of this point:

> He had to work a lot, it seemed, when I was younger, so when open time came on a Saturday afternoon, he made sure that we went out and did something . . . . I'll never forget the few months leading up to baseball season . . . . Occasionally my older brother would come too, but often it was just my dad and me. He would hit ground balls to me and I'd throw them to my brother at first base, or he'd knock the ball into deep center field, allowing me to work on following the ball over my shoulder as I ran like crazy. [My] favorite was when he'd try to strike me out during batting practice, and we'd taunt each other . . . . He'd always try to lure me into a bad pitch not worth swinging at, or get into my head by telling me what he was going to throw next, even though he rarely told the truth. Those Saturdays were the best. . . . As I got older, he'd spend Saturdays watching me play in real games, which never seemed to be quite as fun.

Father play prepares the Next generation

Finally, dad's play can come in the form of passing on traditions and expertise to the next generation. Brian writes:

> I connected more with my dad than with my mom. Dad was a highway patrol officer. He always carried weapons. As a result, I've dealt with weapons my whole life. We spent time cleaning, shooting, and hunting with them. Our camping trips bonded me and Dad and Grandpa, as there were no outside distractions. The fishing and hunting expeditions gave us time to think, ponder, and sit at a campfire. It is my notion that if we could get world leaders out of the leather chairs, some simple time around a campfire with some stars overhead would provide the humility they need to make better decisions. My hunting trips with my dad provided simple teaching and learning opportunities: "This is how you gut a fish. This is the rifle your great-granddad carried when he was in the Calvary. You never point a gun at anything unless you intend to shoot. You always express thanks for a meal and for

the life of the animal who provided meat for your survival." These experiences taught me self-reliance, and my happiest memories are of times when I was old enough, or responsible enough, to be trusted.

Who benefits More?

One of the best reasons for being a playful father, beyond the fact that it helps your kids be happy, healthy, and well-adjusted, is the fact that playing with kids improves Dad's outlook on life as well. Even tired, aching fathers can benefit from five brief minutes of physical exertion after a long day.

Judi's dad was an accountant who put in long hours at the firm. He came up with a novel approach to finding time to play with his kids when he was just too tired to exert himself any more: "Our favorite game was when he would lay on the floor as if dead, and it was our job to try to roll him over. This game usually ended with him trapping us between his legs and tickling us!" Hindsight teaches Judi that her dad was really resting while his kids were trying to push him over. "But it doesn't matter. It was quality play time to us."

Nine-year-old Janna's dad has similar ulterior motives. "My dad's back hurts a lot because he sits at a desk all day, but he loves it when he comes home and I try to balance on top of his back in my bare feet. Sometimes we play 'bull ride,' which is me trying to hold on while he bucks around and tips me from side to side. He says it makes his back feel better."

In other words, fathers who play, and play often, will realize benefits similar to those that their children enjoy:

> Although it has been the subject of little scientific inquiry in young children, free play has the potential to improve many aspects of emotional well-being such as minimizing anxiety, depression, aggression, and sleep problems. In adults, physical activity can decrease depressive symptoms . . . . Studies in older children have shown that improved mood and emotional well-being are associated with physical activity. Mood may be affected not only by the physical activity itself but also by exposure to sunlight if the activity occurs outdoors.[4]

Beyond the health benefits of play, there are also emotional benefits. Not the least of these is the emotional bond developed between fathers and their children. Margaret, who takes a lot of grief from her siblings for being a "daddy's girl," has no regrets about her close relationship. As a rambunctious child, Margaret once met with a serious accident.

> I became unconscious, my heart stopped, and my dad had to perform rescue breathing and CPR for twenty minutes before professional help arrived. Later on in the hospital, I remember waking up and his face was the first one I saw. It was as if I had come back from death, and for some reason, I knew that he was the reason I had lived. There was a very elementary, simple understanding of what he did for me that day to keep me alive, and we talked about how he would be there to protect me and keep me safe. I remember opening up to him and telling him how much I loved him. At that moment, there was an immediate connection, and it was the first time I can remember crying from emotion.

The overwhelming sense of safety and admiration Margaret feels for her father is nearly universal for any child who is cared for, loved, and played with. That is a relationship worth working (and playing) for.

Notes

1. Paquette, et al, www.unites.uqam.ca/grave/prospere/pages/pdf/RTPfinal.pdf.
2. Tamis-LeMonda, *Child Development*, 1806–1820.
3. Paquette, et al, 9
4. Burdette and Whitaker, *Archive of Pediatric Adolescent Medicine*, 46–50.

Chapter 10

Playing with Teenagers

Having fun together without being childish

● ●

Recently, I cornered a group of my son's friends who had gathered in the family room to watch a sporting event. "Since you've been a teenager," I asked, "what is the most fun you have ever had with one of your parents?"

They looked at me for a long time before one of them ventured an answer. "My mom thinks it is fun to race to see who can pull the most weeds out of the garden," he said. There was another long pause, as it became clear that they were sincerely baffled by my question. I could almost see the wheels turning: *Am I supposed to have fun with my parents?*

So I re-phrased my inquiry: "If you could choose to do something with your mom that would be fun for you, what would it be?" After another long, uncomfortable moment of thought, one of them said, "I think I would really like it if she would take me to breakfast." When they really scoured their memory banks, most of them could remember at least one event that had been important to them. One said he liked to go skiing with his dad. Another recalled going to a soccer game with his father and then out for a hamburger. But I was surprised that none of them had a quick response for something memorable his parents had done with him recently.

I know these boys well enough to know their parents are not slackers. Their moms and dads are on the sidelines at least weekly as we watch our sons compete together at sporting events. I see these adults at parent teacher conferences. I get calls from them when the PTA needs volunteers or when the church potluck dinner needs another potato salad. They are busy, committed parents who spend most of their waking moments working, chauffeuring, preparing meals, encouraging hard work, and demonstrating their love and their concern for their children in myriad ways. Why did their children have to think so hard in order to remember the last time they had fun together?

Teenagers are a special breed. We still care for them as much as ever, enjoy them just as much, and worry about them even more than we did when they were little. But it is common to find that teenaged children don't have as much time to connect with parents. They are pulled in too many different directions, due to their expanding independence and the heavier expectations placed on them by teachers, coaches, and society in general. Keeping up with them means parents don't have as much spare time either.

And yet, teens *want* time with their parents. In a survey commissioned by the Clinton administration, teenagers rated "not having enough time together with their parents" as their number one concern—ahead of drugs, alcohol, and violence. Teens are more than three times as likely as their parents to say that finding time together is a problem. Clearly, teens want more time with us than we think they do.[1]

What else do teenagers crave? Can parents supply something that will increase the likelihood that a teen will turn into a successful, well-rounded, happy adult—one of the "first-rate" kids the title of this book implies it is possible to raise? Researchers have pondered the question for years, and while the conclusions vary, several central themes emerge over and over again. In order to thrive, most teenagers need the following:

- A warm, satisfying relationship with a parent or another caring adult
- A parental mentor who models healthy behaviors
- Parents or guardians who monitor the teen's activities
- Rules to obey and expectations to live up to

In this chapter, I hope to show how "playful activities" help parents provide these very real needs.

I suppose it was because I was in the midst of preparing this book that

I started paying attention to when and where my children and I "connect" when we are together. I can share three very different experiences:

Scenario 1

Each of the members of my immediate family was seated in camp chairs around the campfire holding a paper plate with a tinfoil dinner that my twelve-year-old had cooked in a foil packet over the coals (hamburger patty, potatoes, carrots, onion, cheese, and a spoonful of condensed mushroom soup; my potatoes were still mostly raw). My youngest daughter had eaten only one bite of her meal. Instead, her plate held two very burned marshmallows, a square of chocolate, and two sections of graham cracker. One son was strumming a guitar off and on, so that the rest of us had to raise our voices to be heard over the music. As I recall, much of the conversation centered around rock climbing.

Scenario 2

The family had, by sheer coincidence, all converged in the family room. It was nearly 10:00 PM before the last one came in from a late study group. There was a box of crackers on the computer desk and one or two devoured containers of yogurt. Two of my children had been chatting with friends on separate computers, but now they were leaning back in their chairs, sharing a bag of trail mix and discussing the best and worst school teachers they had ever had. I was sorting socks. The eight-year-old had fallen asleep on the couch. Their father had pulled up an extra chair to join them. At 11:30 when the conversation began to wind down, we were hesitant to send them off to bed, because the conversation had been so engaging.

Scenario 3

I was with one of my sons at a nearby restaurant on a morning when he didn't have school. He ordered pancakes, sausage, eggs, bacon, and toast. Then he spent the next hour telling me about his plans for a small business venture he would like to start. I was convinced enough that his idea would work that we stopped on the way home so he could buy supplies for his prototype. Within a few weeks he had orchestrated a deal to borrow four hundred dollars in capital from his dad (which is accruing interest as I am sitting here typing) so that he could have his product made in bulk overseas. He hopes to triple his original investment by month's end.

As I have considered these three scenarios, I've come to some important realizations:

- In all three scenarios, the teenagers drove the conversation, and the parents mostly listened.
- Only one of the three opportunities to "connect" was orchestrated so we could sit down and talk. The other two were entirely spontaneous.
- All three scenarios involved some form of food, and two came about as an extension of a meal.

I have not questioned my children about whether they agree that these scenarios were powerful moments for them. I probably only noticed them because I was watching for them, and yet, as they were happening, there was the sense that something important was going on.

In small focus groups with teenagers and through surveys in which they have shared their thoughts with me, I have had an opportunity to consider how parents "play" with teenagers effectively. One fact has become clear: most teenagers, while they don't often verbalize it, crave opportunities to connect with their parents. More than anything else, they seem to yearn for opportunities for simple, friendly, relaxed conversation. They have an aversion to being grilled about their lives and can see through adult tactics to get them to talk. They far prefer to initiate the conversation themselves and see where the discussion takes them. They especially like hearing about their parents' experiences growing up, as long as the experiences aren't directed toward teaching them a lesson or moralizing about something the teenager should be doing better. Teenagers are surprised and delighted when adults do spontaneous things—things that are out of character. They struggle with knowing how to get their parents to see that they still need hugs and affection, and they especially dream of and appreciate opportunities to spend time with a loving adult one-on-one.

What does the research say about connecting with a teenager?

Researchers are quick to point out that adolescent behaviors often "cluster." For example, teens who are depressed often exhibit other undesirable behaviors. They are more likely to be substance abusers, struggle with anxiety disorders, experiment with risky sexual behaviors, or exhibit poor health habits. Teens who are more stable emotionally tend to be more engaged in extracurricular activities and avoid risky behaviors.[2] Because there are so many negative influences in the lives of struggling teenagers, and so many positive influences in the lives of teens who seem to be doing well, it is impossible to identify one specific experience or characteristic that will help turn a struggling teen around. But research is clear that a teen's relationships with adults are key to being successful.

Youth with frequent, stable, and satisfying youth-parent interactions:

- Have higher levels of reading, scientific, and mathematical literacy
- Demonstrate better self-esteem and mental health, even into adulthood
- Exhibit fewer violent behaviors
- Are less likely to be delinquent or suspended from school
- Avoid or use alcohol, tobacco, and drugs less frequently
- Are less likely to initiate sex or be sexually active
- Experience less emotional distress and have fewer suicidal thoughts and attempts
- Exhibit higher levels of self-confidence, empathy, and cooperation with others[3]

A teenager who has a warm, involved, and satisfying relationship with a parent will not struggle as much as a teenager who does not. I understand that the world is full of parents who have superb parenting skills and seem to have done all of the right things and *still* have teenagers who struggle. But it also seems logical that if you have a teen who is not doing well physically, emotionally, or mentally, one powerful solution might be to put emphasis on enhancing or even repairing the parent-adolescent relationship. One of the best ways to do this is to find a way to play again. Through casual, entertaining, and mutually satisfying "playing" experiences, teens find opportunities to "connect," and these connections are what help them find happiness. Psychologist Dan Kindlon writes, "I know a brilliant therapist, the head of a large hospital-based clinic, who gives the same homework assignment to each parent who comes to him with a tale of a troubled child. He tells the parent to spend one hour that week doing something together with the kid that they *both* enjoy."[4] Often, following that advice solves the problem.

Teenagers I spoke with identified six specific forms of "play" they wish they could enjoy more often with their parents:

1. Eating together
2. Spontaneous fun
3. Family vacations
4. Opportunities to express affection
5. Sharing of responsibilities and interests
6. Opportunities for casual conversation

Eating together

Family meals, one-on-one breakfasts, Sunday brunch, cookies after school, pizza and a video on a Saturday night, a hamburger together after the basketball game—these moments when we are seated together and relaxed, and have satisfied stomachs and time to converse are singularly powerful opportunities for connecting with adolescents.

"My family always has good dinner conversations," writes Cami. "Generally they turn into comedy fests and quoting movies. We always talk about our day and upcoming events during dinner. Mealtimes are a favorite time at my house because we all laugh together. It's where we connect the most as a family."

P.J., who is the youngest in his family, finds that the dinner table is a great place for family bonding, even though he is the only child left at home. "I am the only one they have to spend their time and attention on, but also the only one they have left to discipline and inspect. The way that we have been able to be close is through understanding and accepting our situation. I understand they are losing their last child and it is difficult for them to face. They understand I am growing up and moving to a different stage in my life where I am going to be independent. Realizing this has made us respect and understand each other better as well as enjoy what little time we have left in better fashion. It only gets tough when that perspective is blocked . . . . We go out to dinner a lot because that is what my parents like to do. These times give us a chance to talk and just spend time together. Even with their busy schedules, they usually are around to have dinner at home as a family. Most of the time it's my schedule that is the difficult one to work around."

"If I could have my mom all to myself for one day, I think I'd like to go to lunch and just talk about stuff, life in general," writes Shaylin.

Once when the two of them were having lunch together at a church function, the food reminded Shaylin's mom of the day when she first met Shaylin's dad. "I learned a lot about her and my dad when they were younger."

Bryce is the youngest in a blended family that includes several siblings. "Every night, we eat our meals together at the dinner table. It is a bonding time for us all. We find out how each other's day was and get my dad mad and we all laugh, but not my dad."

Humor and conversation are just part of the appeal of the dinner table. The National Center on Addiction and Substance Abuse at Columbia University has studied teens and substance abuse for more than a decade. In a statement accompanying the results of the Center's research for 2006, Joseph A. Califano Jr., Chairman and President of CASA, wrote:

> This nation's drug problem is all about kids. *A child who gets through age 21 without smoking, abusing alcohol or using illegal drugs is virtually certain never to do so.* And no one has more power to prevent kids from using substances than parents. There are no silver bullets; unfortunately, the tragedy of a child's substance abuse can strike any family. But one factor that does more to reduce teens' substance abuse risk than almost any other is parental engagement, and one of the simplest and most effective ways for parents to be engaged in teens' lives is by having frequent family dinners.[5]

According to the Center, frequent family dinners (five or more times per week) help assure that your teen will be at 70 percent lower risk for substance abuse, half as likely to try cigarettes, one-third less likely to try alcohol and more likely to get better grades in school. Other researchers have identified additional benefits, including less depression, less permissive attitudes toward sex, and an increased tendency to be willing to work up to one's potential.[6]

My parents learned the value of food early, and our meals weren't limited to the immediate family. On Sunday afternoons, my mother regularly feeds as many as forty people. The Sunday dinner table still supplies us with the same great conversations it did when we were younger—only now we bring our spouses and our children along. College roommates are always welcome, as are in-laws, cousins, aunts, and uncles who are in town for a visit. My mom always said that opening her cupboards to the crowds made it possible for her to lure teenagers to our home so that she could keep an eye on what was going on in our lives and in our relationships with members of the opposite sex. Someone asked her once if the open-cupboard philosophy wasn't expensive. Her reply: "It's the best investment I ever made. I sacrificed a lot of peanut butter and jam, but look what I go in return!" Now that we're grown with families of our own, Sunday dinner keeps our growing families connected with each other.

Along with sharing the contents of the pantry, Mom and Dad have always been willing to accommodate the noise and the mess that come with the package. (Of course it helps that Dad is hard of hearing!) When I was a teenager, every week I would invite half a dozen of my friends to get together to make chocolate éclairs or Whoopie Pies (the name of our favorite cream-filled homemade cookies). Next, we invited another half dozen boys over to *eat* éclairs and Whoopie Pies. One of our favorite activities was to gather a group around the piano and sing raucous show tunes (the young man I especially liked and eventually married was a fantastic jazz pianist). Today when I tell my kids how much fun this was, they just roll their eyes, but I have noticed that they have just as much fun gathering a few electric guitars, a drum set, and an amplifier or two and jamming in the living room—especially if there are meatball sandwiches, a bag of Doritos, or fruit smoothies available when the jam session is over.

Whether it's setting aside a time for an ice cream cone, taking a child to breakfast now and then, or just finding the time and the energy to put together yet another meatloaf, feeding teenagers can be time consuming and expensive—just not as time consuming and expensive as putting a child through drug rehab. Someday, if only one meal is memorable, it may all have been worth it.

That's the way it was for Landon. On the last night of their family vacation in Hawaii, Landon and his parents enjoyed a quiet dinner on the beach. "I don't know if it was because of the amazing steak I had, or because of the beautiful sight of the sun going down, but I just remember looking at my parents and realizing how much I really loved them and how much they loved each other."

If you want an opportunity to enjoy your teen, a good meal will work magic.

Spontaneous fun

Lynn's father is an accountant and her mother a homemaker, and both of them are fairly straight-laced, so Lynn especially enjoys it when they violate decorum and do something "weird." Asked to identify her most memorable moment playing with her parents, she wrote:

> Once, after we had worked in the yard all morning, my dad was hosing off a piece of black plastic before he folded it to put away. We were all hot and sweaty, so he invited us to go get our swimsuits, and pretty soon, we were all running and sliding on this wet plastic. My mom hates to get wet, and he knows it, but when she turned her back, he just let her have it. Pretty soon, there was an all-out war. Eventually, my mom disappeared into the kitchen for a few minutes and when she came out, she had two cans of pressurized whipped cream. She gave one to my dad, and the two of them chased us all over the yard, squirting whipped cream at us.

Teens love to have "extreme" fun. Because they are in the process of leaving their childhood behind and are taking on more and more complex roles and responsibilities, playing and having fun are like comic relief in a dramatic movie. Both teenagers and parents need moments to step back from their frantic lives and laugh a little. But maybe there's another reason they value spontaneity so much—it reassures them that adulthood isn't boring. Playing with our teenagers in spontaneous, inexpensive, fun-loving ways helps them learn that when pressure builds, there are safe, uplifting, accessible ways to cope. Parents need these "down times" as much as their teenagers do. In a recent high school survey, one student wrote, "I don't know what I want to be when I grow up, but I know what I don't want to be. I don't want to be like my mom and dad. They seem so sad and scared and stressed."[7]

Parents are not the only ones who are stressed. College deans have names for them: Teacups and Crispies. These are the college freshmen who arrive for their first semester so fragile or so burned out that they cannot enjoy college life. Having just completed three or four years on the tread-mill of academic excellence, extracurricular overscheduling, living on junk food, and being consistently sleep-deprived, they arrive at the university too stressed to cope. One teenager I know created a display picture for his personal instant messaging profile that shows a cartoon image of a boy wearing shorts and a red T-shirt and crouched into a tight ball with his arms covering his head. The caption says, "If your child doesn't look like this when you come home, you have FAILED as a parent."

"The stress that incoming college freshmen are feeling was once reserved for adults who had been toiling in the workplace for many years," writes psychologist Wendy Mogul. "By pushing adult-level responsibilities on our teenagers and acting as if their entire future is riding on every test grade, parents are turning teens into prematurely angst-ridden 35-year-olds."[8]

We need to create scheduled opportunities when we can demonstrate to our teenagers that there is time in life to relax, unwind, and breathe deeply again. In a world where our teens see the media version of themselves bungee jumping, sky diving, hang gliding, and base jumping, they lose sight of the fact that having spontaneous fun doesn't need to be extreme or expensive to be relaxing. "Any time there is a trampoline, my mom turns into a circus performer," writes Bryce. "She does all kinds of flips and has a great time." His admiration of her spontaneity is not limited to the backyard. "She also participates when we go to an amusement park, and she can do the splits," he muses.

Danielle writes:

> I remember this one time that I was with my mother and my brother in the kitchen. I had just bought this Nerf gun from a toy store and I was assembling it. I really don't remember how it started because it was so spontaneous, but all of a sudden we had started this huge Nerf gun war. My brother, who already owned a Nerf gun, was in the family room. My mother and I were on a team and we crouched behind the kitchen counter. We were just pelting each other with Nerf balls and trying out all these "war" strategies to get closer to the "enemy." It was one of the most fun things I have ever done with my mother because we were both really getting into it. I could not believe my mother was being so silly with me.

Kira remembered: "Once in the car on the way to visit my grandparents, my mom handed me a pack of straws and rubber bands and said, 'make something,' and we had fun laughing together at the ridiculous 'structures' we made."

"When my sister and I were young," wrote Wendy, "our mom and aunt would sit on the couch while we sat up on the back of the couch and fixed their hair. We came up with lots of interesting styles and we loved it. When we finished a style, we'd send them to look in the mirror and they returned with admiring comments and, much of the time, laughter. Sometimes they fixed our hair, but we liked doing theirs best.

Here are some more silly and spontaneous games you can play with your teen:

Bring your favorite breakfast cereal

Here's a twist on a tradition created by my sister, Marilee. Get a box of your teen's favorite breakfast cereal in advance. On a clear, warm weekend morning, wake your teen up before dawn and invite them for breakfast—on the roof of your house. Enjoy a bowl of cereal and watch the sunrise together.

Have a mud fight

One summer, my mother arranged for the fire department to hose down a section of dirt in a vacant lot near our home. We invited friends and enjoyed a huge, sloppy mudfight. The experience was so memorable that the local high school adopted the idea, and the annual Homecoming mudfight is a favorite tradition twenty-five years later. If you can find a bare patch of dirt, you can create a smaller version with a garden hose or a few buckets of water.

Build a model together

How long has it been since your teenager glued together a model airplane or put together a puzzle with you? You can find simple craft kits for everything from model rockets to sand art. Usually, these kits are made for kids under ten, but why let children have all the fun?

Go on a shopping spree

Announce to your son or daughter in advance that you are going to clean the garage tomorrow (or do some other odious chore together) starting bright and early. Then, as soon as your teenager gets out of bed, announce that there has been a change of plans. You are going shopping for the best thing you can buy for ten dollars or less. Next, drive to a city, a museum, or a shopping center you have never been to and go window-shopping together. Maybe you'll find a candy shop with caramel apples or some sinfully delicious chocolate. Perhaps you'll run across a beautiful piece of inexpensive jewelry. As an alternative, you can choose a specialty shop and give your teenager a budget to birthday shop for a sibling, or even find a one-of-a-kind Mother's Day gift for your wife. This activity will seem especially random and spontaneous if you are not the parent who normally does the shopping. Could a teenage daughter and her dad have fun on a shopping spree together? It's certainly worth finding out!

Help your teen learn to find down time

Even if your teen is a highly self-motivated individual who wants to be the president of the Russian Club, hold down a part-time job, volunteer at the homeless shelter, dance with the drill team, serve as the yearbook photographer, *and* hold the lead in the school play, loving parents can help a busy teenager create and protect moments for time out. Lest you worry that if you allow her a free moment to goof off, she's not going to do as well on her SAT, consider this advice from what most would consider an unlikely source—the Harvard Admissions office:

- Allow for "down time" during vacations, weekends, and mealtimes. Parents who are in the fast track themselves need some uninterrupted free time to devote to children.
- Bring summer back. Summer need not be totally consumed by highly structured programs, such as summer schools, travel programs, or athletic camps. While such activities can be wonderful in many ways, they can also add to stress by assembling "super peers" who set nearly impossible standards.
- Choose a high school (or a college) not simply by "brand name" or reputation but because it is the best fit. A slower pace or a different academic or extracurricular focus can be a better match for certain students in the long run.[9]

Family vacations

Several years ago, after my parents had become empty-nesters, I decided it would be fun to compile a family history. After soliciting contributions from each of my siblings and their spouses, we started to piece together the most memorable times in being a family. I was not surprised when the topic of choice for the first chapter was family vacations. In it, we chronicled all of the crazy family outings we enjoyed:

- The time we drove to California in a rebuilt school bus that had been painted brown and turned into an RV. Grandpa was driving with the door open because it was so hot, and as we rounded a corner, a drunken bum mistook the contraption for the city transportation system and hopped on.
- The time Dad lost his glasses when we dumped him off his inner tube in the middle of the Snake River.
- The couple who visited Yellowstone National Park for their honeymoon only to be stranded by a forest fire.

If family vacations are such great opportunities for playing together and creating memories, why do so many of us neglect them? Statistical research indicates that in spite of the fact that our incomes have increased and travel is far easier and more economical than it was for our grandparents, fewer and fewer children enjoy this time-honored family ritual. Where teenagers are concerned, family vacations may be the single-most important opportunity we have to make connections and develop relationships. More than one teenager identified the car as their favorite place to connect with their parents. "I always talk to my parents when we are in the car, even if we are just going to get a Pepsi" writes Zac. "I let off my steam and we do some stellar communicating."

What if you're so busy with your son's year-round accelerated baseball schedule that there's no time for an extended vacation? Can't you just count the time in the car driving between tournaments?

"You may argue, as some parents do," write William Doherty, PhD, and Barbara Carlson, "that one-to-one time in the car on the way to children's events can indeed be a connecting form of going out. . . . Random moments of connection while driving somewhere are to be treasured, but you can't count on them as a way to connect with a child—especially now that so many kids prefer to wear their own earphones or watch a video in the backseat of the SUV."[10]

One grandparent told me, "I laughed out loud when I saw an advertisement for a car recently. Two children sat mesmerized in the back of the vehicle, watching a ten-inch screen replay a video about dancing chipmunks, while the car peacefully traversed one of the most visually stunning sections of Yosemite National Park. Doesn't anyone see the irony in this?" Family vacations, and the long moments of travel time that generally go with them, are ideal times to connect verbally and emotionally with our teenagers.

Landon agrees that vacations are his favorite times to communicate with Mom and Dad. "There isn't really one distinctive moment where we just bond or connect, but while I spend more and more time with them, I feel closer to them," he reports.

I believe there are also times that simply being *present* together is enough. Conversation is just a bonus. During a recent vacation, one of my sons humored me with an outing to go stargazing. The rest of the family was sound asleep in the camp trailer, and although I had originally intended to make everyone come along, it was too cold for stargazing to have universal appeal. Instead, my seventeen-year-old and I packed a couple of blankets and a camera and drove until we found a dark stretch of highway. We each wrapped up in a quilt and then lay down in the bed of the truck and watched until our eyes adjusted and the Milky Way came into view. I didn't know what to talk with him about, and he didn't say a word, but he was willing to ride along. It was good to be together, and he even pretended to be pleased for me when I finally succeeded in getting a time-lapse exposure of the big dipper.

My son was willing to humor me, but what do you do when your teenager won't? How do you proceed when she resists your attempts to get her involved in family activities? Dr. Barry Ginsburg, director of the Center of Relationship Enhancement in Doylestown, Pennsylvania, suggests that parents balance their authority with a big dose of cooperation. "In their quest for independent selves, teenagers may reject or be resistant to what they think their parents want them to do. Family events might be fun to them, but may make them feel as though they're being held back from their independence.

"Often these events are in fact boring to the adolescent and mostly for the benefit of the adults. Parents may want their teenagers to go for the parents' own sake, often wanting to hold onto them and not recognizing it," Ginsburg says.[11]

He suggests that if a relationship with the teenager is the primary focus, the real concern is to help your teen see that her needs have been taken into consideration. After you've reassured her that you understand her position, it will be easier to negotiate a compromise, like allowing her to bring a friend along, or agreeing that as part of the trip, the family will do something that is strictly for her.[12] In tough cases, you may have to leave a teenager behind for one trip with the agreement that participating in the next one is non-negotiable. Either way, you don't want to sacrifice family vacations just because a teenager grumbles. They are just too valuable. Let your teenager grumble, and take him along anyway. That's how it works in Zac's family. "After I get over the fact that I have to spend time with them, we always have fun. It's just getting over that, 'Oh man, I have to hang with my parents,' " he laughs.

In families where teens have jobs and other responsibilities that make family vacations difficult to schedule, you might find success in taking vacations that are separated by gender. Mom and the girls spend a few days in the city shopping, and Dad and the boys go backpacking together. For a truly memorable experience with your teen, however, consider having Dad take his daughter and swap the following week while Mom takes her son to a destination of his choice. One of the most delightful vacations I've ever been on involved my husband and me going to San Francisco for a week with one daughter and leaving her siblings behind with Grandma. She and her dad rode the cable car together to Fisherman's Wharf, and she got her first taste of crab. We took an audio tour at Alcatraz, played all day at the Exploratorium (a world-renouned children's science museum), and even had lunch at the Hard Rock Café. None of us will ever forget it. Several years later, the mementos we bought together in Chinatown still dominate her bedroom décor.

Teens I surveyed seemed to be particularly delighted with "unannounced" family outings that had been planned just for them. Cami's parents let their kids think they were taking a short car trip one evening and then purposely passed the freeway exit and kept right on driving—all the way to Disneyland. One of Zac's favorite family outings started out with a similar surprise: "My Mom and dad dressed up like the Tin Man and the Wicked Witch of the West and told us we were going to New York to see the Broadway play *Wicked*. That was a blast!"

Family vacations are also important for helping your teen stretch beyond the limits of his or her day-to-day routines. P.J.'s father took him on a fifty-mile backpacking trek in the Uintah mountains. "We spent a week together in the wilderness, sharing a grueling physical challenge. This really cemented my relationship and respect for my father, which was already great," says P.J.

The cementing of the relationship happened in a similar way for Cami during a cold, wet hike on one of their family trips.

> There were several ice sheets covering the path. We were hiking at night, and it was very scary to cross the ice sheets. At one point, I slipped and fell down the side of the hill. It was really scary, and I was quite frightened afterwards. My dad stayed near me the rest of the hike and helped me across the rest of the sheets. He was very sensitive to me, and even though I felt a little silly because I was having a harder time than the younger kids, he encouraged me, and we made it back just fine. I felt like that was the most connecting experience I ever had with my dad. It brought me very close to him.

Opportunities to express affection

Although teenagers are famous for getting too old and too tough for the hugs and kisses that they enjoyed when they were younger, one of the aspects of a relationship that parents have to work at is the expression of affection. Teens need non-sexual touch from their parents, and playing together gives us many opportunities—touch football games, holding hands and jumping off the dock together, or putting an arm around a child after a hard-fought tennis match, for example. Hugging, ruffling hair, a hand on the shoulder, or even a high-five are all forms of touch that help adolescents know we love them. Teens also need verbal affection. Write a short note to hide under a pillow or in a lunch box to say you think he's great and you were proud of his hard work in the yard last weekend. Paste a sticky note to the bathroom mirror to wish her luck on her math test. Stash a funny card inside her sport bag or backpack. Send her a short e-mail or an animated e-card. Studies show that teens who recalled a parent praising them or giving them a hug during the previous week were more likely to do better in school.

One Canadian study looked at the differences in the way mothers and fathers respond to their children. The results of the study indicated that teen-parent relationships, particularly between a father and his daughter, are a good predictor of adolescent depression. The study also verified that teenaged girls find it more difficult to establish affectionate relationships with a father than teenage boys do.[13] Since girls tend to suffer symptoms of depression more often, psychologist Robin Goodman points to the results of the study as an indicator that dads need to work harder to develop good relationships with their daughters. The good news from the study is that when parents were not good at displaying affection, their efforts to improve led to improvements in the relationship. So another great reason for playing with our teenagers is that it gives us spontaneous, natural opportunities for touch and affection. Even parents and teens with the most difficult relationships can do better as a result. If it's been too long since you said the words "I love you" out loud (and even if it hasn't been long), here are some non-invasive methods you can use to get a new start.

A gift from Dad

What daughter, traveling away from home for her first overnight debate meet, wouldn't have her heart melted by a small card from her father with a ten-dollar bill inside and a note that says, "I will sure miss you. Use this to buy something I would get for you if I were along for the trip. Love and kisses, Dad."

Decorate a locker

Dawn says, "My sons think locker decorating is sissy girly stuff, but I have yet to find one who is disappointed to find a bag full of treats stashed inside on his birthday. Once I put in a brown paper bag with everything my son would need for an ice cream sundae—a parfait glass, nuts, caramel, even cherries. The only thing I left out was the ice cream, and I included a note that said I had some waiting for him in the freezer at home." The counselor in your child's guidance office will probably be willing to supply you with your child's locker number and combination.

Make the night away from home memorable

Once, when I left home for a week to go on tour with a high school orchestra, I arrived at my destination to find that my sister had crammed every nook and cranny of my suitcase with little notes. She waited until after I had packed and then snuck little slips of paper and small treats into my makeup case, the pockets of my jeans, and even inside the lid of my deodorant. Today, when her own daughter is away at night riding the band bus home from a late football game, they will text message one another during the long, dark hours while the bus is making its way back home.

Get "in touch" with each other

Any kind of friendly physical contact can be good for a teen. Arm wrestle while you are waiting for dinner or have a thumb war in the dentist's waiting room. If you are a religious family, holding hands during grace at the table or kneeling shoulder-to-shoulder in a circle for a family prayer can be a warm custom. Our family has a tradition of "prayer hugs" after we say our evening prayers.

Bedtime back rub

When one of my sons injured the muscles in his back during a track meet, the doctor prescribed muscle relaxants and a back rub every night before bed. I enjoyed the conversation as much as he enjoyed having his sore muscles massaged. Offer to give your teen a quick back rub after he stays up late to work on a term paper, or give your daughter a good foot rub after her next volleyball game (it's okay to make her put on clean socks first). It's physical, non-threatening contact that can be very soothing and relaxing.

A trite, worn-out saying is perfectly acceptable

"Bye, Mom. Love you." I hear this phrase from my children as they leave the house every morning. I don't know which of my kids started the tradition, but it has stuck with each of them. My nine-year-old has a complex handshake ritual that we go through every morning. The ritual changes every August to reflect the start of a new school year. Currently it goes like this: She says, "up high" and then pounds her fist on one of mine, then "down low" and hits my fist from below. Then she hooks her thumb into mine and says, "and away we go," and flaps her hand against mine as if our two flapping hands are wings that fly up and apart. If I don't happen to be in the room as she is leaving, she will yell her little rhyme from the other side of the house before she leaves. I think it's notable that I did not create these goofy, trite little phrases. My kids did. I think they want to hear that someone loves them as they're leaving in the morning. It's a good message for us to start our day with. Our cousins have two grown sons who have graduated from high school and live away from home now. Their e-mails home always end with the salutation, "1-2-3, sure love ya!" Since these two young men were toddlers, this is the phrase the family repeated in chorus every night before bedtime. Now, miles away from home, it gives these boys a connection that keeps homesickness at bay.

A warm wake-up call

Anna learned that when her teens overslept and didn't get up when their alarms went off, they were especially cranky in the mornings. She hated the job of standing at the bottom of the stairs yelling for them to "get up right now," so she had to come up with a different plan. These days, if her sons don't come downstairs to breakfast by 6:30, she walks into their bedrooms, waits for them to stand on their feet, wraps a warm blanket around them, and gives them a hug. Already wrapped up and warm, they come to breakfast more willingly. On an especially frigid morning once or twice each winter, she even tosses the blankets into the dryer for a moment before her wake-up call.

Come up with your own code

In the Henderson household, three of anything is secret code for "I love you," so it's a message Mom or Dad can give in front of a group of peers, and no one is ever the wiser. Three beeps on the car horn while the carpool is waiting for one of the kids to finish brushing his teeth, three squeezes on the shoulder as father and son are leaving a football game, or three knocks on the bedroom door when it's time for lights out have become a nonverbal way for family members to say "I love you" dozens of times a week.

E-mail a greeting

Periodically, I get a zany e-card from one of my daughters. Visit a reputable site like www.hallmark.com and click on "e-cards" to find dozens of animated cards you can send for free. Make sure you include a message that expresses your affection.

Sharing of responsibilities and interests

Along with your affection, your teen needs your trust in order to thrive. One of the best ways to play with teenagers is to begin to allow them to enjoy some of your adult hobbies. Just like when they were young and adult jobs like mowing the lawn and polishing the silver looked fun, many of your adult duties are intriguing and appealing to a teen. What game is more fascinating for a sixteen-year-old than being behind the wheel of a vehicle for the first time!

Even extended family members can develop relationships with teenagers by being willing to allow them to help with "adult" tasks or take part in activities that are usually reserved for the grown-ups. I remember how fun it was to include our oldest son in a dinner party with his aunts and uncles. It was the first time he had been considered one of the "adults," and he was clearly pleased.

Jim remembers his uncle inviting him to fly on short business trips.

> Verl had a pilot's license, and I recall going with him in the airplane to bid a construction job in the next state. Once in the air, he would let me or the cousin traveling with us steer the plane. This was great fun! The steering wheel rotated so the plane could be steered, but by pushing it in or pulling it back, you could make the plane dive or climb. Verl would even let us bring the plane in close to the runway before taking the wheel from us to land. Getting to fly with Uncle Verl was a big deal for me. I thought for many years that I would someday earn my own pilot's license too.

My sister Karlyn delights her nieces with regular invitations to "job shadow" her at her salon for an afternoon. They get opportunities to see their fun-loving aunt dealing with clients as a professional, and the day always ends with a facial or a pedicure—at someone else's salon!

Jessica remembers playing board games at her grandmother's kitchen table with her aunts and uncles.

> Most people played individually, but some of the younger kids teamed up with someone older than them because they were too young to play by themselves. I played by myself because I was old enough. While the game was going, we had ice cream and brownies and we laughed and joked while waiting for our turn. It was this "side socializing" that I liked best about playing games with [the adults] in my family. I liked to listen to the conversations between my parents, aunts, and uncles because I thought that they were so witty and smart. Their jokes were so much better than mine, and sometimes I would commit the things they said to memory for later use.

Including children in favorite sports and hobbies can also be a fun way to play together. Linda's father ran a farm and worked nights in a factory, and because her dad was in the fields during the day, she often saw him only on weekends during the summer months. But when she turned twelve, she was invited to become her dad's tractor-pulling buddy.

> Originally, this sport was known as horse pulling. The farmers would have a competition to see whose horse team was the strongest. The horses were hitched to a skid (a platform with no wheels), which they pulled along a dirt path. Every few feet, men were stationed to throw a sandbag or some kind of weight onto the skid as it passed. The team that could pull the skid the farthest with the most weight won.

After horse pulling evolved into tractor pulling, Linda's father joined the circuit in the "stock" class, which meant that the tractor had to be in original condition, with no added power or attachments, and it had to be "field ready." The weight of the driver had to be calculated into the total weight before it could be determined which weight class the entire outfit could compete in. That is how Linda got involved. As a twelve-year-old girl, she didn't add a lot of extra baggage.

> My dad balanced his tractor perfectly for conditions, but he was too heavy to make the weight class he wanted to be in . . . . The officials had no rules about age or sex of the driver, but they required my dad to walk alongside the tractor as I drove for safety . . . . I had been driving tractors on the farm, hooking up and unhooking equipment since I was eight, so it wasn't a problem. I was the only girl and youngest tractor puller on the circuit.

Linda soon relinquished her tractor-pulling spot *and* her dad's one-on-one attention to her younger brother. "I didn't really mind, because by then I was into dating the sons of his tractor-pulling buddies," Linda laughs. But the moment was memorable for both of them. Her dad loved reliving their tractor-pulling days and was still telling their story the week before he died, thirty-seven years later.

The fact that our children are older does not mean they no longer want time to "play" with us. The playing just takes on a different form. What other interests do you have that could include your teenager? Do you play golf? Have you ever taught her how to do the silk ribbon embroidery your grandmother taught you? Is he old enough to help you build a chess set? Would she enjoy helping you redecorate the bathroom? Have you considered taking a stained glass class together? One father I know keeps a tenuous relationship with his rebellious teenage daughter alive by baking brownies or frying donuts with her on Sunday afternoons. Another takes his daughter regularly to go for a drive and get a Pepsi. Yet another dad invites his daughter to accompany him on his delivery route on days when she is out of school. When the work is done, their day together always includes lunch.

Connections between parents and children can also come through shared adolescent experiences. It can be comforting for a child to know that Mom or Dad battled acne, hated their overbite, felt awkward around members of the opposite sex, and didn't get asked to the prom. Our teenagers usually enjoy hearing about our life experiences so they can compare and contrast their lives with ours. Laurel remembers the day her father took her to get her first pair of eyeglasses:

> I'm not sure why my father was the one to take me to the optical shop on the Air Force Base in Texas where we lived because it seemed that my mother always took care of doctor's visits and shopping for the children in our family. Come to think of it, I think she took me to choose the frames, maybe because she wasn't sure what I'd end up with if my father went. However, Dad took me to pick them up and for final adjustments in the fitting. What was memorable was the time together after we left the optical shop. [For the first time, I was able to really see] with clarity and definition—the leaves on the trees, the sharp lines and definition of sidewalks, blades of grass, traffic signs. Everywhere I looked, everything was new, bright and damp from a recent rain. I don't remember exactly what he said, but Dad helped me feel that he understood the experience. He and I were the only ones in my immediate family who needed glasses.

Do you still have a few old forty-eight singles somewhere in the basement? You might be surprised to discover that if you took time to listen, you and your teen have surprisingly similar musical interests. Try this experiment: Tell your teen to bring his iPod to the family room. Lay a blanket and some pillows out on the floor and tell him you want to hear his three favorite songs, and you want to share your three favorites.

If you don't think you can make it through three of his tunes, limit yourselves to one. Just lay on the floor and listen to music together. Being careful to completely withhold judgment, ask him to tell you what he likes about it. Is the beat intriguing? Do the lyrics hit home with him? Next, share *your* favorite song. The task for you is just to listen. Nothing more.

Have you ever considered volunteering with your teenager? Avoid thinking of this as one more of those "it will look good on your resume" experiences. Instead, look for an opportunity for the two of you to work shoulder-to-shoulder changing other people's lives for the better. Is there any better way to learn to appreciate your son's goodness than by watching him gently fold the fingers of a disabled child around a softball at the Special Olympics? Can your daughter help you make blankets for Project Linus? This is an organization that supplies cancer patients, children injured in accidents, or the victims of a natural disaster with a warm blanket to cuddle in. Could you redesign a website for a nonprofit charitable organization or organize a playday for at-risk children in your neighborhood? Visit www.volunteermatch.org to get an idea of what other motivated, helpful people have done and to see if there are immediate needs in your own community.

Here's another idea. Take your teenager on a road trip (one-on-one) to visit your birthplace. Show him the house you grew up in or the elementary school you attended. Buy an ice cream cone from your favorite ice cream shop. Go bowling at the same bowling alley you loved when you were a teenager. Visit the church you attended, or take in a movie together at that old theater and see if your feet still stick to the floor from spilled soda. Show her where you scratched your name into a tree. Plan at least four separate stops at locations of interest your child has never visited. Avoid making this merely one of those outings where you get out of the car to look at a historical marker. Have something interesting and fun to share with your child at each location.

Barbara loved the theater when she was in college, and she still buys a set of season tickets to see plays at the local university. Each month, a different teenager goes along with Mom for a night out. My husband loves basketball and football games at his alma mater. His daughters clamor for the opportunity to join him, and he keeps enough change in his wallet for a treat at halftime. In the days when these purchases stretched our budget almost beyond its limit, I doubted the wisdom of the expense, but game day with Dad has become a favorite father-teen tradition in our home.

While not "playing" in the traditional sense, sharing common interests and learning new responsibilities can be entertaining and fun. And it can also bless parent-teen relationships—even those that seem damaged beyond repair.

Opportunities for casual conversation

As I mentioned at the beginning of this chapter, the times I felt like I really connected with my teens were times when they opened up and simply conversed with me. Casual conversation is supremely important to a teenager, and playing together can be a great catalyst for creating opportunities to chat with one another.

"One night, my mom couldn't sleep," writes Julie, "and I was up late for some odd reason. I talked her into pulling out the blankets and popcorn, and the two of us stayed up most of the night watching old movies. It was so much fun!"

Tanya remembers getting up the courage to tell her father about her first "boy crush"—and expressing the concern that maybe he liked her friend and not her. "I remember feeling very insecure and confused about the situation," Tanya writes. Her father listened intently to her whole story, and when she had finished, he said, simply, "You're beautiful."

"You're supposed to say that. You're my dad!" Tanya argued.

But Tanya also remembers what he said next. Her father reassured her and explained that the best thing to do was to be herself, and eventually, if the young man liked her, he would let her know. That simple advice, coupled with the fact that he didn't lecture her about being too young to get involved romantically, helped Tanya learn that her dad was a trustworthy sounding board—someone willing to listen without lecturing.

When I asked teens what they would most like to do if they had their mom or dad all to themselves for a day, I was a little surprised at the responses. No one said anything like "I would fly cross-country and go to a Broadway play" or "I would make him take me to Aruba to go wind surfing." Instead, these teens listed dozens of simple pleasures—activities that are so common, they might not even be considered out-of-the-ordinary for most of us. One response was typical: "If I had one day with my dad, I would go fishing with him. I would ask him about his childhood and find out how he coped with problems as a boy. If I spent time with my mom, we would visit historical sites and have a good time laughing about my dad."

Here are some more responses teens gave when asked what they would like to do if they had Mom or Dad all to themselves:

- Listen to their stories about when they were younger.
- Ask them for advice.
- Go shopping and out to eat and chat.
- Go to a concert.
- Go for a bike ride all the way around the lake.
- Go out to lunch and talk about stuff.
- Go to a movie.
- Bake something together.

It was interesting that in about 50 percent of the responses, teens most desired a chance to "chill and chat," or in other words, an opportunity for casual conversation. But their responses yielded another interesting aspect of conversation. More than one youth was careful to point out that while they wanted to talk with Mom and Dad, and while they were sincerely interested in getting advice and learning "what it was like when Mom and Dad were younger," they resented forced conversation. The question on the survey they completed was, "Have you ever had a one-on-one conversation when you really communicated with each other? What were you doing before you started talking that made you feel safe about opening up?" Here are some of the responses I received:

- "Most of the time, I feel I can open up to my parents because we have a close relationship anyway. But it is best when I want to *come to them* to speak, when I am trying to think things over—not them asking me questions. It seems to be more effective that way" (emphasis added).
- "One thing that helps me is when my parents share with me their struggles and their issues. Not all of them, but enough for me to know that they weren't trying to hide things from me because I knew they had problems."
- "I feel more comfortable if I *come to them* because I know what the conversation will be about. If they come to me, I usually have no idea what we are gonna talk about" (emphasis added).

- "The times I treasured most with my dad were our 'daddy-daughter dates.' I remember we got to put our date on the calendar, and he took me to breakfast once. What a treat! I don't remember anything we talked about, but I remember wishing and wishing he would take me out again—just me and him. As the pressures mounted, I pulled away as a teenager, but deep down, I still craved a little private date with my dad. I always wanted a moment with him where I didn't have to report on my to-do list but just sit and laugh."

- "I was talking to my mom in the kitchen one day. I really wanted to talk to her about a relationship I was in, but I didn't really know how to bring it up. I was just sitting at the bar stool and she was making dinner. Nobody else was at home, and I knew I had plenty of time to talk to her alone. We were just talking about other things nonchalantly, and I brought it up because I felt like the time was right. I think that if my mom had teased me about the relationship beforehand, I would have had a much harder time opening up to her. I knew that she was willing to listen and give advice."

Apparently, there are two elements at work when adolescents are willing to communicate. One, the teen has something he or she has been mulling over or thinking about and needs a sounding board; and two, the teen finds an opportunity for talk that feels comfortable for them. Most teenagers have to feel absolutely safe before they are willing to risk sharing a confidence—safe from intrusions, safe from being laughed at, safe from being interrupted, and safe from being overheard. In other words, it takes a pretty special venue to get a teen to really open up and communicate, and spending one-on-one time with a teen on a regular, unhurried basis seems to be the most logical way to create the venue. Can you plan opportunities for your teen to talk with you without it looking like the opportunity was planned? Absolutely. But it might be most effective if you schedule regular one-on-one time and just let conversation flow when the need arises. You can do this simply by being "at the crossroads" in a child's life—available when she comes in from school or after a date, nearby at bedtime, accessible during the long drive to a soccer game or a lesson. You can also schedule regular opportunities for talk.

For five years, from the moment she outgrew bedtime chats at age thirteen until she went away to college, Dr. William Doherty enjoyed a weekly date to Dairy Queen with his daughter. "Sometimes Elizabeth had an agenda for these outings, something she was worrying about or curious about. Other times they talked about nothing in particular. But they both knew that these trips were not primarily about ice cream . . . . In January in Minneapolis, they were sometimes the only people at the Dairy Queen on Hennepin Avenue."[14] Playing with teenagers is sometimes less about being physically active and more about being emotionally accessible. And on the other hand, maybe your opportunity to talk will come during a driveway basketball game or on an autumn jog to the park and back. For some teenagers, holding a difficult discussion is easier if you don't have to look anyone in the eye.

Again, natural settings seem to have special appeal to teens who want an opportunity to sound out a parent's opinions. That's the way it was for Kim on her most memorable day of "connecting."

> Sometime during my late teens, my mom and I took a drive to visit a state park a couple of hours from our home. We chatted as the road to the park wound through miles of green hills full of flowering dogwood trees. When we arrived, we watched the bulging waters of a huge natural spring bubble at the head of the river. We followed the river through the park, watching fishermen toss their silky lines in the spring sunlight. Finally, we got out and walked the aisles of an enormous fish hatchery. Hundreds of fish writhed and flapped as they competed for the tiny pellets of food we threw in.
>
> Then Mom and I walked over to the river and took off our shoes. We stepped into the current, the water rushing gently past our legs. There in the warmth of the sun and the cool of the water, conversation flowed easily. I had always had a good relationship with my mom, but was never one to share the details of my life and feelings with her openly. But for some reason, there in the woods, I wanted to talk; and I dared ask a few questions and answer some as well. Two of the questions I remember asking her were, "What do you fear most in life?" And, "If you could re-make one decision in your life, what would it be?" She answered and explained, and then asked me the same things back. We waded and talked and waded and talked. There in the water, a wall began to erode in my

soul, and I realized I could *talk* to my mom. We went home refreshed, connected, and contented.

Eating together, having spontaneous, purposeless fun, going on family vacations, sharing hobbies and interests, allowing youth to feel the weight of our adult responsibilities, and creating venues for conversation might not be considered "play" in the typical sense of the word, but in fact, they are all superb play methods, and every one of them is effective for helping build those critical relationships with teens. And while the heaviest cost to you will probably be in terms of sacrificing your time, it's comforting to know that the keys to "eroding the walls in our teens souls" are so accessible, so simple, and so doable.

Reader's Homework

Based on what you have read in this chapter, what ONE idea for playing with children appeals to you most as something that you could feasibly do in your own home? (This can be an idea you read about in the book, an idea of your own that came to you as you were reading, or something you remember experiencing as a child).

Write your ONE idea here:

_____

_____

If you'd like, record this idea in the "Gallery of Ideas to Try" at the end of the book.

Notes

1. "The White House Conference on Teenagers: Raising Responsible and Resourceful Youth," clinton3.nara.gov/WH/New/html/teenconf1.html, 1.

2. Moore and Zaff, www.childtrends.org/files/K7Brief.pdf, 1–2.

3. Blum and Rinehart 1997, allaboutkids.umn.edu/cfahad/Reducing_the_risk. pdf; Moore and Zaff, Childtrends Research Brief.

4. Kindlon, *Too Much of A Good Thing*, 99.

5. Califano, www.casafamilyday.org/PDFs/FDIIIreport06.pdf, 1.

6. Kindlon, *Too Much of A Good Thing*, 198.

7. Mogul, www.nais.org, 4.

8. Mogul, www.nais.org, 5.

9. Fitzsimmons, Lewis, and Ducey, Harvard College Admissions, 3.

10. Doherty and Carlson, *Putting Family First*, 80

11. Ginsburg, www.aap.org/pressroom/playFINAL.pdf.

12. Waldrop, teenagerstoday.com/resources/articles/outings.htm.

13. Bushnik, dsp-psd.communication.gc.ca/Collection/Statcan/89-599-MIE/89-599-MIE2005002.pdf.

14. Doherty, *Putting Family First*.

Chapter 11

All Children Must Be Accompanied by a PLAYING Adult

How grandparents who play bless the next generation

• •

The most conspicuous feature in my Grandma and Grandpa Whiting's backyard was a giant swingset. Hand-welded from leftover pipe scrounged from the shop and workyard that were headquarters of Grandpa's construction company, the swingset was a one-of-a-kind play structure, crafted as a favor to Grandpa by one of his employees. The top spar that supported the swing was well over ten feet above ground, so if you could get a good running push from a willing uncle, the drop you would feel in the pit of your abdomen as the swing completed its first arc and started hurtling toward earth again challenged the sturdiest of stomachs.

Grandma's house was a haven for a special kind of play because it was there that we were able to gather with our cousins—friends we only played with once or twice a year—to create memories and forge relationships that still enrich us, even now that Grandma and Grandpa are gone. What was interesting about Grandma and Grandpa was that they were seldom "active" players. Instead they were "facilitators of play."

Because they were willing to create opportunities for us to gather, were willing to put up with the mess and the noise, and saved a lot of interesting junk for us to play with, Grandma and Grandpa's house holds dozens and dozens of play memories for me that I can connect directly to them.

I can only remember one time Grandma actually came and played *with* us. There were sixteen "girl cousins" among her granddaughters, so when we got old enough, Grandma scheduled what we called Girl Cousin Parties. She would push the quilting frames and the ping pong tables aside in her cluttered basement rumpus room and make space for all of us to sleep together in one huge, giggling slumber party. One weekend, after we'd woken up late and sat on the stairs to eat our Apple Jacks and poached eggs (we couldn't all fit into Grandma's kitchen at once), we spent the morning playing the typical slumber party games with each other.

My oldest cousin, Pat, was usually the source of these games that delighted the rest of us, and because Pat was judicious about being sure no one was treated cruelly, we could play together for hours. On this particular day, we coaxed Grandma down from the kitchen to join us and proceeded to take her for an "airplane ride." We blindfolded Grandma and stood her on top of a sturdy board that several of us supported with our hands. Two other cousins allowed Grandma to place her hands on their shoulders for support. Once the airplane ride started, these two cousins crouched down slowly, giving Grandma the illusion that we were raising her several feet into the air. Pat narrated a detailed "flight" over the top of the Swiss Alps and across the Amazon River, until our plane encountered "engine failure." The cousins holding the board began to rock it back and forth while Grandma fought valiantly to keep her balance, but alas, the plane eventually had to crash land, and when Pat screamed "Jump, Grandma, jump," Grandma did.

Her reaction was everything we could have hoped it would be. We're probably lucky she didn't collapse on the spot from heart palpitations or a broken hip, but Grandma was so delighted with the joke that it has been a favorite memory for each of us.

Grandma's playful spirit was the source of dozens of great playing experiences I had in her home as a child. She was hard of hearing, which probably helped. She joked that when she invited us over for slumber parties, she could simply take her hearing aids out at bedtime and never be disturbed again. In the summertime, she'd have Grandpa start a fire in the backyard fireplace and slather us in her own homemade, stinky, oily mosquito repellent. She'd usually have a few fireworks or sparklers for us to play with as it got dark, and then she'd produce marshmallows, roasting sticks, and a boxful of stale graham crackers. At bedtime, she showed us how to arrange our sleeping bags on the lawn in spokes like a wagon wheel so that all of us could have our heads in the center where we could talk and giggle for as long as we pleased. Sleeping just a few feet away from us, with her bedroom windows wide open, she had the illusion that she was supervising.

The "boy cousins" had similar goofy gatherings that included competitions to see who could drink an entire gallon of milk without vomiting, slam-dunk the most balls, or jump out of trees onto the next-door neighbor's trampoline without major injuries and without parents being any the wiser. Sometimes the girls stayed upstairs and the boys down, and sometimes, since there was a fifteen-year span in our ages, the gatherings were purely age-based (older cousins to the pool, younger cousins to the ditch in front of Grandma's house to wade and eat popsicles). Because we lived in different states, we'd never have known each other so intimately without Grandma's carefully planned parties and reunions. No matter who was in town, Grandma could always get up a good party simply by providing space for us. She helped us create friendships that continue to bless us into adulthood.

Grandpa was also a good sport. Long before any of us were old enough to drive legally, he'd pile several of us into his old Plymouth Valiant and take us to the church parking lot to drive around in circles until we ran out of gas. On another occasion, he took us to the sand dunes where we spent the morning filling our socks full of sand and launching them as far down the dune as they could fly.

What intrigues me still about playing with Grandma and Grandpa is that the kind of play we remember best could be duplicated by any grandparent, although the equipment used, the location, and even the methods vary depending on the circumstances of individual grandparents. Without even knowing it, Grandma and Grandpa had a knack for providing the right "equipment" for our play. In Grandpa's basement office, we were allowed to swivel in the office chairs, pretend to type at the typewriter, open and close the drawers of the file cabinets (as long as we didn't disturb the files inside), and call each other on his phones. (He had a regular home phone line and a second line that connected to the construction yard.)

Upstairs, Grandma had closets filled with her old formals and evening gowns and lots of beautiful stiletto-heeled shoes. We were free to try them on as long as we were careful. She even had several hat boxes full of the stylish hats she had worn during the nineteen-forties and several more she had inherited from her own extended family and preserved. The bedroom vanity had a comb and brush set and a few bottles of perfume that my aunts had left behind when they married and moved away, so the upstairs bedrooms were a haven for playing house. One of our favorite games was "hotel." One of us would be the guest and another would provide "maid service." Essentially, we'd spend the afternoon taking turns messing up the beds and throwing pillows on the floor, then waiting while "maid service" cleaned everything up, only to switch places and do it all again. Of course, we'd never have considered this kind of activity fun if it had involved making beds in our own bedrooms.

The playtimes we enjoyed had nothing to do with advance planning. Grandma and Grandpa simply allowed us access to things in their home that were interesting to us. When necessary, they made rules about where we could and could not play, but other than that, they just provided the space and let our imaginations run wild. The house and closets provided hours of fascinating "looking."

We loved to travel between the floors of her house via the laundry chute that connected the upstairs bathroom to the laundry room a floor below. As a child of the Depression, Grandma never threw anything away, so there were many interesting trunks and boxes full of broken porcelain doll parts and delicately crocheted hankies. The cupboard in her sewing room was filled with tiny drawers that could be opened individually. Each one held a different treasure—tiny pearl beads, strips of gold and silver braid, silk fringe, colorful ric rac and lace, and hundreds of interesting buttons. Grandma cut off and saved all buttons, even the buttons from the family underwear. I especially loved the silk kimonos and cloth dolls Grandma had received from her pen pals in Japan and Greece and the file folders full of photographs of our parents—blond when we had never known them to be blond, skinnier than we had ever seen them, and awkward and buck-toothed (which was soothing for those of us who were also awkward and buck-toothed at the time).

It was Grandma's habit, periodically, to invite two or three of us at a time to spend a weekend with her. I did not consider at the time how these visits might have inconvenienced her, but I know how thrilled I was to get the invitation. One weekend, she helped me and my sister learn to piece and tie our first quilts. Another time, she taught us how to properly set a formal dining table. Once, she pulled out a box full of calligraphy pens and ink and showed us how she made the beautiful, flowing lettering on her Christmas cards and invitations to club meetings. In one easy lesson,

I developed an instant desire to reform my own penmanship—a task my fifth-grade teacher had been unsuccessful at promoting after a whole year of trying. On another rainy afternoon, she taught me how to crochet a lace edge around a pillowcase.

If it was summertime, she might give us a few coins and let us walk to the corner market a block away to buy a small treat—a privilege that felt recklessly adventurous at the time. In the evenings, she and Grandpa took us to the local art museum or for a drive to get a hamburger and a rootbeer float. Having Grandma or Grandpa all to ourselves even made it easy to put up with the "educational" outings, like taking a tour of the two local graveyards to see where ancestors were buried, or driving through town to look at all of the trees that Grandma's great-grandfather had planted more than a hundred years before, or visiting the withered great-aunt who lived next door and told the same stories over and over again. What I know now about playing with Grandma is that it was probably a serious undertaking for her. She was passing on to me some of her generation's wisdom—wisdom she knew I would need but had nowhere else to learn. She was wise enough to just let me think we were having fun together, and because of that, most of the lessons took.

The case was different with my maternal grandparents. There were no cousins because they had only one child, so we got their total attention. Because it was an all-day trip to drive to their farm, our summertime visits doubled as family vacations. Grandpa built his own RVs, long before RVs were popular. He'd cut the top off an old school bus; put in a stove, sink, couch, beds, shower, and other amenities; and panel the outside. You'd never guess it was a bus in a former life. A tinkerer by nature and an inveterate tease, he kept things lively. Grandpa was never quite ready to go when we arrived, so we spent the first day, or more, watching Grandpa's legs as he lay under the bus, trying to get something or other in working order and listening to Grandma complain about how long it was taking. This was unnerving for her, but for children, the farm was its own adventure. There was always a rusting hulk of a school bus or a broken-down ambulance parked in one of the fields. These would eventually become another RV, but in the meantime they provided hours of fun for us. The engine might not run, but usually the battery had a little juice—at least enough to provide a day's entertainment as we blinked the turn signals, opened and closed the bus doors, shifted gears, and fiddled with the mirrors.

It would be impossible to recount here the playthings available to be discovered on a twenty-five acre farm.

Eventually, Grandpa would get "the bus" running, and we'd head for the mountains. When we got to camp, Grandpa disappeared almost immediately, usually with one or more of us in tow, to try out the nearest fishing hole. Grandma stayed behind to hug the baby, sweep the forest with the camper broom, and worry about Grandpa when he didn't come back when he said he would—there was always one more fish to outwit. I remember the first fish Grandpa "helped" my older brother catch. Grandpa wrapped it in newspaper for him, and he held it all the way home. When Grandma offered to cook it for him, he replied, "My fish doesn't want to be cookded; he only wants to be holded." I don't remember that we ever caught a lot of fish, but we had hours of great times tying flies, wading in Idaho streams, ganging up on and dunking Grandpa, singing around the campfire, and eating Grandma's good food. My grandparents weren't wealthy, but it simply didn't matter.

Grandmas and grandpas are living in a different world now, just like the rest of us. If you are a grandma, you are as likely to drive an SUV and work as a stockbroker as you are to invite ladies to Club and write to Greek pen pals. If you are a grandpa, you may have traded in your spacious basement for a condominium and your fishing pole for a computer. You probably get your "bottled" peaches from the grocery store just like the rest of us. You might be a grandpa who still putters in the garage on weekends, but it's just as likely that you prefer road biking.

Inviting your grandchildren over for a weekend is complicated because they're as likely to live halfway across the nation as they are to live in the same town or state. On the other hand, you may be *raising* your grandchildren instead of inviting them for a family reunion now and then. You needn't despair if you can't provide the same opportunities my grandparents provided me. The memories you create for your grandchildren will be unique to you and unique to your life experience. They will be every bit as memorable for your grandchildren. The specifics of grandparenting may be different than they were a generation ago; the potential impact of a playful grandparent, however, has not changed. Your efforts to bless the next generation are timeless, whether you teach a grandchild how to print calligraphy on linen envelopes, or whether you prefer to send greetings via e-mail.

The methods of play that are available to you are infinite. A few are suggested here that have impacted the children I know. Hopefully, these ideas will help you generate play opportunities of your own.

Long-distance love

Creative grandparents have invented dozens of ways to connect when their opportunities for face to face visits with a grandchild are limited because of the distance between them. I know one little boy who has a great time playing Battleship with his extended family members via cell phone. Because he is on the same network, he can talk as long as he wants without incurring expensive long-distance charges. He can be in his living room in Seattle and call out, "C-4," and on the other end, an aunt or a grandpa who is a thousand miles away can respond, "You just sank my battleship!" Online gaming services might be an option if you want to play chess or Scrabble with a grandchild. Set up a weblog that you both contribute to weekly, learn how to instant message one another (your grandchild probably already knows how), or create a family website. E-mail a different Sudoku puzzle every week and challenge your grand-child to finish it before you do.

Emily Todd suggests other options. One grandfather tape recorded a detailed description of the process he uses to bake bread and sent the cassette to his grandsons so they could duplicate the procedure at home. Try creating your own children's storybook based on one of your own childhood experiences (you can self-publish and illustrate your book, or choose a professional publisher to bind it for you). Don't underestimate the value of being a pen pal to a grandchild. My grandma used to mail me small cards with vocabulary words she had encountered that she thought I should learn. The first package included a pick from a florist's bouquet that could hold the card upright. Grandma told me to stick it in a flower-pot in my bedroom where I could see a new word every day.

Another grandmother encourages letter writing by holding an annual contest to see which grandchild could send her the funniest letter, the lon-gest letter, the letter with the most embarrassing experience, and so on. Of course, she offers prizes. If you want to strike up a letter-writing relationship with a grandchild, send your own letter first and include a self-addressed, stamped envelope, requesting that in their return letters they tell you some-thing you don't know and ask you something they want to know.[1]

Read Me a Story, GrandMa

Grandchildren love reading with Grandma or Grandpa. In our home, we are blessed to have a grandma who has extended bedtime stories beyond her own couch. As a former educator, she has kept up with the best children's and young adult literature, and my children look forward to receiving a great hardback book (often something they request in advance) as birthday and Christmas gifts. As they've grown older and have outgrown board books or Mrs. Piggle Wiggle, I have set their books aside in sturdy, waterproof containers so that each of them will have a ready-made library of their own favorites someday when they begin reading to their own children. If you give books as gifts, consider writing the name of the child, the date, and the occasion for the gift on an adhesive sticker or book plate to be given along with the book. (Don't attach the sticker. Just give it along with the book in case your grandchild already has the book and wants to exchange it for something else). Another alternative for faraway grandmas and grandpas is to include a recording of your own voice reading the book aloud to your grandchild. If expensive hardback books aren't in your budget, look for paperback versions of great books and cover them with clear contact paper. They'll last through the next generation and beyond.

Store a few GrandMa and GrandPa boxes for iNstaNt eNtertaiNMeNt

Essentially dramatic-play boxes, "Grandma and Grandpa Boxes" are simple plastic storage containers that contain a variety of props related to a specific theme. When they visit, grandchildren can choose a box and enjoy lots of fun pretending with Grandma or Grandpa. When playtime is over, all of the props simply go back into the box until the next visit. The possibilities for Grandma and Grandpa Boxes are endless. Try two or three of these:

Flower Shop Grandma Box: Collect a few of your old flower and garden magazines, a few child-sized garden tools, garden hats and child-sized garden gloves, a watering can, empty seed packets, an assortment of old plastic flowers, small baskets filled with styrofoam squares (for arranging flowers), and a few unbreakable vases. If you are more adventurous, your flower shop box can contain potting soil and seeds so that you and a grandchild can plant something together.

Repair Shop Grandpa Box: Save some of your old, broken appliances for a grandchild to take apart and study (remove the electrical cords for safety). Include a clipboard, pliers, safety glasses, a hard hat, an apron, play tools, an assortment of colored wire, nuts and bolts that can be screwed together, scrap wood and nails for pounding holes, and a battery-operated screwdriver.

Hair Salon Grandma Box: Don't throw away your old foam hair rollers or your broken-down hair dryer! Cut the cord off an old blow dryer or curling iron, and include a few perm rollers with paper strips. Add a plastic smock, some old towels, a shower cap or hair net, and an assortment of dollar-store ribbons, bows, and hairclips. A spray bottle full of water and a brush and comb will round out your supply. If you are planning to play along and supervise, you could also include some nail polish, cotton swabs, and polish remover, or even some washable makeup.

Camping Grandpa Box: Find a small tent at a garage sale—one you don't mind setting up indoors, if needed. Add a working flashlight, a fishing vest, and a play fishing pole. A sleeping bag, binoculars, a fly swatter, and sunglasses are good props. For your pretend cookout, supply a small wire grate and a spatula with some plastic hot dogs, hamburgers, or fish to cook over the pretend fire. Paper plates, cups, and utensils are also a fun addition.[2]

Let your grandchildren learn about your current or former profession by salvaging some of the supplies you used in your work every day. Were you a dentist, a letter carrier, a restaurant owner, a schoolteacher, a computer programmer, or a veterinarian? What props could you supply that would help your grandchildren learn about the way you made a living?

Create playful holiday traditions

Leola remembers celebrating Easter with her extended family. Her parents reserved Sunday for their religious observance but spent Saturday playing together.

> The Easter bunny left eggs and the coloring kit before we woke up on Easter Saturday. Our mom supervised as we boiled eggs, then helped us color them. When they were all finished, we took our eggs and joined Mom's sister and our cousins on a nearby hill. We had a really enjoyable time rolling our eggs down the hill and chasing them. When the eggs

cracked, we'd take them to Mom and she kept them. When
we children had worn ourselves out running up and down the
hill, we'd go home and make deviled eggs and a potato salad
while Aunt Ruth did the same. When the food was ready,
we'd all get together again and go for a picnic lunch.

One grandma has an annual Easter Egg hunt that includes finding
dollar-store prizes hanging from the trees and bushes, hunting for candy-
filled plastic eggs, and making fondant-filled chocolate eggs or chocolate bunnies (she purchased molds at a local candy supply store). Another
family has a tradition of "stuffing Santa's underwear." Grandpa models a
pair of his long red underwear (a one-piece extra large union suit), and
family teams take turns competing to see which team can stuff grandpa's
underwear full of the most balloons without popping any.

As families grow, the "big holidays" like Hanukkah and Easter can
get complicated to celebrate as an extended family. Consider creating your
own tradition surrounding one of the "quiet" holidays instead. Celebrate
Cinco de Mayo by inviting your grandchildren over for piñata-smashing
(or mail a piñata and supplies to them). You can attract the attention of
a college-age grandchild by sending a package for a holiday they don't
expect you to celebrate. How about a box full of entirely green stuff (green
toothbrush, green gum, a few packages of broccoli soup mix, or even a
little green cash) for St. Patrick's Day?

If you are a petite grandma, try throwing a "taller than Grandma"
party every time one of your grandchildren passes you in height, or make
getting taller than Grandma a special occasion that is celebrated with a
one-on-one "grown-up" outing to a fancy restaurant or a concert.

Another friend suggests making up a long-distance family celebration if you can't get together for a reunion or special holiday. Celebrate
your own "Johnson Day" or "Smith Day" by planning your celebration
together, executing activities in your own local areas, and then posting
photos and individual family experiences to an online weblog or family
website. For example, if your celebration is "Jones Family Feed the Animals Day," you can share photos of the kids in Florida swimming with
dolphins, the kids from New Hampshire feeding ducks at the local park,
and the family from Texas visiting the giraffe exhibit at the zoo.

Note: To create a free weblog, visit www.google.com, click on
"even more" in the list of choices and look for the program "blogger"
in the menu list. There are several great family website options. The site
www.myfamily.com is easy to use and is economical.

Pass on your own legacy

Brian describes his grandparents' simple but profound impact in his life:

Everyone's childhood should be simple. Mine was. My grandma and grandpa were self-employed. They built and recovered furniture. Grandma did most of the sewing, and Grandpa did most of the woodworking. They let me get my hands on both. One of the powerful lessons they taught me about customer service included a zip top bag. When Grandpa was re-covering a couch, you could find lots of things lost in the crevices. It might be a dime, or a few bills, or just some buttons or other odds and ends. Whatever we found, Grandpa bagged up to return to the customer. It was my belief that Grandpa just liked to watch people's faces when he handed them the bag and said, "This is yours, and I'm giving it back to you in case you want to put it in the new couch to make it feel like home." Customers were always amazed that he took the time to return their property, usually worth less than two dollars. It was a great lesson in treating clients with honesty.

If Grandma and Grandpa were already working when I got to their house, one of them would stop and give me an important job to do. In reality, it kept me out of their way, but they made me feel like my service was vital. My job, as I was taught, was to help the customer. Usually, my task was to make covered upholstery buttons (something I was good at because of my attention to detail—I was always careful to be sure the buttons lined up with the pattern in the fabric instead of making buttons whose stripes ran the wrong direction). Now and then, I was assigned to make shoe shine kits for Grandpa's male clients. Using leftover foam rubber, wood pieces, and fabric, I would wrap foam around a board and tack the upholstery fabric down on the sides. It was a great lesson in giving people their money's worth and then some.

Other times, I would go with Grandpa to haggle over the price of the material at a local fabric barn. Bolts and bolts were stacked pyramid style. This way, random bolts could be pulled out without the whole stack falling down.

Once we found the fabric a client had chosen from a swatch in a book in Grandpa's office, we would carry the fabric to Grandpa's van and finish the trip with a stop at Farr's Ice Cream. I don't remember what they said to me. I just recall the time they spent with me. I don't remember having any of the self-esteem issues that I see most kids go through now. As I once heard a psychologist explain it, I got lots of good attention, so I didn't crave the bad kind. Unless you count the time my sisters painted my toenails pink while I was sleeping, I was not ever teased or poorly treated by others. I think my grandparents helped me feel confident about who I am.

Working with a grandparent truly qualifies as play for most grand-children. My dad makes sure his grandsons get lots of one-on-one time in his woodshop. They each know how to run the belt sander, the drill press, and the table saw. Grandpa Jim has taught each of my children how to pound a nail straight and why drilling a guide hole makes it easier to set a screw. Over the years, woodworking projects have ranged from building bows and arrows out of wood scraps to turning baseball bats on the lathe. My sons have had Grandpa's personalized instruction as they've made inlaid chess tables, shelving for sprinkler parts, and even jewelry boxes for girlfriends. My daughters have carved their initials out of wood and learned to repair faulty electrical sockets.

Grandpa's patience is legendary. "I remember him teaching me to always hold the knife a certain way so I would be safe while I was carv-ing," recalls one son. "One time, he was helping me, and I didn't follow his advice. The knife slipped and I sliced Grandpa's finger. He didn't even flinch. He just got a Band-aid and we went back to work."

Children as young as age four have learned how to make their own batch of cookies in my mother's kitchen, and she's tutored her teenage grandsons in the process of preparing everything from clam chowder to caramels. Cooking with Grandma is play, while Mom somehow always makes it feel more like work. It is not uncommon to find Grandma out-side sitting in the sandbox or upstairs playing with the dollhouse when grandchildren come for a visit.

Be youNg at heart

Jess writes:

> No matter how tired or busy my grandma is, she always seems to have endless energy to devote to us as grandchildren. At seventy, if no one else wants to play cars, Grandma will crawl down on her hands and knees to build the best track. My favorite memories are out on their boat on breathtaking lakes in Canada. It never mattered what the water temperature was, or how many times she'd already been in the lake. She was always happy to jump in again. Even in her sixties, she would cliff jump with us, rope swing, water ski, and swim. She would always buy me books that we'd read together, and she managed to always make me feel like the most important person in her life. I remember being asked to write about my best friend in grade school. I wrote about my grandma. Even when she lived in a different country, she would always ask about each of my friends by name (she must have had them all written down somewhere), how my test went the day before, how my talk in church went, etc. I think everyone needs one grandparent to make them feel incredibly special!

The sight or even the smell of old-fashioned yellow roses in the spring reminds my mother of her own grandmother:

> I see Grandma digging out a yellow rose bush that persisted in growing in one of the best spots in her garden. She hated yellow and she hated that rose bush. But every spring it sprouted anew and every spring Grandma dug it out—again. That scene has become an icon of the kind, uncomplaining, but persistent grandmother who took life as it came, the good along with the bad and made the best of it. Best of all, she loved me—unconditionally. I don't remember that she ever told me so. I just knew. She was careful not to step on my pretend children, Gagen and Rye, or sit in a chair they already occupied. She let me wade in the irrigation ditches in her garden and feel the cool mud squish between my toes. She helped me pick green apples and ate them with me on the spot; in fact, she carried a small salt shaker in the pocket of her apron for just such an occasion. Her mulberry tree was

another favorite attraction; you could simply see the whole world from its upper branches, or so I thought. Hollowed out, too-large zucchini from her garden became battle-ships to float in the ditch. I was her traveling companion whenever we visited cousins, and I was also her theater partner. She couldn't remember the way home when she came out of the theater, invariably turning the wrong way; so when Grandma took in a show, I got to go along to make sure she got back home. The grandmother who loved me dances through my every childhood memory. How lucky I was."

Buy experiences, not things

Maybe what your grandchildren need most of all is not another Barbie doll or Lego set but rather Grandpa himself. A young child would relish a one-on-one trip to the zoo. An hour alone with Grandpa at the park or lunch that includes both Grandpa *and* a chocolate shake would easily qualify as a child's most memorable birthday party.

Older grandchildren will clamor for an opportunity to be your golf partner, your fishing partner, or your chauffeur through a local national park. The venue is not critical. It is the one-on-one time that matters.

One grandmother provides each of her granddaughters with supplies for a craft project in place of a Christmas gift. Each package includes an appointment with Grandma to work on the craft together. Another grandmother sends tickets to a play, concert, or ballet and takes the child out to dinner on the evening of the event. Try to choose something your grandchild will enjoy, but don't stress about it too much. The musical selections aren't what will be memorable, and Shakespeare will only be interesting to them if it is important to you. If you love a good football or basketball game, your grandson will get all the entertainment he wants just watching you cheer.

Make your home a playtime haven

I remember the day I cleaned my oldest son's bedroom for the last time after he moved to his own apartment. After I had put the last pizza crust in the trash, emptied the sock drawer, and dusted the dresser, I stood in the doorway with my hands on my hips and thought to myself, "Well, at least it will stay this way this time." Somehow, it was no consolation. What a tragedy it would be if keeping your home organized, your windows free of fingerprints, and your carpet nap all vacuumed in the same direction took precedence over letting grandchildren into your life to make a mess again.

Make yourself a list of the things that would make you cry if they got broken or destroyed, and when the grandchildren come, gather your treasures and store them in a safe place. Now you can relax about being a grandparent. If you don't want the carpets dirty, put down some throw rugs. If you don't want the petunias smashed, go to the park to play ball. If you don't want the living room messed up, create space in a bedroom or clean out that little nook under the stairs where you can close the door and leave the clutter until after the kids go home.

Freeze a few meals in advance so you have time to spend playing with your grandchildren instead of being stuck in the kitchen cooking for them when they drop in. Keep a cake in the freezer or a box of granola bars in the cupboard for unexpected visits. Use paper plates some of the time so you can play Monopoly after dinner instead of washing the china.

If you feel guilty about your "failure" to play with your children, now is your chance to make up for it by lavishing playfulness on your grandchildren. Leave the dirty pans in the sink if you can. Buy that trampoline for the backyard if you think it will help. Pretend this visit from your grandchildren will be the last chance you ever get to connect with them. Someday it just might be.

What's iN it for you

Like playful relationships between parents and children, a playful grandparent-grandchild relationship is a reciprocal blessing.

Chris remembers one important conversation he had with his grandfather as they were eating together at their favorite Chinese restaurant. "I asked him if he would be there to see me play in the major leagues when I got there (this used to be my dream). He told me he would, and then I quickly replied that he had better stop [using substances that were hazardous to his health] or else he wouldn't be alive to watch me . . . I remember him looking me straight in the eye and promising me that he would quit that very moment."

Julie's vivid childhood memory of a day she spent with her grandfather when she was four is a good example of the "staying power" of the lasting and warm memories created for children and grown-ups alike when they find time to play together.

> Grandpa and I were great pals, at least that is how I always felt about him. He must have been amazing, because I have many wonderful and vivid memories of him, even though he died shortly before my fifth birthday.
>
> When I was four years old and he was fighting his battle with cancer, I went to go stay with him. At the time, I had a nurse suit of my own that I wore with pride. I brought it with me so I could take the best possible care of him.
>
> I wanted to make him as comfortable and as strong as possible. The softest thing I could think of was tissue. I can remember him sitting in his recliner holding perfectly still while I covered him from head to toe in unfolded tissues.
>
> To make him even more comfortable, I turned on the TV to find a program I was sure he would enjoy more than that "dumb news program" that he always got stuck watching. I found some cartoons instead. Then, I went to the kitchen to get him a bowl of ice cream. He and I would take turns eating the spoonfuls of ice cream that I scooped up, all the while being careful not to disturb the tissues. I can still remember the twinkle in his eye.

I believe that one of the supreme benefits of grandparenting is the fact that a grandparent can shower a child with happy experiences and unconditional love, unfettered by the need to provide continual discipline (hopefully, Mom or Dad take care of that part).

If you have worked to develop a reasonably warm relationship with a grandchild, the result will likely be that your opinion will matter to him when no one else's does, your influence can steady her when no one else's can, and he or she will listen to your advice when everyone else's is ignored. That is a relationship worth playing for.

Notes

1. Todd, *FamilyFun Magazine.*
2. Myhre, *Young Children,* 6–11.

Reader's Homework

Based on what you have read in this chapter, what ONE idea for playing with children appeals to you most as something that you could feasibly do in your own home? (This can be an idea you read about in the book, an idea of your own that came to you as you were reading, or something you remember experiencing as a child).

Write your ONE idea here:

_____

_____

If you'd like, record this idea in the "Gallery of Ideas to Try" at the end of the book.

Chapter 12

Making Space
for Play

Finding a way when play is a challenge

- -

Regina did not become concerned about the development of her oldest son, Keaton, until other children his age began talking and he did not. Happiest when he had a very strict schedule, Keaton would get extremely agitated whenever his routine was interrupted or when his surroundings were unfamiliar. A visit to the neurologist confirmed that Keaton had autism. But there was another surprise. As he observed Keaton's younger sister who was also at the appointment, the neurologist made a pronouncement that rocked Regina's world. Emma was autistic as well. Regina returned home with the prognosis ringing in her ears: "Keaton will never progress beyond his current developmental age of three. Emma will have similar difficulties. You cannot ever expect your children to interact with you or to progress normally." Within months, Regina's third child, Benjamin, was diagnosed with autism as well.

Others thought Regina should be overwhelmed that she was raising three autistic children, but with characteristic resolve, she created a new mantra for herself: "This is just our 'normal.' Hiding under the bed because she didn't want to interact with others was Emma's 'normal.' Becoming agitated when we went to someone else's house was Keaton's 'normal.' In my heart, I believed that these children were blank slates just like every other child. It was up to me to decide whether living a life of not being able to interact was their 'fate' or whether we should try something else."

After copious research, Regina determined to trust her instincts and find another way. "They were not in some world of their own," insists Regina. "They simply did not know how to do the things that are intuitive for other children." The obvious beginning point seemed to be to teach them how to play. "I found that the ground was the best classroom I could have. At first they did not want me around. I would not push my way in or become overbearing. I would just follow them from room to room until they were ready to play. Patience, patience, patience was my best ally. I decided that since play and imitation are the cornerstones for any communication later in life, they just needed to learn the skills they lacked. They needed to learn what comes naturally for other children." Regina credits patience, good training, observation, and a lot of prayer for her successes.

She began by just being in the same room—on the floor with her children. Little by little, the games increased in complexity. One of the favorite games was to play with bubbles, which didn't require touching, overstimulation, or noise—all three are unsettling for a child with autism. The children loved music, so Regina played music almost constantly. From there, the children progressed to developing their gross motor skills. She purchased a small indoor trampoline, and later, an outdoor version. She learned to keep her distance and just watch her children play until they were ready for her to join in. She could tell by their nonverbal cues—pacing, shaking their hands, and making noises—when it was time to back off.

"I had a wagon I could fit all three children into, and we went for miles and miles of wagon rides," Regina said. Bicycles were the next hurdle to tackle. Today, Keaton and Benjamin each ride a bicycle known as a Tri-Fecta—essentially a large, adult-sized tricycle. Emma, who hasn't quite mastered the bicycle, rides along in a rickshaw so that the entire family can go on outings together.

Simple songs like "Patty Cake" and "Head, Shoulders, Knees, and Toes" were important for teaching the children about their bodies and helping them learn to imitate—a skill they needed in order to learn to walk, to talk, and to function better in mainstream society.

As with all autistic children, Regina finds that a very structured schedule is imperative. She used PECS (Picture Exchange Communication System) when they were young. A picture represents each component of the daily schedule: playtime, snack time, music time, and everyone's favorite—adventure time. Every day there is a new "adventure"—a hike, a trip to the swimming pool, a bike ride, a trip to the library, a visit to a nearby children's garden, or playing in the children's fountain at a local shopping center. Adventure time can also be something as simple as putting pillows and blankets on the lawn in the backyard and listening to music or painting.

Regina's exhausting schedule leaves her little time for herself. "When I became a single parent, I lost who I was for a while," admits Regina. Now that she is remarried with two additional children who are not disabled, the pace of her life has not slowed. One of her main concerns is finding time to play with the two youngest children. She plans additional activities that are developmentally appropriate for them, knowing they need her time as much as Keaton, Emma, and Benjamin do. "I really don't have time for myself, even now that I am remarried, and I don't know when I will. I just have to face life with the realization that moments are must moments—no matter how bad. This has kept me calm when things are most insane. The children do go to sleep eventually, and that gives me time to fall in love with them all over again."

She admits that there are also days when she has a good cry or shuts herself into a room and screams into a pillow. When reminded that those of us who are *not* raising disabled children do that, Regina responded with typical optimism: "Yes. That is just our 'normal.' Everybody has a different normal. The most important thing I have learned in all of this is that this is a season in time. It is very hard to give up so much of my time, and my effort does not always give me the growth that I would hope. Success is measured by months and years in our family, not by days and weeks. My children will not remember how many races I have run, how many bike miles I have put in. They will remember the time I have spent with them playing."

When asked if she had advice for other parents who struggle, Regina said, "All children progress differently. If you have a child who is disabled, and you never manage to get her to talk, you are not a failure. That is her normal. She is where she is able to be, and if she is happy, that is the only thing that is important."

Was play important? For Regina and her children it has been impera-tive. "Without the time I have put into teaching them to play, I would not have children, autistic children, who will seek me out to play and share a hug. I was told never to expect this. They are not 'in their own world.' They just had to be played with until they could share mine."

Is play THAT powerful?

The rest of us can learn a lot about what is important by considering Regina's advice. On a cold winter evening, I was sitting in a meeting with a group of other women who were discussing a plan of action for improv-ing the lives of the children in our neighborhood. As a committee, we had brainstormed for some time and each of us had proposed several options for programs we could put into place or policies we might implement that would help parents understand the importance of helping their children succeed academically, get along better with their peers and families, and develop themselves physically, spiritually, emotionally, and socially. But there was one good woman serving on the committee whose children were grown, and she had a better idea. "All these parents need to do is play more often," she suggested. As we batted around what I considered to be more ingenious and profound ideas—after-school programs, publications we could create and distribute, classes we could sponsor, her voice was steady and persistent. "They just need to *play* with their children," she insisted.

I have come to appreciate her wisdom. I did not buy into the idea at first. It was not until I started to try to convince others to play more often that I realized the wisdom of that path myself. Perhaps it took writing this book to convince me personally that the impact of simple play could be so wonderfully profound. I have learned this: Of all of the programs and policies, of all of the classes and curriculums that promote the idea that we can improve our relationship with our children and help them become the responsible adults we hope to raise, there are few activities that will have as weighty an impact as simply spending time with them—high-quality, playful, engaging *time*.

As I've worked at implementing my own advice, I have discovered that while playing is simple, finding time for it is not. When I began writing this book, I became, for the first time, what society knows as a "working mother." I have attempted to compensate by getting up earlier and going to bed later, or by multi-tasking more effectively (I will drive you to your dance lessons and read this research in the car while I wait). I have also had to eliminate outside conflicts (I will only attend your home games—not the away games), and I have had to call upon outside sources for support (if you people are hungry, then you *will* come in this kitchen and help me chop vegetables). Meanwhile, the weeds in the flowerbeds are flourishing, the dust continues to accumulate, and other projects have simply been filed away where I will not have to see or deal with them until another day. I came home late one evening recently with a throbbing headache (a result of too little sleep), with a looming writing deadline, dishes in the sink, and quarreling children, and thought to myself, "I could not possibly consider playing with my children if I felt like this every night." This experience helped me develop a newfound appreciation for those of you who are single parents, working parents, and parents of disabled or challenging children. I have more respect for your burdens. I admire your courage and your stamina.

With the challenges and painful struggles of parenting in mind, I am compelled to attempt to offer some small ideas I hope will help you in your effort to harvest a few extra moments for playing.

1. For busy parents: Mark a space on your calendar

- When someone calls to schedule a meeting with me, I am pretty good at honoring my commitment to attend.
- There is a block of time set aside in my schedule every Sunday when I attend worship services.
- In the last year, my children have only missed their piano lessons once, due to an unavoidable conflict.
- I get my hair cut every six weeks.

All of these activities have one thing in common. Each of them occurs on a regular basis because they are important enough to deserve a spot in my schedule and on my calendar. If parents are sincerely committed to playing with children, there will be at least some spaces on the calendar that are "reserved" for time with a child. Some of us who have the opportunity to be in the companionship of children on a daily basis can snatch moments now and then, as it's convenient. Those of us with busier schedules have to be more precise.

While part of the joy of playing with children has to do with the fact that playing can be purely impulsive, with no goals or deadlines attached, it is also true that if we wait for those moments to come along, we'll get precious few opportunities for play. Parents I have spoken with have lots of strategies for creating space for play. Maybe some of them will help you:

Have an annual planning session and block out playtime first

One family I know has a planning party on New Year's Day. They order pizza and then pull out a big wall calendar and identify all of the dates the kids will be out of school for the next full year. Those are specifically reserved for family time. Next, the family schedules a block of time for their annual family vacation—an outing that will take at least a week. Then, Mom and Dad schedule their own date nights with each other— usually Friday evenings—and two weekend getaways just for the two of them. Finally, they allow each child to choose four evenings during the year (two with each parent) when they will have Mom or Dad's undivided attention for an activity of the child's choice. This family goes as far as assigning a budget amount for each activity, and then the total budget is divided up and a monthly amount is direct-deposited from the family paycheck into a "recreation" savings account. Next comes the fun. The family brainstorms about all of the great activities they could participate in, either together or in smaller groups, and the ones that sound great get top priority. They can be written on the calendar months in advance.

The beauty of annual planning is threefold:

1. Having a written plan significantly increases the likelihood that the chosen activities will actually occur.

2. You can say no to almost any engagement if you know far enough ahead of time that you have already scheduled a high-priority family activity at that time. Even business trips can take second seat to a family vacation if you've scheduled far enough in advance and warned your employer you will not be available during that week.

3. Annual planning gets you "looking." If you decide you want to attend a cultural event in December, you can start looking for great tickets in September before they are sold out. You can book vacation flights when they are cheaper, schedule a horseback ride in a national park when space is still available, and even start collecting milk cartons in June to use in the frozen ice castle you plan to build together in February.

Choose a "Family Night"

In 1915, leaders of The Church of Jesus Christ of Latter-day Saints instituted a church-wide program aimed at helping parents build unity in their homes. In 1970, the Church made the program more formal by encouraging families to set aside Monday for Family Home Evening. All church activities that had previously posed Monday night conflicts were suspended so that families could be together in their homes on Monday night. While many LDS parents use Family Night as an opportunity to review doctrinal teachings, church leaders also remind members that formality is to be "strictly avoided." Instead, Family Night should include opportunities to build relationships and have fun. (See www.lds.org/hf/display/0,16783,4235-1,00 for activity ideas published by the Church.)

Other agencies have created programs using similar wisdom. Dr. Alvin Rosenfield has encouraged a nationwide "Family Night" in an effort to show parents and their families how refreshing scheduled time together can be.[1] Visit www.nationalfamilynight.org for more information and to see what other parents have done to celebrate their family night, whether it is just a once-a-year event, or something that happens every other Friday.

"The key to success for Family Night is to be a stickler," writes one mom. "There are times when we allow other activities to intrude—for example if one of the kids has a school concert we can all attend. But the rest of the time, everyone is expected to be at home on Family Night and we don't allow exceptions. We protect this family time as if it were sacred, and it probably is."

2. For parents who are trying to do too many good things: Cut back

Cutting back is the most obvious solution but not the easiest one to implement. Cutting back means different things to people. For some, it means eliminating one after-school activity for a child. For others, it means completely revamping a lifestyle: downshifting to a smaller, less expensive home, cutting back on the amount of work you bring home in the evenings, or finding employment that requires less business travel. Cutting back requires sometimes painful soul searching both for the parent and for the child. And so you'll know that I have struggles cutting back too, I offer the following example:

Our conscientious, driven, third-born son struggled with boredom in the fourth grade. Knowing his abilities and wanting the best possible experience for him, we had specifically requested a teacher for the following year who would really challenge him, and then we looked for outside opportunities for him to develop skills the school couldn't teach. As a result, he was taking piano lessons and was involved in Tae Kwon Do twice a week. He went to Cub Scouts once a week and joined an advanced soccer league as well. He was a healthy, strong kid, and I was a stay-at-home mom with free time in the afternoons, so why not?

As a "kindness" to his mom, my son was getting himself up at 6:00 in the morning and making breakfast for the family so that I would have time to finish my early-morning workout. This was not an assignment from me; it was just a good-hearted service he performed because that's the kind of kid he is.

Then, during the last two months of school, his teacher challenged him to be the first student ever to complete a "genius project." This was a time-intensive, self-directed learning project that included interviewing experts in the community, reading books, doing experiments, creating audio-visual projects, and so forth. His subject of choice was natural disasters, and his presentation included everything from building a working model of a tornado with miniature fans and a dry ice cloud, to assembling a 72-hour survival kit for each member of the family, to developing a PowerPoint presentation on different kinds of natural disasters. It was just what he needed to inspire him academically. Unfortunately, the project coincided with soccer season, preparation for the end-of-year piano recital, and testing for the next rank in Tae Kwon Do.

One evening, when he'd had a particularly long day, I noticed that he had been in the bathtub for an unreasonable amount of time. It was near bedtime, and I thought he should be in bed doing his thirty minutes of required reading for school, so I pounded on the bathroom door and told him to get out. When there was no response then and still no response five minutes later, I pounded on the door again. When he still didn't answer, I instantly panicked.

Luckily, a level-headed sibling produced a meat skewer to poke into the lock (saving my husband the burden of breaking down the bathroom door), and I burst into the bathroom to find him sound asleep, with his ears submerged just below the water line so he could not hear us pounding or yelling.

It was quite a wake-up call. I realized that despite my best intentions, I had become a "hyper-parent." Dr. Alvin Rosenfield coined the term "hyper-parent" to describe parents who sign children up for a slew of after-school activities, thinking that doing so is in a child's best interest. These parents end up feeling frustrated and trapped by the burden of maintaining a schedule that is unrealistic, and their children suffer physically, mentally, and emotionally as they try to manage an overscheduled lifestyle so that they can keep up with Mom and Dad's expectations.

When we took time to really talk to our son about his schedule, it was clear that Tae Kwon Do was not nearly as important to him as it had been to us, and allowing him to quit, while it was a bit painful (we had already invested so much time and money, and he was so close to earning his black belt), it was like taking a nice deep, relaxing breath—it turned out to be a relief for all of us.

I should point out that when I signed my son up for his after-school schedule, each opportunity was chosen with a specific outcome in mind. What I did not anticipate is that combined with all of the activities I signed his siblings up for as well, my own schedule was thrown off balance. I resented the time I spent in the car chauffeuring, and then I felt ashamed for feeling resentful. So even if my son had been able to manage his schedule, I had failed to measure the impact on *me* and the consequent impact on the rest of my family. My teenaged children, in their effort to match my pace and live up to my expectations (or even expectations they created for themselves, based on my example) have had moments when they were excessively sleep-deprived, under-nourished, and over-stressed. That is not what I intended when I urged them to sign up for AP classes, get a job, and join the track team. Maybe parents who read this book can learn from my mistakes.

It is true that some children need to be pushed into participation in worthwhile activities, but parents can and must be better monitors. We have to be rigorous about questioning the value of creating burdens that neither we nor our children can effectively manage. And when we make the mistake of hyper-parenting, we need to have enough integrity to allow ourselves to lighten up and offload the extra baggage.

3. For Frantic Parents:
Discover your Personal Plimsoll Line

Samuel Plimsoll, a British politician and social reformer who lived in the 1800s, got fed up with unscrupulous ship owners who purposely overloaded their vessels in an attempt to collect insurance money when the vessels sunk at sea. Hundreds of crew members lost their lives unnecessarily. Through Plimsoll's efforts, commercial ships were eventually required to have a "load line" or "Plimsoll line" painted on the side of the ship. As a ship is loaded to its full capacity, the hull of the ship settles lower and lower in the water. The purpose of the Plimsoll line is to give both captain and crew a visual indicator of the ship's maximum safe depth. Once the Plimsoll line was developed, it was obvious to anyone who cared to look whether or not the load the ship was carrying was appropriate to the ship's capacity.

Your family can develop a "Plimsoll line." It is the indicator that "the maximum possible load" has been met or exceeded. When my children were very young, the library book due date was my Plimsoll line. When my life got so hectic that I didn't have time to get the library books returned on time, I knew that it was time to regroup and cut back. It was a strange measure, but it was very reliable. Establishing a Plimsoll line is essentially a way to create an early warning system that tells you when your life is out-of-balance so that you can react in time and fix the problem. This early warning system is important because when you exceed your maximum possible load, playtime will be one of the first things you eliminate from your schedule in order to compensate.

Here's an example: My current Plimsoll line is my morning workout. When my life gets so busy that I have to let something go, exercising is easy to give up, both because it takes a fairly big chunk of time and because I don't especially like doing it. But because exercising is part of how I maintain a healthy stress level, my whole family knows when I am not getting enough of it. And when I am not getting my exercise, it's a fair bet that I have overloaded my schedule and my children will not get family meals, a bedtime story, or time at the park either. When I go for more than one or two days without exercising, a little alarm goes off in my head that says, "You are overdoing it again." It doesn't stop me from overdoing it, but it does help me be aware, which I hope sometimes acts as an antidote to overscheduling myself in the first place.

Maybe your Plimsoll line is the number of times you hit the "snooze" bar on your alarm clock in the mornings (when you are overdoing, you deprive yourself of sleep and your body knows and fights you). Maybe it is substituting fast food for a home-cooked family meal (when you are overscheduled, you don't have time to shop, so there's nothing in the house to eat). Maybe it is keeping the gas tank half-full (when you are too busy, gassing up the car drops low on the priority list until it becomes a crisis). Maybe it's the weekend date with your spouse. If you really want to find more time for playing, choose a regular playtime activity that both you and your children enjoy that will become your new "Plimsoll line." It can be a nightly game of catch, a piggy back ride at bedtime, or wrestling in the living room after work. When you notice that playtime activity disappearing, you'll know it's time to regroup and get your priorities straight again.

4. For parents caught in the time squeeze: Capitalize on a captive audience

Recently, my youngest daughter was stuck at home with a brief illness. She was too sick to go to school but felt too well to stay in her bed sleeping all day. While I did not have time to sit with her all afternoon (the option she might have preferred), I did have time to scrounge around the house to look for a project that would entertain her with a little help now and then from me. Armed with a package of modeling clay and a stack of Dr. Seuss books for inspiration, she went to work creating her own made-up Dr. Seuss character. She started out with sketches of three or four ideas on a piece of paper and then set to work inventing. Each time I was summoned to bring a glass of juice or check her temperature, she invited me to "sit down and roll a few worms" with her. Her delight was contagious, but it was clear that her preferred design was going to require some additional buttressing if it was going to stand up alone. So putting on my "parents are allowed to play too" hat, and gathering a little bit of floral wire, some duct tape, and a soldering iron, we managed to create a wire frame that would stand upright (sort of) while she covered its belly with ring after ring of brightly colored clay.

She has a good attention span, but I was surprised to see her sculpture maintain her interest for nearly three full hours. I wondered at the time whether she would have kept at it nearly as long if she hadn't been confined to the couch, or if I had refused to take the time to suggest options that made the project into a conquerable challenge. Either way, we now have a delightful keepsake to show for the day's work.

Snatching a moment for play when your child is a captive audience is not difficult, but it sometimes takes a little advance planning. I have known mothers who keep a set of jacks or a jumprope in the glove compartment of the car or a set of UNO cards in their purse so that they can be ready at a moment's notice to turn waiting time into playtime. Long car rides, waiting for the meal to be delivered at a restaurant, waiting at the doctor's office, and even sitting in the barber's chair makes your child fair game for a game. You can also try these suggestions:

- Purchase a simple book of car games, buy a pad of crossword puzzles, or sneak some of the cards out of your favorite trivia board game and keep them stashed under the front seat of your car.
- Make a "sick box" of quiet games, puzzles, and easy craft projects for children who are home for a day and stuck in bed.
- Take advantage of time in the car between appointments, and have a game plan in mind. Keep a book of "lateral thinking puzzles" in the glove box, have a favorite sing-along CD on hand, or pack a bag of twisted pretzels and see if you can form every letter of the alphabet just by biting the pretzel in the right place.

What other opportunities can you create for one-on-one play with a captive child? One wise mother even found an excuse to turn a punishment into a good memory. After being warned never to walk home from school via the "dangerous" route, which involved crossing several busy streets, Erica decided to disobey one day so that she could walk home in the company of a friend. Normally, her parents did not resort to grounding as a punishment, but this time the infraction was severe:

> My "grounding" experience was an interesting one. My mom told me I couldn't play with friends . . . . When my brothers' and sisters' friends came over, though, I was so sad, so my Mom played with me. We drew pictures on the sidewalk with chalk, jumped on the trampoline, and played with dolls. I was so happy despite my "grounding." I thought I was the

coolest kid in the world who had the coolest mom. I realize now that I must have terrified my mom, and perhaps that was the reason she took two hours out of her day to play with me.

5. For exhausted parents: Find games you can play in your sleep . . . almost

With three young children at home, Kim knows that some days she will be too tired to play. Her solution has been to invent games that can be played by exhausted parents from the comfort of the couch or their own comfy bed. Here are her favorites:

Retrieve the Retriever. While you lay down on the bed, have your child fetch a small stuffed dog or other animal. Then have your child leave the room while you hide the dog. The easiest way to hide it is to throw it across the room and let if fall into a semi-concealed spot. Then call for your child to return to the room, and let the hunt begin! Use the good old-fashioned "hotter" and "colder" hints to prompt your child's search, and cheer when your child finds the dog.

I'm Thinking of Something. This is a great game for younger or older children. Think of an object in your mind. (It could be anything—a peach, a windmill, a volcano, a tractor, a stingray.) Once you've got the object in mind, say, "I'm thinking of something . . ." and add on a clue to help your child guess what you're thinking of. For instance, if my object were a stingray, I might say, "I'm thinking of something that lives in the ocean." And then I'd add on clues such as "I'm thinking of something that lives in the ocean . . . that can hide in the mud . . . that can hurt you if you get too close to it . . ." until the child guesses what I am thinking of. Then it's the child's turn to choose an object and give the clues. (This game is great to play while lying down on the bed, cuddling on a blanket under the stars, or on a wearisome car trip.) You'll be amazed at the ideas and the clues your child comes up with!

Open Sesame. This classic game lives on as a staple for tired but playful parents. Lie on your side with a pillow under your head and wait for your child's magic command: "Open sesame!" Then raise one leg, and try to catch a wriggling child as she darts between your legs. For extra fun, add sounds effects like the creak of an old door or the zip of a spaceship entrance with each scissoring of the legs.

I was a little surprised to find how many other tired parents had invented similar games. Steamroller and Bull Ride were introduced in chapter 9. (Steamroller is a limp father-figure resting on the floor, waiting to see if his children can jump over him without getting caught. Bull Ride involves having a child ride on your tired back while you stretch out the kinks from a day of sitting in an office chair.) Here are a few more ideas contributed by other pooped parents or remembered fondly by the children who played them:

- **Target Practice:** Chris reports that his favorite game to play with his dad when he was young was when he and his brothers would hold a pillow in front of themselves like a shield while their father tried to hit them with something soft, such as a foam ball.

- **Popcorn Machine:** Gather up all of the soft balls in the house (or use crumpled newspaper or rolled-up socks out of the mismatched sock bin) and lay them on top of the tired parent's stomach. Mom or Dad will rest quietly for a few moments and then shout "Pop" and throw all of the balls up into the air, like air-popped popcorn. The children will then run to retrieve the balls and replace them for the next round.

- **Bear Trap:** A tired dad can lay on the couch under a blanket with only his hand exposed. A child who ventures too close will soon find that the "bear trap" slams shut on unsuspecting arms and legs at will and must be pried loose before the bear under the blanket attacks.

- **Tortilla:** One child sets a kitchen timer for fifteen minutes, and while the timer is ticking off its required "quiet time," Mom can relax under her favorite fleece throw. When the timer rings, it is time for one of the children to climb under the blanket with her, and then they both roll off the couch and continue to roll into a "tortilla." If Mom prefers, she can stay on the outside of the blanket and use the "tortilla" to roll up extra ingredients (children). As she does, she can name off the contents of her wrap: "I need to add some shredded cheese (child #1) and some guacamole (child #2). When she is finished adding the desired ingredients, she can then "nibble around the edges" (gently tickle, nibble, or kiss exposed arms, legs, and necks).

6. For single parents: Embrace your ironic advantages

In speaking of the special challenges of single parents, authors William Doherty and Barbara Carlson identify an "ironic advantage" enjoyed by single parents: "*They cannot compete with two parents in today's rat race of childhood, so they are free not to try.* Far from feeling sorry for single-parent families who keep a modest outside schedule, the rest of us should learn from them," the authors conclude.[2] My interviews with children raised in single-parent households have yielded a surprise. Single parents sometimes just do a better job of playing with their children. By using the same resourcefulness that helps them put food on the table and manage household responsibilities that are normally shared, single parents seem to have special gifts when it comes to creating meaningful playtimes.

Becky grew up in a single-parent household but recalls fondly how her mother found time for play even amid the challenges of raising a family alone.

> My father died when I was one year old, leaving my mother to raise five children on her own . . . . After my father's death my mother took me from my crib and I slept with her until I was ten years old and she remarried. I can still remember wrapping my arm around my mother's neck (nearly choking her) every night as I fell asleep feeling safe and secure.
>
> After having family prayer, I would watch my mother kneel and have her personal prayers. My mother took in jobs like cleaning houses, ironing several big bags of clothing a week, driving a school bus, and other jobs that made it possible to take me with her. She took me everywhere with her until I was old enough to start school and then got a job in a doctor's office. In some ways, I believe [our] relationship was little closer than the other kids' because we had all that bonding time together.
>
> I remember that she tried to act as a father would in taking my brothers rabbit hunting and shooting guns with them. She encouraged and supported them with any sports they wanted to do. I remember my mother always getting out with us and playing baseball with us. I believe because of this my brothers went out for baseball in high school.
>
> She would always save milk carton tops and on Saturday afternoons would take us to the movies. (Back then, you could get into the matinee shows with an Elsie the cow milk

carton top.) Some of my most cherished memories are listening to my mother sing when she was cooking or cleaning.
Many times we would both be in the kitchen cleaning or she
would be teaching me to cook and we would sing together.
She taught us songs that her mother and father would sing to
her when she was a child and I have taught them to my kids.
We didn't have much money, but I remember my mother
would occasionally load all of us kids in the car and we would
go to the A&W for a nickel ice cream or we would go to the
Drive Inn Movie. We would bring our pillows and blankets
and laugh and play games before the movie started.

Becky is quick to add that her mother's example of sacrifice, love,
devotion, and faith helped mold each of the children in the household
into caring, responsible adults. Through her ingenious management of
her time and because she was willing to take advantage of inexpensive
play opportunities, she had a powerful impact on her family.

One child psychologist has pointed out that well-educated mothers
get particularly frustrated when they have to spend a lot of time in the
car chauffeuring. If you are a well-educated parent, and a single parent,
consider the heightened value of your precious spare time. You may get
more for your money if you lavish those precious moments on your children rather than spending them sitting in a car driving them across town
so that someone else can do the teaching.

7. For all of us: Create family rituals and traditions

Regularly scheduled family traditions can be the perfect catalyst for
playtimes, and because they are often attached to a specific holiday or
event, it is easy to make them a priority. These family rituals can be as rich
and varied as the families who create them, and children will remember
them fondly. Here are a few examples of playful traditions and rituals
incorporated by other families:

- Every fall, on the first day back to school, one mother
  takes her children out for a special dinner to celebrate
  the start of the new school year.
- One husband and wife planted a tree in their front yard
  and took a photo in front of it. Every autumn, the family
  poses for a new photo. The event is capped off by "tree

games" such as seeing who can climb the highest in the tree. At the end of the evening, all of the leaves from the tree (and others in the yard) are raked into a single, huge pile and parents and children alike jump in.

- One family reserves every Saturday night for pizza and a movie.
- The first weekend in October is "Cider Fest" for members of the Blackwell family, who gather every year to harvest the last of the apples and press about eighty gallons of cider.
- One family collects a Christmas ornament from a souvenir shop every time they travel somewhere together as a family. These all go on a special Christmas tree every year at the beginning of the holidays. The ornaments still bring back memories long after the T-shirts from the vacation are reduced to rags. The family schedules a special holiday evening for decorating the "vacation tree" and playing holiday games together.

In an engaging essay on the importance of family rituals, author David Frum tells of the strange family ritual associated with his extended family's visit to a small summer cottage. It was his father-in-law's practice to stop the car before they arrived at their destination and dare each family member to dive off from the bridge into the canal.

"He always led the way," Frum writes. "He would climb onto one of the posts of the guardrail, stretch, and then dive headlong into the canal below. The kids would follow more or less reluctantly, feet-first. To this day, my wife says that whenever she has to do anything frightening, she tells herself: 'Well, it's easier than going off the Baysville bridge.' "

Frum continues by saying that while he doesn't necessarily advocate jumping off bridges, the tradition has served his family well. Each successive jump has helped them become more and more courageous—a characteristic they need in their post-9/11 childhood. "Danger comes unbidden," writes Frum. "And from now on, it will strengthen them to say, 'I jumped off the Baysville bridge—I can handle this.' "[3]

Family rituals have a way of strengthening all of us. And so does play. Whether you are the single mother struggling to help your sons make the baseball team, the parent of an autistic child whose playing needs are completely nontraditional, or a busy parent trying to decide whether a bike ride or a presentation to the board of directors should have more priority, don't give up. You can find a way to make space for play.

Reader's Homework

Based on what you have read in this chapter, what ONE idea for playing with children appeals to you most as something that you could feasibly do in your own home? (This can be an idea you read about in the book, an idea of your own that came to you as you were reading, or something you remember experiencing as a child).

Write your ONE idea here:

_____

_____

If you'd like, record this idea in the "Gallery of Ideas to Try" at the end of the book.

Notes

1. Rosenfield, *The Overscheduled Child: Avoiding the Hyper-Parenting Trap.*
2. Doherty and Carlson, *Putting Family First.*
3. Frum, www.findarticles.com/p/articles/mi_m1282/is_16_55/ai_106672819.

Epilogue

Several months ago, at the beginning of this book-writing venture, I sat in the publisher's office to sign a contract to write a book about playing with children. That day, the newspapers carried a headline about a young man who had killed five innocent citizens in a shooting rampage at a shopping mall. "Apparently no one ever played with that young man," the publisher observed.

Just yesterday, as I put the finishing touches on the last pages of the manuscript for *Piggyback Rides and Slippery Slides*, I opened a magazine and looked for the first time at the faces of the thirty-two individuals killed during a shooting rampage on the campus of Virginia Tech. Again I heard the words in my mind: "Apparently no one ever played with that young man." The timing of these two horrific crimes in relation to my own experiences of researching and writing about ways to help our children be mentally stable, contributing members of society has been disquieting. Would life be different now for these two troubled young men, their thirty-seven victims, and hundreds of friends and extended family members if some caring adult had simply found space to play with a reserved, withdrawn young boy more often?

In just a few days, summer will begin, and we will pull the Allred Family Summer Box out from under a bed and take a look at what is inside. It is filled with mementos we saved from some of last summer's playing experiences. Here are some of the things my children are going to find in the box when they open it and begin remembering:

- A museum brochure from a farmhouse built in 1904 where we watched a volunteer making an old-fashioned rag rug

- A program from an outdoor musical
- Two brown pill bottles full of fragments of topaz we chipped out of some boulders on a rock-hounding expedition
- A dried stem of yarrow blossom and a small white snail shell we found at the side of a trail in a canyon near our home
- Ticket stubs to a major league soccer game
- A map for the location of some Native American petro-glyphs that are preserved in a section of a geological formation known as the Waterpocket Fold
- Three small seashells

As we finger these mementos again, I'm hoping a flood of happy memories will return for my children: the jokes their uncle told them while they were waiting for the musical to start, the sound of the drums and the airhorns the first time the soccer ball whooshed into the back of the net, the way cold orange crème soda tasted at the end of a long day of hiking among towering sandstone cliffs. This summer we will fill the box again, not out of a sense of duty, but because playing together is so much fun, and because, as physician Hillary Burdette reminds us, the brain "naturally reinforces behaviors that make it healthy."

I am not a child psychologist. I don't have a PhD. I am not an expert or even a specialist. I'm just a mom. But if my twenty years' experience as a mom qualifies me to say anything, I hope it qualifies me to say this: Playing together matters.

Last summer, on the final day of our family vacation, we took an opportunity to rent some snorkels and fins so our children would have a chance to experience what I consider to be one of life's most exhilarating recreational activities. I was disappointed when our youngest daughter refused to swim beyond the first ten feet of the shoreline. No amount of coaxing could convince her to try. Her fins pinched her feet. She kept swallowing salt water. Her mask fogged up. Her complaints went on and on, so there she sat in the hot sand, a small, curled-up ball of frustration.

Her dad had a solution. He helped her take off the uncomfortable fins. He helped her adjust the air pressure in her float vest so that her body would quit rolling to the side. He showed her how to clear her mask, and then he lifted her onto his shoulders and piggybacked her across the sharp rocks she had spent the last hour tripping over as the tide washed her feet out from under her. Then, lowering her into the water, he swam next to her, holding one of her hands, and then called to me to hold the other. At first, we had to promise not to take her out very far, but as we swam farther from shore and the sand receded away below us, she began to see why we wanted her to come and play so badly: Dark spiny anemones, orange sponges, damsel fish, brain coral, sea fans, star corals, angelfish, and parrot fish drifted in an explosion of color just beneath us. Later, she wrote of the experience:

> I was too scared to go into the deep water and look at the fish. I wanted to, but at that time I didn't know how to swim. When my mom and dad said that they would take my hands and go out with me, I said I would try. I felt comforted when they took me out because they were right next to me holding me. We saw a school of fish, blue fish, and plenty of coral and sponge. We saw this spiny anemone. It was the best trip of my life!!! It was a lifetime of fun!!! I had so much fun with snorkeling that when I went back to the hotel, I got my snorkeling stuff and snorkeled in the pool until it was time to go to sleep.

If I could offer a metaphor for the benefits of playing with our children, I suppose this would be my favorite. Side by side, we take hold of their hands and lead them to places they can't go on their own in order to give them opportunities to see and do things they would never be able to experience otherwise. In the process, we give them the courage and the skill they need to venture out successfully on their own. The experts from the American Academy of Pediatrics remind us:

> Although no one can be sure what skills will be needed, certain character traits will produce children capable of navigating an increasingly complex world as they grow older. These include confidence, competence or the ability to master the environment, and a deep-seated connectedness to and caring about others that creates the love, safety, and security children need to thrive. In addition, to be resilient—to remain optimistic and to be able to rebound from adversity—young people need the essential traits of honesty, generosity, decency, tenacity, and compassion. Children are most likely to gain all of these essential traits of resiliency within a home, when parents and children have time to be together, and to look to each other for positive support and unconditional love.[1]

Let me tell you about some children whose family members have already caught the vision of playing together. One youngster wrote that her favorite family activity is helping her mother make caramel sticky buns for breakfast Easter morning. Another reported that her favorite thing to do is learning Tai Chi with her grandmother. One family has the tradition that the children race to see who can be the first to hug Dad when he comes in from work at night.

What if you were the child who was blessed to have parents who like to jump off the dock with you at Echo Lake? What if you were the child who loves family slumber parties by the lighted Christmas tree, or the child who loves sitting at the player piano and singing with his grandmother, or the little boy who has Oreo-stacking contests with his dad, or the teenager whose mother is teaching her to decorate cakes, or the seven-year-old whose mother painted a target on his bedroom door so they could take turns throwing sticky frogs at it every night before bedtime, or . . .

Playing together has paid great dividends for my family and me. Playtime, Family Home Evenings, family meals, and family vacations, together with our religious devotions, have brought harmony into our home and have helped us appreciate one another. It has helped make our home a refuge from the storms that seem to rage all around us. I am committed to the belief that play helps us offer our children security and hope for the future. The problems, when we have them, will be more manageable if we have learned how to play. Find a child you love and say, "Come play with me!"

Note

1. Ginsburg, www.aap.org/pressroom/playFINAL.pdf, 12–13.

Gallery of Ideas

Here's a six-step plan for putting your playing ideas to work

A. Write five of your favorite ideas for playing with your children here:

1.
2.
3.
4.
5.

B. Put a star by the one that will be *easiest* for you to accomplish

C. In the space below, write a date you would like to set aside time for your starred activity.

_____

D. On a scale of 1 to 5, rate how *important* it is to you to accomplish this activity with your child. (1 = it's no big deal whether I do it or not. 5 = this is extremely important to me.) If you haven't rated your activity with at least a 3, you might want to choose one that you're more passionate about.

E. Once you've carried out your plan, write a paragraph about how the experience went, what you would do the same if you were to do it again, and what you would do differently.

F. Choose another activity and do it all again!

Resources

Parents who are interested in learning more about benefits of play, or who want more ideas for fun playtime activities, can begin with some of the following resources:

- The Alliance For Childhood maintains a website with a great resource page. Visit www.allianceforchildhood.net/pdf_files/restoring_play_resources_110506.pdf.

- FamilyFun Magazine
  To subscribe, go to familyfun.go.com.

- The International Play Equipment Manufacturers Association www.ipema.org

- The National Institute for Play nifplay.org

- The Strong National Museum of Play strongmuseum.org

Bibliography

American Academy of Orthopaedic Surgeons. Online. "Adolescent Sports Injuries: Pain is Not a Gain!" Available from http://www6.aaos.org/news/Pemr/press_release.cfm?PRNumber=546; accessed February 27 2007.

American Academy of Pediatrics, Committee on Sports Medicine and Fitness and Committee on School Health. Online. "Organized Sports for Children and Preadolescents." Pediatrics 107, no. 6., 2001, 1459–1462. Available from http://aappolicy.aappublications.org/cgi/content/full/pediatrics;107/6/1459; accessed February 22, 2007.

Azar, Beth. "It's More Than Fun and Games." American Psychological Association. Monitor on Psychology. Vol. 33, no. 3, 2002. Available from http://www.apa.org/monitor/m ar02/morefun.html; accessed March 7, 2007.

Berk, Laura E., Trisha D. Mann, and Amy T. Ogan. "Make-Believe Play: Wellspring for Development of Self-Regulation," *Play = Learning*, ed. Dorothy G. Singer, Roberta Michnick Golinkoff, and Kathy Hirsh-Pasek. New York: Oxford University Press, 2006, 72–100.

Blum, Robert W. and Peggy Mann Rinehart 1997. Online. "Reducing the Risk: Connections that Make a Difference in the Lives of Youth." The National Longitudinal Study of Adolescent Health (Add Health). Available from http://allaboutkids.umn.edu/cfahad/Reducing_the_risk.pdf.

Brown, Pei-San, John Sutterby, and Candra Thornton. Online. "Dramatic Play in Outdoor Play Environments," *PTO Today*. Available from http://www.ptotoday.com/articles/article.php?article=0901play3.html; accessed March 7, 2007.

Bruner, Jerome. "Play, Thought, and Language." *Peabody Journal of Education*. Vol. 60, No. 3, The Legacy of Nicholas Hobbs: Research on Education and Human Development in the Public Interest: Part 1. (Spring 1983), 60-69.

Buckley, Christopher. "Shouts and Murmurs—Memo from Coach," *The New Yorker*, October 1997. Noted in Rosenfled, Alvin M.D., and Nicole Wise. The Overscheduled Child. Available from http://www.decatursports.com/articles/memo_from_coach.htm; accessed March 6, 2007.

Burdette, Hillary L. M.D, M.S. and Robert C. Whitaker, M.D., MPH. Online. "Resurrecting Free Play in Young Children: Looking Beyond Fitness and Fatness to Attention, Affiliation, and Affect." *Archive of Pediatric Adolescent Medicine* 2005, 159:46–50. Available from http://pediatrics.aappublications.org/cgi/content/full/119/1/182; accessed February 9, 2007.

Bushnik, Tracey. Online. "Youth Depressive Symptoms and Changes in Relationships With Parents and Peers." Children and Youth Research Paper Series. 2005. Available from http://dsp-psd.communication.gc.ca/Collection/Statcan/89-599-MIE/89-599-MIE2005002.pdf; accessed April 26, 2007.

Califano, Joseph A. Jr. Online. "Accompanying Statement," The Importance of Family Dinners III. National Center on Addiction and Substance Abuse at Columbia University (CASA) September 2006. Available from http://www.casafamilyday.org/PDFs/FDIIIreport06.pdf; accessed October 20, 2006.

Doherty, William J. and Barbara Z. Carlson. *Putting Family First*. New York: Henry Holt and Company, 2002.

Fiese, Barbara H. "Playful Relationships: A contextual Analysis of Mother-Toddler Interaction and Symbolic Play." *Child Development*, Vol. 61, No. 5 (Oct. 1990), 1648–1656.

Fitzsimmons, William, Marlyn McGrath Lewis, and Charles Ducey. Online."Time Out or Burn Out for the Next Generation." Harvard College Admissions. Available from http://www.admissions.college.harvard.edu/prospective/applying/time_off/timeoff.html; accessed March 3, 2007.

Frost, Joe L. Online. "The Dissolution of Children's Outdoor Play: Causes and Consequences." International Play Equipment Manufacturer's Association website, 2006. Available from http://www.ipema.org/Documents/Common%20Good%20PDF.pdf; accessed February 28, 2007.

Fitzsimmons, William, Marlyn McGrath Lewis, Charles Ducey. "Time Out or Burn Out for the Next Generation." Harvard College Admissions, 2006. Available from http://www.admissions.college.harvard.edu/prospective/applying/time_off/timeoff.html; accessed March 3, 2007.

Frum, David. "A Great Leap Forward," *National Review*, September 1, 2003. LookSmart Find Articles.

Gill, Tim, 2005. Online. "Let Our Children Roam Free," *Ecologist Online*, September 23, 2005. Available from http://www.theecologist.org/archive_detail.asp?content_id=481; accessed April 3, 2007.

Galyer KT and IM Evans. "Pretend Play and the Development of Emotion Regulation in Preschool Children." *Early Childhood Dev Care*, Vol 166:93–108, 2001.

Ginsburg, Kenneth R., MC, MS Ed. and the Committee on Communications and Committee on Psycosocial Aspects of Child and Family Health. Online. "The Importance of Play in Promoting Healthy Child Development and Maintaining Strong Parent-Child Bonds." The American Academy of Pediatrics, 2006. Available from http://www.aap.org/pressroom/playFINAL.pdf; accessed October 20, 2006.

Hair, Elizabeth C., Ph.D., Justin Jager, and Susan B. Garrett. Online. "Helping Teens Develop Healthy Social Skills and Relationships: What the Research Shows about Navigating Adolescence," *ChildTrends*, July 2002. Available from http://www. childtrends.org/Files//Child_Trends-2002_01_01_RB_TeensSocial%20Skills. pdf; accessed February 5, 2007.

Haight, W.L., and P.J. Miller. *Pretending at home: Early development in a sociocultural context*. Albany, NY: State University of New York Press, 1993.

Hirch-Pasek, Kathy and Roberta Michnick Golinkoff, with Diane Eyer. *Einstein Never Used Flash Cards: How our Children Really Learn—and Why they Need to Play More and Memorize Less*. New York: Rodale, 2003

Kellner, Alex. Online. "You Are Where You Eat: Thinking About How 'Dining Out' Really Affects Us," 2007. Available from http://www.gwu.edu/~uwp/fyw/euony-mous/Kellner.pdf>; accessed February 28, 2007.

Kindlon, Daniel J. *Too Much of A Good Thing: Raising Children of Character in an Indulgent Age*. New York: Hyperion, 2001.

Kremer-Sadlik, Tamar and Jeemin Lydia Kim 2007. "Lessons from Sports: Children's Socialization to Values Through Family Interaction During Sports Activities," *Discourse & Society*, Vol 18(1):35–52.

Louv, Richard 2005. *Last Child in the Woods: Saving Our Children from Nature-Deficit Disorder*. North Carolina: Algonquin Books, 2005.

Luthar, Suniya S. and Shawn J. Latendresse. Online. "Children of the Affluent: Challenges to Well-Being," *Current Directions in Psychological Science* 14(1): 49–53, 2005.

Lynn, Karen. "'I Have Work Enough to Do' (Don't I?)," *Ensign*, 1981, 40.

Mayo Clinic Staff. Online. "Childhood Obesity," 2006. Available from http://www. mayoclinic.com/health/childhood-obesity/DS00698; accessed February 27, 2007.

Meyerhoff, Michael K. Ed.D. Online."Playing Games: Perspectives on Parenting—Social Skills and Personal Development—Brief Article," *Pediatrics for Parents*, October 2001. Available from http://www.findarticles.com/p/articles/mi_m0816/ is_10_19/ai_82470764; accessed February 28, 2007.

Moore, Kristin Anderson, Ph.D. and Jonathan F. Zaff, Ph.D. Online. "Building a Better Teenager: A Summary of 'What Works' in Adolescent Development," ChildTrends.org, November 2002; accessed April 7, 2007

Moore, Melisa, M.A. and Sandra W. Russ, Ph.D. "Pretend Play as a Resource for Children: Implications for Pediatricians and Health Professionals." Developmental and Behavioral Pediatrics Vol 27: 237–48, 2006

Mogul, Wendy. Online. "Helping Teenagers Develop into Happy Adults," National Association of Independent Schools. Available from www.nais.org. http:// www.nais.org/publications/ismagazinelist.cfm?Itemnumber=147073&sn. ItemNumber=145956&tn.ItemNumber=145958; accessed March 3, 2007.

Myhre, Susan M. "Enhancing Your Dramatic-Play Area Through the Use of Prop Boxes." *Young Children* 48 (5): 6–11, 1993.

National Association of Early Childhood Specialists in State Departments of Education. Online. "Recess and the Importance of Play: A Position Statement on Young Children and Recess," January 29, 2007. Available from http://naecs.crc.uiuc. edu/position/recessplay.html; accessed February 26, 2007.

The National Center on Addiction and Substance Abuse, www.casafamilyday.org

National Youth Sports Safety Foundation. Online. "Sport Parent Code of Conduct," 2000. Available from http://www.nyssf.org/sportparentcodeofconduct.html; accessed February 28, 2007.

Neuschütz, Karin. *The Doll Book: Soft Dolls and Creative Free Play*. Translated from the Swedish Lek Med Mjuka Dokor by Ingun Schneider. New York: Larson Publications, Inc., 1982

Newman, Susan Ph.D. Online. "Bedtime Rituals That Forge Warm Memories." Available from http://sheknows.com/about/look/6130.htm; accessed November 7, 2006.

Office of Dietary Supplements, National Institutes of Health. Online. "Dietary Supplement Fact Sheet: Vitamin D," 2005. Available from http://ods.od.nih.gov/factsheets/vitamind.asp#h4; accessed April 6, 2007.

O'Neill, Mary. Online. "Double the Pleasure, Double the Fun." Available from http://www.allforchildren.org/mystories.php?id=8; accessed November 7, 2006.

Paquette, Daniel et al. Online. "Prevalence of Father-Child Rough-and-tumble Play and Physical Aggression in Preschool Children." Available from http://www.unites.uqam.ca/grave/prospere/pages/pdf/RTPfinal.pdf; accessed March 23, 2007.

Pellegrini, A.D. and Peter K. Smith. Online. "Physical Activity Play: The Nature an Function of a Neglected Aspect of Play." *Child Development*. Vol. 69 No. 3, 577–598, 1998.

Rosenfield, Alvin and Nicole Wise. *The Overscheduled Child: Avoiding the Hyper-Parenting Trap*. New York: St Martin's Griffin, 2000.

Rothenberg, Stephen, Psy.D. Online. "Playing with Self Esteem: The Importance of Social Skills." Nonverbal Learning Disorders Association. Available from http://www.nldline.com/dr.htm; accessed 28 February 2007.

Russ, Sandra, Andrew L. Robins, Beth A. Christiano. Online. "Pretend Play: Longitudinal Prediction of Creativity and Affect in Fantasy in Children." *Creativity Research Journal*. Vol 12 No. 2, 129–139, 1999. Available from http://www.findarticles.com/p/articles/mi_m1282/is_16_55/ai_106672819; accessed April 15, 2007.

Segal, Marilyn and Don Adcock. *Just Pretending: Ways to Help Children Grow Through Imaginative Play*. New Jersey:Prentice-Hall, 1981.

Sexton, Thomas. "Teens eat more veggies when parents are at the table," *Psychology Today*. September/October 2003:24.

Shonkoff, Jack P. M.D. et al. Online. "Young Children Develop in an Environment of Relationships." Working Paper by the National Scientific Council on the Developing Child, 2005. Available from http://www.earlychildhoodnm.com/Documents/Early%20Ed%20Center%20Report.pdf; accessed November 10, 2006.

Singer, Jerome. "Epilogue: Learning to Play and Learning Through Play" in *Play = Learning*, edited by Dorothy Singer, Roberta Michnick Golinkoff, and Kathy Hirsh-Pasek. New York: Oxford University Press, 2006, 74–100.

Singer, Dorothy G. and Jerome L. Singer. *Make Believe: Games and Activities to Foster Imaginative Play in Young Children*. Illinois: Scott, Foresman and Company, 1985.

Tamis-LeMonda, Catherine S. et al. "Fathers and Mothers at Play with Their 2- and 3-Year-Olds: Contributions to Language and Cognitive Development," *Child Development*. November/December 2004, Vol. 75 No. 6, 1806–1820.

Temple, Jennifer L. et al. "Television Watching Increases Motivated Responding for Food and Energy Intake in Children." *American Journal of Clinical Nutrition*. Vol. 85:355–361, 2007.

Todd, Emily B. Online."How Long-Distance Grandparents Stay Close." *FamilyFun Magazine*. Available from http://familyfun.go.com/parenting/child/skills/feature/famf199611_grandma/famf199611_grandma.html; accessed March 29, 2007.

Torgan, Carol, Ph.D. "Childhood Obesity on the Rise," *The NIH Word on Health*, June 2002. Available from http://www.nih.gov/news/WordonHealth/jun2002/childhoodobesity.htm; accessed February 27, 2007.

Trelease, Jim. *The Read-Aloud Handbook*, Fifth Edition. New York: Penguin Books, 2001.

Waldrop, Sharon. Online. "Teen-Friendly Family Outings." Available from http://teenagerstoday.com/resources/articles/outings.htm; accessed April 26, 2007.

"The White House Conference on Teenagers: Raising Responsible and Resourceful Youth," May 2000. Available from http://clinton3.nara.gov/WH/New/html/teen-conf1.html; accessed April 10, 2007.

Videon, Tami M. Online. "Parent-Child Relations & Children's Psychological Well-Being: Do Dads Matter?" *Journal of Family Issues* January 2005, 26 and 55. Available from htcpp://jfi.sagepub.com/cgi/reprint/26/1/55; accessed February 5, 2007.

Wolf, Bonny. Online. "Commentary: Value of family meals together," NPR, December 11, 2005. Available from www.npr.org/templates/story/story.php?storyId=5048043&ft=1&f=1057; accessed October 20, 2006.

Zabel, Brett. Online. "China Has More Students than we Have Students and Other Interesting Facts," Chris Knudsen on Life, Business, and Entrepreneurship blog, comment posted October 5, 2006. Available from http://www.chrisknudsen.biz/?p=147; accessed 3 March 2007.

About the Author

Lynnae W. Allred was born to two fun-loving parents who raised her in an era when seasonal work for children included tasks like building snowmen, making flower leis out of Catalpa Tree blossoms, playing Kick the Can in the backyard, and eating homemade doughnuts and caramel apples. It has been her life's work to give the same kind of childhood to her five children. She has yet to serve on the board of directors for a powerful corporation, but she has developed expertise in decorating birthday cakes using Cheetos, building pinewood derby cars, writing obituaries for pet fish, negotiating with toddlers who want ice cream at 3:00 AM, repairing "backed over" tricycles, editing student body campaign videos, and creating sculptures out of chicken wire, smashed aluminum cans, and papier mache. Her personal interests include writing, needlework, photography, camping, music, reading, biking, and skiing.

0 26575 70534 8